Sugababes

Sugababes

The story of Britain's most amazing girl band

Emily Sheridan

JOHN BLAKE

Published by John Blake Publishing Ltd,
3 Bramber Court, 2 Bramber Road,
London W14 9PB, England

www.blake.co.uk

First published in paperback in 2007

ISBN: 978 1 84454 421 9

British Library Cataloguing-in-Publication Data:

A catalogue record for this book is available from the British Library.

Design by www.envydesign.co.uk

Printed in Great Britain by CPD, Wales

1 3 5 7 9 10 8 6 4 2

Papers used by John Blake Publishing are natural, recyclable products made
from wood grown in sustainable forests. The manufacturing processes conform
to the environmental regulations of the country of origin.

Acknowledgements

Edited by Ian Garland
Thanks to Michelle Perry (research) and
Graham Smith (editing)

Contents

Who are Sugababes?   ix

1. Keisha's Childhood   1

2. Mutya's Beginnings   9

3. Heidi's Atomic Life   17

4. Siobhan's Suga-Free Childhood   27

5. Amelle's Life Before the 'Babes   33

6. Sugababes: Ver 1.0   41

7. Getting in (One) Touch with the Charts   53

8. Situation's Heavy   69

9. Sayonara, Siobhan   83

10. Hello, Heidi   93

11. Becoming Number One 'Freaks'   105

12. Three's A Crowd?   149

13. Time Out, Please?   171

14. Year of the Cat … Fight   189
15. Babes Growing Up   205
16. Everything's Changing   215
17. Babes are Back!   227
18. Minus Mutya, Add Amelle   243
19. Growing Even Taller   251
20 What Siobhan Did Next …   273
21. Sugababes and their Sugapies   283
Epilogue   289
Sugababes Discography   293

Who are Sugababes?

It's 2007 and the Sugababes are the most successful female act of the 21st century. They have enjoyed 17 UK hit singles, including four Number Ones, and have had four albums in the Top Three, including their last original disc, *Taller In More Ways*, which entered the charts at Number One.

Although the face of the Sugababes has changed a little over the years, the group have now been releasing songs for seven years. It's no mean feat when you consider the Spice Girls only lasted four and a half years and their rivals All Saints as little as three and a half years. The only girl group of the past 10 years that the Sugababes can stand next to in terms of chart longevity is pop quartet-turned-trio-turned-duo Eternal, who split just two years before the Sugababes broke into the British charts with their catchy debut 'Overload' in September 2000.

sugababes

Sugababes have always stood apart from their chart rivals because they couldn't be pigeon-holed. While Atomic Kitten and Girls Aloud have been placed firmly in the pop genre, and All Saints and Mis-Teeq were definitely R&B, Sugababes had their own brand of music. As Mutya Buena once put it, 'I don't think we have any rivals because we like to do things differently – we don't stick to one category of music.'

Sugababes are a major success story and continue to grow in strength. Because they started so young, they have grown up side by side with their fans – allowing their music to evolve along the way. But things haven't always been easy for the band and their story is a rich one. They have had to overcome years of negative press centred round rumours of bitter infighting and the unexpected departure of two band members, as well as being dropped by a record company. Other acts would have fallen by the wayside, but not this sassy, tough and talented trio.

CHAPTER 1

Keisha's Childhood

LIKE MANY YOUNG girls, Keisha Kerreece Fayeanne Buchanan dreamed of being a singer. Unlike the sexy, confident pop star we know today, Keisha used to sing in her bedroom with the door closed. Born on 30 September 1984, at Paddington Hospital in London, Keisha was one of two children raised in a single-parent family. Money was in short supply and Keisha knew her mother couldn't afford for her to have singing lessons or to send her to a stage school like Sylvia Young's in Marylebone, London. One day, her mum gave the seven-year-old a tape recorder and microphone set so the youngster could live out her pop-star dreams at home. Keisha would spend hours locked in her bedroom singing at the top of her voice and playing back her songs.

'I've never really thought, I wanna be in a band, I *always* just wanted to be a singer. My mum couldn't afford to send me to any stage schools so she used to give me this little tape-recorder thing to tape your voice. She just encouraged me to practise my vocals every single day so I used to always have the mic. I never went around the house singing to the family; I normally sang in the privacy of my own room.'

From the tender age of four, Keisha was a huge fan of Michael Jackson and she loved to listen to his *Bad* album on repeat. She enthused, 'I've got every album of his, but the reason why I like *Bad* is because it's got "Liberian Girl" on it. When I was younger, I wasn't sure if he was singing about someone who works in a library or a Libran, which is my star sign, but I assumed he was singing about me. I love him!'

Like many young girls, though, she lost interest in her hobby: 'I remember at one time, when I was about eight, I was like, "I don't wanna do this any more." And I just gave up singing for like a year. All of a sudden it just came back on me when I met Mutya.'

Long before she decided she wanted to be a singer, Keisha dreamed of being an actress. At six years old, she auditioned for a part in *EastEnders*, but sadly, 'nothing came of it'. A year later, when she was a huge fan of Aussie soap *Neighbours*, she even named her dolls after two of the characters, Chrissie and Caroline Alessi. At primary school, chatty and confident Keisha stood out from the crowd. She was thrilled at being chosen to play Sita in a production of *Rama and Sita*, an Indian love story. Later she said, 'That's the biggest part I ever got – I always wanted to be the star of the show.'

Having switched from drama to music, Keisha now plans to try her hand at acting when her time in Sugababes comes to an end. But acting and singing aren't her only talents – her double-jointed ears mean she can do party tricks! She explained, 'I can fold my ears inside out! I've got practically no bones in my ears, so I've been able to fold them in since I was small.'

Keisha grew up with her mum Beverley Buchanan and brother Shane, who is two years older. She saw her truck-driver father Andrew Brown occasionally, but was closer to her Jamaican grandparents. Her mum took on two jobs, so the Buchanan kids were often cared for by their grandmother fondly dubbed by Keisha 'my second mum'. The grandparents taught their grandchildren about their Caribbean home and instilled a strong sense of heritage pride within them, so much so that, when Keisha received her first proper paycheque from Sugababes, she bought a leather jacket with the Jamaican flag across it.

Keisha's mother and grandparents were practising Christians and made sure the youngsters learned about the Bible while growing up. She recalled, 'I always used to watch Jesus films. I really love Bible stories, and I was reading one about this guy who had leprosy, and Jesus healed him, which was amazing.'

To this day, her faith remains important and she credits her religion with keeping her strong during the hard times in the group – 'My mum has definitely kept me sane and my faith has taught me not to be afraid and to be happy, and that's what I try and do. I want to have a better relationship with God and read my Bible more. I always take it with me, but I only get a chance to read it every couple of weeks. I think it is really important to go to church.'

Like many siblings, growing up, Keisha and Shane had a

turbulent relationship. Keisha remembers arguing over silly things like where to hang the decorations on the Christmas tree. A sensitive child, she used to spend hours writing her thoughts and dreams in a diary, as well as writing poetry. However, when Shane found her book of secrets, he realised he had power over his sister. Keisha said, 'Whenever he wanted something from me, he'd bribe me by saying he'd tell our mum about something he'd read if I didn't let him have his way. I've not had one since.'

Despite this, Keisha's lyrical talents blossomed years before her singing voice. She loved writing poetry and found it easy to express herself through words. As she explained, 'I used to write lots of poems. It happened when I got frustrated or angry. I'd just put everything down on paper – what I felt and stuff. That kind of helped me express myself. I'd then give a melody to the words and slowly arrange the poems into songs. I wasn't an average child.'

When she was nine years old, the family moved from Kilburn to Kingsbury in northwest London, where Shane had been born in 1982. Keisha was enrolled at Roe Green Primary School and Shane joined Year Seven at Kingsbury High School near by – where Keisha would follow several years later.

When she joined Roe Green, Keisha met Mutya Buena. Instantly recognising her from an appearance she'd made on Michael Barrymore's *My Kinda People*, she was starstruck. Within a few days, Keisha was part of a gang. Mutya, Keisha and their friends were all fairly tomboyish and loved playing sports. She recalled, 'We'd play a bit of football with the boys, then go swimming. There were at least 15 of us hanging around together.' Keisha also joined the local Brownies group, which boosted her confidence and social skills: 'For me, it was really about the bonding and it's really important when you are younger to interact with kids your age because then you learn a lot about yourself.'

Despite the family's lack of money, the Buchanan children had a happy childhood. Keisha fondly remembers one particular Christmas when she and Shane didn't expect to have any presents because money had been especially tight. With two cleaning jobs, their mum barely had time to shop. Keisha said, 'I remember Mum flicking through the Argos catalogue with us and I was seeing all these gifts, knowing that she wouldn't be able to afford to buy us anything. By Christmas Eve, there was nothing under the tree … The next morning there were 50 presents there, the pile was halfway up the tree! I've never forgotten that.'

Keisha credits her down-to-earth attitude to her modest childhood. For the first few years of Sugababes, she was amazed when people expected her to have left her old friends behind. In 2003, she admitted, 'It's really funny because everyone is asking me, "Are you a millionaire yet?" Well, I'm still living in the same house I've lived since I was nine, so no, not yet. Kingsbury just feels like home; I really love the atmosphere here. My friends know how it is in the real world. If you wanted trainers or a mountain bike, you knew you couldn't just have it, that you had to earn your own money.'

In September 1996, a few weeks before Keisha turned

12, she and Mutya moved on to Kingsbury High School. Out of all her subjects, it was perhaps no surprise that she enjoyed the performing arts and physical education, especially hockey, netball and rugby. She said, 'I've always been really active and used to be in both the rugby and hockey teams at school. To me, it's not a big deal or an effort to exercise or eat healthily, because I enjoy doing it.'

But Keisha never revealed a big interest in more academic subjects such as science and maths. In English, the only book she enjoyed, besides the Bible, was CS Lewis's masterpiece *The Lion, The Witch and The Wardrobe*, which included Christian themes. When they made the movie in 2005, she was thrilled: 'I love *The Chronicles of Narnia*, don't get me started. *The Lion, The Witch and The Wardrobe* is the best. I've got it on DVD.'

Keisha and Mutya used to hang out with a big group of friends, who would meet outside the local newsagents on weekends. They would play football, hang out in the park or talk about boys and music. The two girls began listening to R&B, in particular female soloists such as Faith Evans, Aaliyah, Mary J Blige, Whitney Houston and Brandy. Keisha affectionately labels the stars her unofficial singing teachers, saying, 'You don't need to have a singing teacher. When I was growing up, I listened to a lot of Whitney Houston, Faith Evans, Brandy, Aaliyah – they teach you how to sing. It's important to train yourself vocally every day.' For Keisha, Aaliyah became a fashion icon: 'She was so unique. Even though her music was quite hip-hop and R&B based, she still always managed to look feminine. She always looked great, even wearing baggy jeans.'

When her idol was killed in a plane crash in the Bahamas in August 2001, she was deeply saddened and it was to be a bad week for her when Siobhan Donaghy decided to leave Sugababes, too.

CHAPTER 2

Mutya's Beginnings

AS A YOUNG GIRL growing up in Kingsbury with four older brothers, clearly Rosa Isabel Buena needed to do something to get some attention. Born on 21 May 1985, from the age of three, she began to sing and she'd show off her voice at any opportunity. While her older siblings Charlie, Kris, Danny and Roberto teased her mercilessly and demanded she stop singing, her parents Rose and Roberto Junior recognised their little girl's talent. Rosa was the first daughter in the Buena family and was given the nickname 'Mutya' by her father, which translates as 'Princess' in his native Filipino.

When Rosa was joined by twin sisters Ligaya and Dalisay in 1991, her Irish housewife mum had to concentrate on the two babies, so her father (a travel agent) decided to enter the six-year-old into a Filipino Fiesta concert, providing her first stage experience. Mutya said, 'I started off singing little songs for my family and my brothers used to tease me – I used to get told to shut up. My dad got me on to the stage from when I was around six. I performed in front of a couple of thousand people; it was a Filipino Fiesta thing. Since then, everyone kinda loved me and I was performing all the time.'

After the success of the concert, it became clear to Mutya's parents that their child had a real talent. Using his business contacts, Roberto Junior arranged for his eldest daughter to perform at Filipino events all over Europe. Mutya was delighted: not only was she getting the chance to sing to thousands, she also missed 'boring' school occasionally. Her biggest pre-Sugababes' moment came in 1992 when she was chosen to sing on Saturday-night TV king Michael Barrymore's *My Kinda People* primetime show in which the funny man travelled the length and breadth of the UK, looking for raw talent. Every week, his TV crew would set up in a shopping mall and invite local shoppers to show off their entertaining skills. When ITV came to Mutya's local area, producers were quick to spot her talent among the thousands of other hopefuls and soon she was showing off her big voice in front of a potential 13 million viewers. While other young boys and girls chose traditional children's songs, Mutya knew she had an unusually large voice at such a young age and instead she opted for Whitney Houston's power ballad 'Greatest Love Of All'. Houston released the song in 1986 – when Mutya was less than a year old – and it went on to top the US charts, and made it into the UK's Top Ten. At the recording of *My Kinda People*, Mutya realised she had found her calling. The shopping-centre crowd cheered after she finished and she loved the feeling of being on television. On her return to Roe Green Primary School the following Monday, her friends were so excited for her.

Mutya knew from an early age she wanted to be a singer when she grew up, but never imagined she would fulfil her dream so young. She said, 'I didn't think I would have started so young. I probably would have thought I would have started my career when I was 18 or 19, but I was 13 when the band started.'

What she didn't know when she sang her heart off on Saturday-night TV was that one of the audience members watching at home was to play a big part in her musical future. Eight-year-old Keisha was mesmerised by Mutya's performance and realised she wasn't the only young girl who could sing. Keisha recalled, 'I saw this little girl, she was Filipino, long hair, big frilly dress. I liked her instantly when I saw her because she was the first person I saw that was my age and could sing as well.'

Two months later, Keisha, Shane and Beverley moved to Kingsbury and Keisha enrolled at Roe Green, where she was stunned to discover she was in the same class as 'the girl off the telly'. As she explained, 'About two months after that, we moved northwest and basically we were put in the same class. When I first met her, I thought she was the most famous person I had ever met because I had seen her on TV before I actually met her in person.'

Mutya was equally intrigued and within days the youngsters formed a friendship which would prove incredibly fruitful. Describing the moment they met, Mutya said, 'The first time I met Keisha, I was in primary school. I must have been about seven or eight. I remember watching this new girl come in and sit at the back of the classroom. It only took me two days before we started properly chatting. The first few days I was like, "Hmm, who's this girl?" but afterwards everything became cool. We started up a little gang called the "Love Gang", just talking about little girl things. I don't know why we were talking about those things at the age of eight. But, from there on, we started singing.'

As the girls' friendship continued, they followed in the footsteps of their older brothers and started at Kingsbury High in 1996. By this point, Mutya had younger brother Bayani. Her mum stayed at home and raised the children, while her dad Roberto worked long hours to pay the bills. Mutya admits life was tough growing up on a council estate, but her parents had strong morals that they instilled into their nine children. Despite Rose and Roberto Junior's attempts to shield their children from the outside world, it was impossible to protect them from everything. Hanging out around the estate with her friends, Mutya was in tune with local gossip and goings-on and she was aware of the area's drug-dealing and gang behaviour. While the Buena family were well liked, with many friends and family, this didn't mean Mutya could always feel secure in the area. Several times in her teenage years, she fled dangerous gangs or strangers. She recalled, 'I've had to run for my life a couple of times, which was very scary. I've been followed and a group of boys tried to drag me off once, too. There were two girls and this big group of boys crowded round of us. A 13-year-old girl was raped in broad daylight, too, close to my home. I felt really threatened as a female. You can be ugly or pretty, but, because you are a girl, blokes think they can approach you.'

Growing up on an estate and having to cope with her older brothers' bullying gave Mutya a thick skin and contributed to the tough street image she projected during her time with Sugababes. Although her older siblings, Charlie, Kris, Danny and Roberto, were rough with her in her early years, she believes their mean behaviour was for her own good and toughened her up in preparation for the outside world and the music industry, in particular. She revealed, 'Every time they saw me they'd punch my arm. They wanted me to be stronger which is handy in Sugababes. There are people who hate me just because I'm in a band. You have to keep looking behind your back in case there's someone standing there with a knife.'

While Mutya insists she wasn't a naughty child, she was often in trouble with her mother owing to her sweet tooth (which was to come into play when the girl group were looking for a band name) and her girlie obsession with hair and make-up. Long before she had the legitimate reason for missing school to go to the studio, the young teen was skipping classes to hang out with her cousin Penny at Andy's Barbers in Wembley. Mutya used to spend hours at the barbers styling her hair and just listening to the conversations Penny and her work colleagues would have with the customers. She admits the chat was often inappropriate for her young ears, declaring, 'The conversations we had in the shop were so funny, really nasty. They talked about really, really rude stuff. I told them, "I'm too young to hear it", but they wouldn't listen.'

Back home, Mutya would cause chaos in the kitchen trying to create her own beauty treatments out of *Sugar* and *Bliss* magazines. While her mum's back was turned looking after the twins and Bayani, Mutya raided her cupboards for eggs, honey, carrots and yoghurt to make her youthful face look even more luminous. 'I used to follow recipes from the magazines. I used to always get them wrong and start adding in sugar and weird stuff – it was almost edible.' Inevitably, the fun ended when Rose entered the kitchen to find it in a mess. 'My mum used to make me clean it all up afterwards.' Mutya also experimented with cucumbers on her eyes and, to this day, she swears toothpaste is a good cure for spots. She explains, 'I don't get many spots, but, when I do, I put toothpaste on them. It depends what brand because they've got different chemicals in them – Colgate and Aquafresh are the best.' Mutya was so fond of skincare and cosmetics, she freely admitted that if Sugababes suddenly ended, she would 'be a beautician or a sales person – I always love a good deal.'

Her love of hair and make-up continued well on into the days of the band, where she established herself as the Chameleon-like member, thanks to her different looks. In the video for Sugababes' debut single 'Overload', Mutya showed off a crimped bob but, just six months later, her hair was an elfin crop in the promo for 'Run For Cover'. In Heidi's video debut 'Freak Like Me', Mutya was back to the bob again, this time with 1920s-inspired finger waves. Her craziest video look ever is generally considered by fans to be their second release from *Angels With Dirty Faces*:

'Round Round' when Mutya danced round in a PVC mini-dress with plaited ponytails randomly placed on her head. In 2003, she admitted to a slight addiction for dyeing her hair, saying, 'I'm always changing my hair colour. I've had blue hair, blonde hair... At the moment it's pink.' Later that year, her hair went red, then blonde again in 2004. In her last ever video – 'Ugly' – with Sugababes, Mutya showed off perhaps her most beautiful screen look. Wearing a fitted black dress and baby pink shrug, with long curly strawberry blonde locks, she appeared to be telling her fans she'd grown up, paving the way for an exit just two weeks after the single was released in the UK.

While Mutya was free to experiment with hair and make-up, she also opted for more permanent piercings and tattoos. Although proud of her body art, she was horrified when BBC DJ Sara Cox claimed live on her *Radio 1 Breakfast Show* that Mutya had had her nipples pierced. She fumed, 'Sara said it live on the radio but it's not true. I've got 12 piercings, just on my face. I had my stomach done but I've taken it out – I like to be different.'

After having pierced ears as a child, Mutya began piercing her nose and just above her lip in 2002. Mutya has four holes in each ear, as well as the piercings on her tongue, the right side of her nose and just above her lips. Her tattoos include a red rose on her left breast, a curvy lady on her right leg and her late sister Maya's name appears on her hip. There's also a Chinese symbol and her daughter Tahlia's name on her right arm, her family name 'Buena' on her left arm, a heart on her right hand, 'Only God can judge me' is written across the back of her neck and there's a lion on her back.

sugababes

Contrary to the tough image projected by her during her time in Sugababes, Mutya is actually a friendly, genuine person. Despite her upbringing on a Kingsbury council estate, she's just a normal Christian family girl: 'I've been brought up very well considering where I live. There are drugs and violence all around.'

In 2007, as Mutya attempts a solo career, she also hopes the media and fans see the real her. 'I'm only a bitch to people who treat me like an idiot. I was a moody teenager, but I'm 21 now – I don't want to cause trouble. If nothing else, it's harmful to your career. Sometimes I think I'm too nice – if a nasty thing is said to me, I ignore it. I want people to get to know the real me.'

CHAPTER 3

Heidi's Atomic Life

UNLIKE HER LONG-TERM Sugababes' bandmates Keisha and Mutya, Heidi Range was groomed for the stage from an early age. While undergoing a traditional Catholic-school education, she was enrolled in a string of after-school dance and music lessons. When she joined Sugababes in September 2001, Heidi's stage-school training was clear to see from her constant smiling, as she stood next to the scowling Keisha and Mutya. During performances to promote their first album *One Touch*, Sugababes – along with former band member Siobhan – were renowned for their awkward stage presence and lack of movement. When Heidi joined, the girls started dancing in their videos. In the video for 'Freak Like Me', Heidi was officially introduced to Sugababes' fans dancing with a crowd of boys in a grimy nightclub.

Heidi came into the world in Walton, Merseyside, on 23

sugababes

May 1983, to her support-worker mum Karen and builder dad Paul. The little blonde baby joined her three-year-old sister Hayley, who was to become her best friend and confidante. Heidi was a confident, happy child. In nursery school, she was renowned for her love of singing and dancing and she was always entertaining her friends.

At the tender age of three, she made her stage debut in Liverpool's famous Neptune Theatre on Hanover Street. The Grade II listed building, which opened in 1913, has hosted stars such as Jenny Seagrove, Lenny Henry, Steve Coogan, Jenny Agutter and Kate O'Mara. Heidi and her classmates were chosen to sing Noel Gay and Ralph Butler's wartime children's song 'Hey Little Hen' in front of the 390-strong audience. Their teacher had been working on the tune and accompanying routine for weeks and the children's parents were waiting in their seats ready for the big performance. Dressed in a red leotard, young Heidi couldn't wait for the show; unlike her classmates, she loved the feeling of hundreds of people watching her. When the music began to play, she stepped forward and sang her heart out while the other pupils mumbled shyly in the background.

Heidi admits that her memories of that time are pretty hazy, but her mum Karen has filled in the blanks. Heidi said, 'I was one of those little brats probably, who loved being on stage. I wore a little red leotard with a little bow on the bum. My mum said that all the other kids that were supposed to be doing it with me were just standing there and weren't saying anything. And there I was, standing there at the front doing the routine and screaming it out!'

Heidi's parents realised their daughters loved the arts

and enrolled them at the Elsie Smith Dance School when Heidi was three and Hayley was six. There, they would learn a range of dances after school finished. While Karen and Paul were keen to support Heidi and Hayley's enjoyment of singing and dancing, they also made sure their girls were given moral guidance by regular Sunday visits to their local Catholic church. When Heidi was confirmed she chose the name 'India' as her confirmation name. Although the singer is often known as 'Heidi India Range' on Sugababes' fansites, she admits that 'technically it isn't my real name'. To this day, she remains spiritual.

After her confirmation, Heidi was chosen to star in the Christmas play at school, but was devastated when she was given the role of an angel. She laments, 'I was always an angel. I wore my confirmation dress, but I always wanted to be Mary.'

Heidi was raised on her parents' music: blues, jazz and Motown, with influences evident in her singing voice. Her mother Karen loved to play Tracy Chapman and UB40, which Heidi still listens to today. She was encouraged to sing at home and, one Christmas, her parents bought her a karaoke machine, but she admits the choice of music on the player wasn't fantastic: 'The only karaoke tape had things like "Living Doll" and "The Great Pretender."' Heidi's first music loves were Madonna, Bananarama and New Kids On The Block. Thanks to her older sister Hayley, she was introduced to pop music at an early age and loved dancing around her sitting room to the latest chart hits. She recalled, 'I was more into people like Madonna when I was young, with her cool clothes and trying to copy her dance moves.'

As well as a passion for the arts, Heidi loved animals and desperately wanted a pet. When she was eight years old, dad Paul brought home a spider monkey he had bought at a local market. Young Heidi was ecstatic and rushed back from school every day to play with it. She recalled, 'He was really cute and used to peel grapes. He'd sit by the fire to warm himself and he'd answer the phone.'

But just two months later, the ape bit Heidi so the family decided to rehouse the creature. Despite the misadventure, she remained an animal lover and was thrilled when she bought a pug puppy called Buddy, aka Boo, in late 2004.

After learning the basics at the Elsie Smith Dance School, ten-year-old Heidi moved on to the Premier School of Dance and Drama in Aintree. She learned a combination of song, dance and drama – skills which would all be useful for her future in Sugababes. In September 1994, she enrolled at Maricourt Catholic High School in Maghull – two miles from her Aintree home. At school, she was a conscientious, quiet student, who only really came out of her shell when she was performing. While she never had a great passion for her subjects at school, she couldn't wait to return to Premier every week. When her parents' marriage sadly fell apart, Karen continued to take Heidi to her lessons.

After her parents' divorce, Heidi and Hayley continued to live with their mum and Paul moved out of the family home. Karen's mum, who Heidi calls 'Nanny V', helped out with caring for the children and the girls still saw their dad regularly – Heidi always gives him a mention in Sugababes' album credits. Karen was determined that Heidi should carry on with her after-school activities and continued to take Heidi to her lessons.

Following the divorce, Heidi, Hayley, Karen and Nanny V closed quarters and became a very tight family unit. The four women were incredibly close, so, when the time came for Heidi to leave the fold and move to London to join Sugababes, it was tough for the whole family.

Heidi received positive feedback from her teachers at Premier, in particular her dance teacher Sharon Collins, who taught the future Sugababe for three years. Collins said, 'Heidi was always a bubbly, lively child and it was obvious she was talented. She was a very good singer – very expressive – and always enjoyed everything we did. She was also very pretty and stood out from the crowd. Her mother always made sure she attended classes, even when times were hard. But with Heidi's hard work and dedication it's not surprising she got to where she is now.'

So fond of Collins was Heidi that she paid 'special thanks' to her in the sleeve notes of *Angels With Dirty Faces*.

During her teen years, Heidi saw a lot of the country travelling with her dance school and also with the Zodiac Roadshow dance troupe. Despite her multiple talents, she loved music best and realised she could become a professional singer after a successful performance at Liverpool's prestigious Philharmonic Hall. Premier had organised a show there and 12-year-old Heidi was given the chance to sing in front of hundreds of people. The feeling she got on stage was electric and convinced her even more that her future lay in music. Two years later, in 1997, she competed against 12,600 wannabes in a nationwide competition to find the Pepsi Stars of Tomorrow.

Despite these triumphs, Heidi's mum insisted that she should concentrate on school so her education didn't suffer. While Karen was convinced of her daughter's talent, she knew the road to fame would be hard if not impossible and so she made sure Heidi had a back-up plan. Heidi also loved physical education and, thanks to her lifelong dance training, was very good at gymnastics. Her future bandmate Keisha now claims Heidi is 'very flexible'.

In summer 1998, Heidi sang in a choir alongside Liz McClarnon at the annual Summer Pops festival in Liverpool. The two girls – who had a two-year age gap – were both students at the Shelagh Elliot-Clarke Stage School in the city centre. It was at the school that their singing teacher Sharon Ashton told the two about an audition for a new girl group. Former Orchestral Manoeuvres in the Dark frontman Andy McCluskey was looking for a female singing trio and, after a series of auditions, he recruited Liz McClarnon (17), Kerry Katona (18) and 15-year-old Heidi for 'The Automatic Kittens'.

Soon enough, Heidi was constantly rushing from the school to the studio to record a series of demos and to perform at small gigs. She recalled, 'They'd have to put a big jacket over my school blazer because I would turn up straight from class and perform in my school uniform.'

While there was a good buzz around the group and McCluskey was convinced they would soon be signed to a record label, Heidi was unhappy. While she loved listening to Soul and R&B, she found the Kittens' music too pop for her liking. She had also begun to find the confidence to write songs, but wasn't able to sing them. The Kittens' songs were all written by McCluskey and his former OMD bandmate Stuart Kershaw. During her time with the group, Heidi grew close to Kerry Katona and to this day they remain friends. She enthused, 'I was the baby of the bunch but Kerry really took me under her wing and looked after me – it was almost like having another mum.'

After eight months, Heidi decided to leave The Automatic Kittens. It was only a month away from her GCSEs and she knew it wasn't worth sacrificing her education for a group she wasn't enjoying. While she got on well with Katona and McClarnon – despite the age gap – she wasn't excited about the material they were singing. She wanted to sing soulful ballads and show off her vocal range. In April 1999, she left the group and was swiftly replaced by 16-year-old Natasha Hamilton – and the band's name was changed to the catchy 'Atomic Kitten'.

Heidi admitted, 'I was 15 and even then I knew it wasn't for me. I thought it all through; I decided their type of music just wasn't right for me. I wanted to go in a different direction with music and have a bit more control over what I was doing. It's a tough business too. If I had stayed with Atomic Kitten, I would have ended up releasing my first single when I was 16 and I don't think I would have been prepared for what was going to happen to me.'

Instead, that summer she completed 11 GCSEs and was pleased with her grades: two As, three Bs and six Cs. Despite all the distraction earlier in the year, she had still managed to study hard. Afterwards, while working at

Barratts shoe shop, Heidi thought about her next move. She didn't want to do 'A' levels because she knew qualifications wouldn't prove her singing ability or further her career. Working in the city centre, Heidi quickly realised her future didn't lie in retail either: 'The outfit was bad – a navy-blue polyester skirt to just below the knee, a red polyester shirt, American Tan tights and these horrible shoes! They didn't even have any air-conditioning in the shop and it was boiling. The manager used to come round every hour with his chart and say things like, "You're tenth because you've only sold a certain amount of sundries."'

Barratts wasn't Heidi's only venture into retail – she also worked part-time at Karen Millen in the city centre, where she loved the staff discount and working in the store kick-started her love for fashion. She recalled, 'I used to work there part-time to get some money to pay for trains to go to auditions in London. One thing I used to hate was that I didn't finish work on a Saturday until about 7pm and it didn't give me enough time to go home and get ready to go out on Saturday night with my friends.'

Wondering when she was going to get her big break and feeling slightly miserable, Heidi spotted an advertisement in *The Stage* for an 'all-singing, all-dancing pop group'. The 16-year-old quickly sent her résumé and photo to Pete Waterman's former songwriting/production partners Mike Stock and Matt Aitken and was soon called down to London to audition. Though impressed with her singing and dancing, the famous duo decided she was too young for their group Scooch and instead cast Natalie Powers, Caroline Barnes, David Ducasse and Russ Spencer, who were at least four years older. However, they had spotted her solo-artist potential and kept her details. Meanwhile, that July, Heidi's former bandmates Katona and McClarnon became Atomic Kitten and signed a record deal with Innocent Records. Upbeat Heidi refused to feel envious and kept her faith in God that her time would come too.

In December 1999, Atomic Kitten's debut single 'Right Now' entered the charts at Number Ten. While she was genuinely happy for the girls, the disco-pop infusion track was not to Heidi's taste at all. While her former bandmates' careers were going well, it wasn't long before she herself was approached by Stock and Aitken, who wanted to develop her as a solo artist. Heidi moved down to London for a short time to record a series of demos, but, because her schedule was much more relaxed, she often returned home to Liverpool to see her family. And she couldn't contain her excitement when, in 2000, Stock and Aitken took her to glamorous Los Angeles to work with American producers.

In 2001, her work with Stock and Aitken was slowing down and Heidi began to realise the project might not fit into her path to success after all. She was living back in Liverpool, where she had got herself a job as a hostess at the trendy Pan American bar and restaurant at the Albert Dock. The venue was situated eight miles away from her Aintree home and Heidi admits a majority of her £4-an-hour salary went on taxi fares. Each night she would stand on the door of the bar, flashing her big smile and offering menus to customers.

In February of that year, Atomic Kitten achieved their first Number One with 'Whole Again'. Heidi's friends and family were concerned she might be upset, but she insisted her love of music was so deep she couldn't have compromised her feelings to be in Atomic Kitten. She said, 'People were going, "Oh, you must be gutted" – but I wasn't. It was the right decision to leave. When they became Number One, everyone asked me if I was jealous and I wasn't because I'd made my decision. I was happy for them. I'm pleased that Atomic Kitten has been such a success – I know how hard the girls have worked.'

At the end of the summer, Heidi accepted the lead role in the *Sleeping Beauty* pantomime at the Lowry Centre, Manchester. It didn't involve singing, but she was on stage, her favourite place to be, and the money was better than bar work. She was preparing to work at the Pan American up until she went to Manchester, but fate intervened.

In late August 2001, Heidi remembers being at her lowest. She was bored of being a hostess and her upcoming job in panto wasn't exactly the stuff of dreams. Not only this, but her anti-social hours meant she wasn't spending as much time as she would like with her friends. She recalled, 'The week before I joined Sugababes, I was fed up in my job. It was about one in the morning and I had a ten-minute break. I went outside and sat on a bench and I was crying because I really wanted to be a singer. I was fed up with my job and had no money. I was praying to God and I said, "Please, God, I just really want this and I've worked really hard for it."'

A week later, she took a call from music lawyer Sarah Stennett – part of the management team for Sugababes – and her life was transformed. Heidi's prayers had been answered: 'God sent me Keisha and Mutya!'

CHAPTER 4

Siobhan's Suga-Free Childhood

SIOBHAN EMMA DONAGHY came into the world on 14 June 1984 to Irish airport worker Linda and Northern Irish plasterer Charles. When the young redhead arrived at Perivale Hospital that summer day, she had two sisters waiting: four-year-old Roisin and two-year-old Bevin. Siobhan was the latest member to join the huge Donaghy and Davern – her mother's family – clans, which were based in County Tyrone, Northern Ireland, and County Laois in the Republic. Out of the original Sugababes, Siobhan had the most conventional upbringing. She was raised by both parents in leafy Ruislip and had a Catholic education. After spending her early years at the local St Swithun Wells Roman Catholic School in Hunters Hill, Ruislip, she moved on to Douay Martyrs Roman Catholic School in Ickenham – five miles away from the family home – in 1995. It was during her time at Douays that she formed friendships with Zoe Dowsell, Amy Nolan, Bell, Shona Matthews and Hannah

Moss and credits the girls with supporting her during tough times in Sugababes.

Siobhan was brought up listening to a wide variety of music, which later showed through in her solo material. Her parents' record collection comprised of reggae and rock, including The Rolling Stones, The Who, The Beatles and The Kinks. She kept abreast of the current chart music by listening to her older sisters' albums and loved listening to American singers – Madonna, Whitney Houston, Mariah Carey and Michael Jackson. Like many teenage girls, she was obsessed with the *Dirty Dancing* movie and soundtrack, too.

Siobhan was a shy child, but loved singing in the privacy of her bedroom. Only her family and close friends knew about her singing voice. Although her future bandmates knew from an early age that they wanted to be singers, Siobhan had no idea what she wanted to do. She liked music, art and photography, but hadn't determined a career path. During her time in Sugababes, her interest in photography was stimulated on photo shoots, but she never fulfilled that passion. In 2001, she said, 'All the photographers I meet teach me some things about the camera and they say I can do work experience with them. Now that's a chance that not many people get.'

Shortly before leaving school, Siobhan was given the chance to take media studies classes, where she cultivated a love of film, which remains to this day. She enthused, 'I loved *The Simpsons* and it was brilliant to see how cleverly the show is put together. All the scenes from cult movies made me enjoy it even more. I love *The Italian Job*.'

As well as music, Siobhan had a great passion for animals. While she didn't go as far as becoming vegetarian, as a teenager she refused to eat red meat and would often rant about animals in captivity. She said, 'I'm not vegetarian, but I eat organic and everything free range.'

For her debut solo album *Revolution In Me*, she wrote a song called 'Iodine' after finding out the chemical was used to help remove feathers from turkeys to prepare them for Christmas dinner. She used this ideology in the song to protest about the control held worldwide by US President George W Bush following the September 11 attacks. She explained, 'I read this article about turkeys and found out the iodine used burns their skin. They're pumped full of hormones and killed at six weeks old. It is horrible! I thought it was awful and people should know about it.'

While Siobhan today seems like a distant memory to Sugababes fans, the redhead played a more important part in the band than many realise. In 1996, the shy Ruislip teenager was introduced to west London DJ/producer Ron Tom, brother-in-law of her best friend. She heard he was in the music industry and asked him if she could sing for him. Fortunately, he agreed and, stunned by the 12-year-old's voice, he signed her to his management company Metamorphosis. Years later, she admits luck played a huge part: if she hadn't met Tom, she might never have realised she could make music for a job. 'It's so bizarre, I grew up not wanting to be a singer and then when I became a singer I wasn't writing songs and suddenly I'm this songwriter. My life could've been so different. What if I'd never had that chance meeting with my first manager and I sang him some random song? I think, What would I be doing? and then I think, God, I am so lucky.'

Siobhan admits she lacked confidence in her vocal abilities and her dad Charlie was distrustful of the music industry. She said, 'I didn't really know what I wanted to do with my life at that stage. I knew I loved singing and I kind of went along with it. I haven't got pushy parents. My mum was like, right, you want to be a singer we'll support you. My dad didn't want me to do it. I was like, "Fucking Dad, trying to spoil it for me!" but he didn't like the industry and didn't want his 12-year-old daughter doing it.'

She and Tom fought hard to convince Charles that his daughter had talent and that she would be well looked after.

Tom played a part in the All Saints' beginnings when he partnered original members Shaznay Lewis and Melanie Blatt with Simone Rainford to become All Saints 1.9.7.5 – named after the All Saints Road, the Notting Hill location of his studios, and the year of the trio's birth. After recording some demos with the three-piece, he took a tape to ZTT Records, who had had success with Frankie Goes To Hollywood, Seal, Lisa Stansfield and Kirsty MacColl. Although they were quick to sign the girls, the label dropped Lewis, Blatt and Rainford after a poor response to their singles 'If You Wanna Party' and 'Silver Shadow'. Rainford left the band and Lewis and Blatt went on to join forces with sisters Nicole and Natalie Appleton to become simply All Saints, who were a huge success for London Records when they released 'I Know Where It's At' in 1997.

During her time with Tom, Siobhan opened her mind to many different types of music. When Sugababes first formed, she had a fleeting interest in garage but her heart lay in the more alternative sounds of rock and hip-hop. Thanks to her parents, she had been introduced to the music of Jimi Hendrix, James Brown, Bob Marley, Joni Mitchell and Lynyrd Skynyrd. Siobhan also listened to hip-hop artists such as De La Soul, Fugees, LL Cool J and Salt 'N' Pepa. She said, 'When I was 12, I was obsessed with music. I'm into a lot of guitar-based rock sounds and I'm into hip-hop as well.'

However, her taste in music would prove to be just one of the many things Siobhan didn't have in common with her Sugababes bandmates...

CHAPTER 5

Amelle's Life Before the 'Babes

WHILE THE OTHER SUGABABES tasted fame at a young age, Amelle Emma Berrabah had to wait 21 years for her dreams of fame to become a reality. She was born in Buckinghamshire on 22 April 1984 to father Mohammed and mum Yamina. Her Moroccan-born parents moved to England in the 1970s and brought up their family in Aldershot, Hampshire – a town well known for its army base. When Amelle was born, she joined older sisters Zakiya, 11, Nora, eight, Laila, two, and her brother Khalid, nine. But, two years later, her status as baby of the family was usurped by the arrival of little sister Samiya.

Life was hard for the Berrabah family. As a traditional Moroccan man, Mohammed was expected to provide for his large family and, during Amelle's childhood, he often worked two jobs to pay the bills. The family ran and lived above a kebab shop in the town centre, so their living quarters were fairly cramped. Besides the Moroccan influence in the family business, Mohammed and Yamina were keen to make sure their children knew about their roots and so they exposed them to Moroccan culture at every opportunity. Amelle grew up listening to a combination of music from her parents' native country and the latest chart sounds that her teenage siblings were listening to. In the early 1990s, she became a fan of Take That and, in particular, had a huge crush on Gary Barlow. Little did she know in 13 years she would be sharing the same stage … and falling out with the singer. Amelle insists she has never fallen for one particular genre of music because she was exposed to many types, thanks to her older siblings and parents. She explained, 'There were so many different musical tastes influencing me and I like so many different types of music that I couldn't really pinpoint specific artists. If you like the sound of something, you like it and that's that. So many different songs have shaped the way I am that I wouldn't know where to start.'

Like her older siblings, Amelle started at The Connaught School in Tongham Road, Aldershot in 1995. The school was around the corner from the town Lido, where she spent a lot of her after-school time. She said, 'We'd go there every day. I was really sporty so I'd play a lot of tennis, basketball, and I lived opposite a park so we'd hang out there.'

Early on, Amelle and Samiya showed an interest in the arts and they were always singing and dancing in the house. The sisters used to make a stage out of the furniture and put on shows for their parents and siblings. Amelle knew her parents couldn't afford singing lessons so she made a special effort to participate in music and drama at school. 'I used to really like school. I used to love getting involved with all the sports – they were happy days for me.' While her parents supported her interests, her father stressed the importance of an education. Amelle recalled, 'My dad thought I should have a back-up career.'

During her first year at The Connaught, Amelle entered a school talent competition, where she bravely tackled Mary J Blige's ballad 'I'm Goin' Down'. At the age of ten she was introduced to the American singer's music and to this day, she remains a huge fan. She enthused, 'If I saw Mary J Blige, though, I'd collapse on the floor. I love the way she writes, how she tells a story about her life and all the rough times she went through. She's just got this aura. I really respect her as a singer. I suppose it's a bit mad for someone that young to be into Mary J Blige … I loved that song.'

When Amelle was 13 years old, she had her first taste of working life when she got a job in a local café called Journeys. She disguised her age and was employed as a waitress at the weekends. She admitted, 'I really enjoyed it. I got £18 a week. I started work early and lied about my age.' After two years' waitressing, Amelle took another job working for a loan company at a call centre. At the time she was in the first year of GCSEs and, while she detested the job, she needed the money. 'You'd just have to repeat yourself over and over again, "Good afternoon, Amelle speaking. How can I help you?"'

In summer 2000, Amelle finished her GCSEs and left school with an A and five Cs. She then had to decide what to do next and, when she heard about the Academy of Contemporary Music (ACM) in nearby Guildford, Surrey, she was desperate to go there. When she realised the school was fee-paying, Amelle tried to secure a scholarship. While she had been fairly quiet during her five years at The Connaught School, Amelle had begun to grow in confidence and, although she realised her academic record wouldn't get her into the ACM, she knew she could sing. She was thrilled when she won a scholarship and was offered a place on the vocals course. On completion in 2003, she was to receive a Diploma in Contemporary Music and a BTEC National Certificate in Music Practice. When she started the course, Amelle was in her element. Compared to music facilities at The Connaught, the ACM was very advanced. She was given the opportunity to record in the studios, to organise her own gigs and to study the art of songwriting. The course was very industry based and gave Amelle essential skills she would later use in Sugababes.

As the ACM was ten miles away from Aldershot, Amelle continued to work at the call centre to fund her travel expenses, but the job still held no interest for her. One day, she decided she couldn't take it any more and quit: 'Every day, during my hour break, I used to think, Shall I come back? One day I just walked off and never returned.' After her dramatic exit, Amelle tried an array of jobs, including cleaning and bar work. She admits, 'I've had every job under the sun.'

During her time at ACM, the Berrabah family were rocked by the death of her father Mohammed. For some time he had been suffering from cancer and sadly it had spread too far for effective treatment. Mohammed died in March 2002, just a month before his 57th birthday. Amelle was devastated, but his death made her only more determined to be a success so that he would have been proud of her. But, soon after Mohammed's passing, the family were horrified to find their mother Yamina also had the disease. Fortunately, after a course of chemotherapy, she fought the illness and made a full recovery.

Nearly a year later, Amelle entered the *Top Of The Pops*' 'Search for a Star' competition, co-sponsored by the Academy and Jiant Productions. The winning singer would go to America to become part of a transatlantic pop group. On the day of the finals, which took place in February 2003, she and her family travelled up to London for the audition in Leicester Square. Amelle was one of 15 singers at the final and was stunned when she was chosen as the winner. She gushed, 'I didn't think I would get that far really so I was just really pleased with myself to be in the final. When they went on to announce the overall winner, I was crying and everything.'

Following her win, Amelle started working with songwriting/production duo Pete Kirtley and Tim Hawes. The plan for a five-piece group fell by the wayside, but Amelle had other ideas: she soon introduced her sister Samiya and they formed a group. Amelle explained, 'My sister and I were trying to come up with a band name and were just writing down loads of names. I said Boo 2, half as a joke and the managers just went for it.'

Jiant spent over a year with the sisters, writing songs for them and cultivating their image. Pete Kirtley said, 'We spent a year initially training her, writing songs for her, in the studio every day, including dance lessons five days a week before we showcased her.'

Boo 2 recorded a five-track sampler, including the songs 'Headbash', 'Naughty But Nice' and a cover of Queen's 'Bohemian Rhapsody'. When the siblings weren't in the studios, they were up in London, hanging outside the headquarters of all the record companies, handing out their CDs. Amelle recalled, 'I would wait outside EMI for, like, six hours and give my CDs to people in the industry. It did get to the point where I thought I wasn't going to make it.'

Entertainment lawyer Sarah Stennett (who also happened to be part of Sugababes' management team), an associate of the Jiant team, introduced Amelle and Samiya to A&R Worldwide, an artist-management group based in Beverly Hills, California. As Pete Kirtley explained, 'Sarah was blown away by Amelle and suggested we contact Sat Bisla (founder of A&R) with a view to signing in the US. During the following two years, we continued to write and produce an album's worth of material. We were very close to signing to three majors in the US and two in the UK, but timing and luck weren't on our side.'

At one point, Telstar – home to Mis-teeq and Artful Dodger – were interested in signing Boo 2, but the company went into liquidation. Amelle and Samiya remained hopeful. A&R Worldwide organised for Boo 2 to perform at a string of showcases in front of record-label executives. Though some companies expressed interest, it still failed to develop into any deals, but it was during one of their showcases in late 2003 that Sugababes' manager Mark Hargreaves saw the Berrabah sisters in action and was impressed.

After all the work with Jiant and A&M, interest in Boo 2 died down and the siblings returned home to Aldershot.

Although they were still trying to get signed with the record labels up in London, they were beginning to lose faith. Amelle said, 'There was some interest in America but it didn't work out. Nothing was happening – we'd had interest which had gone, and it was a bit like being on a rollercoaster. We were thinking about splitting up. I thought, God, I'm 21 now – I thought I'd be successful by now.' But little did she know that she was about to receive a call that would change her life forever.

CHAPTER 6

Sugababes: Ver 1.0

RON TOM HAD been managing Siobhan for two years when he discovered 13-year-old Mutya. Tom ran into Mutya's father Roberto in a supermarket and discovered they had talented teenagers in common. In a 2003 interview with *The Face* magazine, Siobhan joked, 'To this day I don't know how the f**k they got on to the subject of his daughter being able to sing.'

Despite the year age gap, in the initial stages, they appeared to get on well. Tom arranged for the girls to sing at a music-industry showcase, where they both sang a capella versions of Mariah Carey songs. In retrospect, Siobhan believed her performance was 'crap'. During her two years with Tom, she had slowly begun to grow in confidence with her singing, but soon realised she had a lot further to go after watching Mutya sing with self-belief. Siobhan admits, 'I used to get so nervous that I couldn't sing, my voice would just crack up. Mutya was like this fantastic, full-on R&B singer, but I'm not good under pressure. In my room, I could belt it out, but then put me in front of people and I just couldn't.'

The pair recorded a song called 'Do You Want To Date?' which Siobhan described as 'funky'.

Soon after, Mutya brought her 13-year-old school pal Keisha into the action. The three girls sang together for Tom and Sugababes were born. With three different-sounding and physically different singers, Tom realised he had found an original pop act which could really shake up the charts.

In 1997, the charts were dominated by the Spice Girls, All Saints and Boyzone. Although All Saints were a credible pop act, dancing and their looks played a part in their success, while Boyzone and the Spice Girls' image seemed to play a bigger role than the music, and, where they failed to win over music critics, they won over millions of fans. But Tom wanted an act which was about music over personalities and the mix of Keisha's Jamaican origins, Mutya's Irish-Filipino background and Siobhan's Irish heritage would make Sugababes a true representation of multi-cultural London. He was eager to rush the girls into the studio – but first he had to persuade the trio's parents that juggling school to make music was a worthwhile sacrifice.

Keisha admitted, 'Initially our parents were sceptical about us forming a group for real. It would be the last thing you'd want for your child, to see them suffering a breakdown or the other terrible things that can happen to kids in this business. But, once they met the good people we've got round us, they were chilled about it.'

After their parents gave permission, the recording studio became a part of the girls' daily lives. They would be picked up from Kingsbury High and Douay Martyrs, often by Keisha's mum, Beverley, and driven to the studio, where they would sing until the early hours. Keisha recalls, 'I remember going into the studio and literally leaving the studio at six o'clock in the morning … and going from the studio to school, leaving school, two hours afterwards, going back to those studios.'

But this was not forever and Ron Tom and the girls' parents made sure the girls did not overdo it. The trio were keen to record a single and release it immediately, but Tom assured them there was no rush and that they should take things slowly. In retrospect, Mutya knows he made the right decision: 'At the beginning, we were all like, "Let's do a single, let's do a single." But we were eased into it and, frustrating though that was at the time, it was the right time to come out – we wouldn't have been ready any earlier.'

During their studio time, Mutya and Keisha were isolating Siobhan with a made-up language called 'Ski', which they had been using since primary school. Over time, Siobhan learned to understand it, but couldn't speak it. While it was just a way for the girls to communicate secretly – a louder equivalent to whispers in the playground – the producers were unimpressed by their childish language and attempted to ban the bizarre speech. Mutya explains, 'It got banned from the studio because we were talking about our managers and our producers. One day they just came and said, "That's it, you're banned from the studio if you talk in that language." And we said, "OK" but then we carried on doing it and we got in trouble once, really badly.'

Despite teaching Siobhan how to understand it, Mutya and Keisha banned her from speaking their same language. Siobhan recalls, 'I wasn't allowed to talk it because I couldn't do it fast enough, and I'd let people in on how it was done. If they had something to say about someone, they would say it in "Ski" because they knew I could understand what they were saying. If they had anything to say about me, they would just come out and say it.'

While Tom thought he had found a harmonious group of girls, privately tensions were growing between Siobhan and Keisha. Despite their shared love of singing and the fact that both girls were raised as Christians, the two were very different. Siobhan had been brought up by both parents in affluent Ruislip, while Keisha's mother sometimes carried out two jobs as she raised her two children alone in tough Kingsbury. And, while Keisha loved listening to UK garage, R&B, hip-hop and gospel, Siobhan opted for the rockier sounds of Lenny Kravitz, Aerosmith, The Rolling Stones, The Beatles, The Kinks and The Who. Laidback Mutya was friends with both girls and, long after Siobhan left the group, she refused to badmouth her, and the two remain in contact to this day.

Siobhan revealed, 'I knew we weren't going to get on from the moment we met. After Keisha joined, it was always three's a crowd and I was always the one left out. We had nothing in common at all and we went on not to get on.'

On the flip side, Keisha believed Siobhan was jealous of her. In 2004, she told the *Mail On Sunday*, 'I think she holds it against me that I was in the band. I was reading a magazine when Mutya was in the studio singing. The manager asked me to sing something for him and he said, "Wow, I want you to get in and do this track today." I think she felt intimidated, like I was pushing in.'

After Siobhan's shock departure in August 2001, it was predominately Keisha who discussed her exit, while Mutya appeared reluctant to comment.

On the way to the studios, sweet-toothed Mutya and Keisha always insisted on stopping at the newsagent to pick up some sweets to give them energy for the gruelling recording sessions. Their love of candy inspired Tom to nickname the trio 'Sugar babies'. Although they didn't mind the name in the early days, when the time came for their demos to be shipped around record companies, the girls were looking far into the future and thought the name would sound too young a few years down the line. Keisha explains, 'Our manager used to always just say, "Ah, these are my little sugar babies." When we were about to get signed to the record company, we said, "Before you sign us, can you drop the 'babies' and keep it as the 'babes', so, when we get older, babes will be known as maybe not so cute, but sexy, more so than the babies part?"'

In a 2001 interview, Siobhan admitted she wasn't crazy about the name, explaining, 'It's supposed to present us as clean and fresh. Given the chance, we would call the band something else, something a bit more grown-up. But then again, The Beatles is a stupid name for a band. What does it mean? But now it's cool and credible.'

Mutya would also have changed the name if she could, but found a positive way to interpret its meaning. She said, 'We were young when we chose it. We had other names, but everyone liked the idea of Sugababes. It works in our favour because the music isn't poppy, but our actual name is quite poppy, young and girlie. But, when you hear us, you realise we're quite different. But we wouldn't choose the name now, definitely not. I thought of the name Q-Tz, pronounced "cuties". Everyone was like, "No, no, no." There were other names they came up with, too. I go on the internet a lot to chat to our fans and there are some girls in Germany and they kept emailing me, asking what names they could use and I just gave them Q-Tz. They said thank you and now they use the name Q-Tz.'

Meanwhile, back at school, the bandmembers were growing apart from their friends and missing out on regular teenage life, such as school discos and trips. Keisha was devastated when she went from being one of the leaders of the in-crowd to an outsider. Speaking in 2006, it's clear she hugely regrets missing out on her teen years and regularly urges her fans to stay in school: 'I sacrificed my childhood for the Sugababes. I missed out on doing all the things other kids my age took for granted, like going out and hanging around together. I missed the school discos and being able to see my friends from one day to the next. When they were going out places together, I was always working in a recording studio or catching up on my school work.'

As big sister to Dalisay and Ligaya, Mutya was

determined they would receive the full education she missed out on. She said, 'If my sister wanted to get into the music business now, I wouldn't let her. I don't think it's right when you're 12 or 13. We were working from that age and, although music is all I've ever wanted to do, it did take over the whole of my education.'

After creating around 60 demos and several albums, Tom shopped the recordings around to record companies and was delighted when London Records – home to his former act All Saints – agreed to sign Sugababes in 1998. Despite the fact Mutya, Keisha and Siobhan were young teenagers, they were fiercely independent and outspoken and objected to their studio roles of singers – they wanted in on more action. They convinced Tom and the producers they could write their own lyrics and so the Sugababes' songwriting method was born. Even now, the girl group admit they aren't involved on the instrumental side of their songs, but they play a huge part in the vocals and prefer to write their own lyrics.

When the group first launched in 2000, Siobhan praised their producers for giving them the opportunity to write: 'At first, we didn't realise we had writing ability. But in the past year the producers we've been working with have encouraged us to write our own material and we write everything now. We write about things people can relate to. "Overload" is about when life gets a bit mad and things get on top of you.'

The composition of 'Overload' was a mass of ideas in the studio and the outstanding track was composed in just two hours. Mutya recalled, 'On "Overload" I just threw in a few lines. It was easy. When people ask you what's "Overload" about, everyone says, "Ummmm." It's about feeling overloaded, either about school, boys or peer pressure, anything. Anything that's overloading you, that's what it's about. The producers said just throw in what words you can and we'll see what we can make out of it. The track was finished within two hours; that's why it sounds really raw.'

During their time in the studio, Sugababes recorded two other albums of material, which weren't deemed good enough for *One Touch*. Mutya believed the unreleased albums were 'Good, actually. Obviously, when you listen to it, our voices were a lot younger, but the actual lyrics and melodies and all that stuff was really good.'

Sugababes' fierce independence and refusal to become pop puppets unlike many groups before them impressed the executives at London. Introducing the band in industry bible *Billboard*, marketing director Randy Nichols enthused, 'We don't want them to get pigeonholed as a teen act because they're so much more than that. We don't want another bubblegum pop act.'

London bosses enrolled the writing and production skills of Cameron McVey, who produced the All Saints' eponymous debut album in 1997. McVey and the girls clicked immediately and he gave them the confidence to add their own input.

McVey brought his wife, singer Neneh Cherry, and their children down to the studio, much to Sugababes' delight. When the 'Buffalo Stance' pop star first walked into the studio, the girls were star-struck. Mutya recalls, 'Neneh Cherry came down to the studio a few times to say hello and see what we'd been up to. Cameron showed her the tracks of what we'd been doing and she loved it. When we came down first, we were like, "I can't believe it's Neneh Cherry." I used to listen to her when I was younger.'

Mutya calls McVey's style 'funky and different', adding, 'he listens to what we want to put into the music.'

Keisha enthused, 'Working with Cameron was funny, he's kind of like a big kid. He's not mature whatsoever.'

Seeing the music industry from the inside for the first time, Keisha admits she was young and naive; she had no idea so many pop acts were manufactured. She explained, 'When we first started, I just thought you wrote your own stuff. We assumed everyone did and it became a big deal: "Oh, they write their own stuff."'

With the group signed to London and their debut album beginning to take shape, the girls' home and school lives were becoming increasingly difficult. In total, they spent two years in the studio making demos and, eventually, *One Touch*, which left their school friends highly sceptical of their reason for staying away from the classroom. Keisha recalls, 'Some of the kids at school thought we were lying. They thought we were taking too long, never thought anything would come of it. They don't realise how much work goes into it.'

It was soon evident that the girls would have to leave school and have private tutors to help continue their education. Siobhan was in year nine when she left – when her friends were beginning to think about what GCSEs to take.

Sandra Khan, Mutya and Keisha's head of year at Kingsbury High, gave the pair permission to leave school early in year ten, when they were 15 years old. Khan had watched the girls' interest in music grow steadily from their first term at Kingsbury in autumn 1996. Mutya and Keisha were so focused on singing that they didn't pay much attention to other subjects, although Keisha admitted a fondness for drama. Khan said, 'It was obvious they were both going to end up in singing careers. They attended singing lessons outside of the school and neither of them was very academic. In fact, when I visited their primary school to see the children who would be moving up to the school, they both stood up and sang a song for me.'

Keisha remembers her last day at school very well. Like many teenagers, she found education boring and with her friends she loved to mock the teachers. When she realised she was going to leave school two years earlier than everyone else, she was ecstatic. After picking up the last of her books and projects, she strode out the front gates on to Roe Green Park, leaving her childhood behind. But, when she returned to Kingsbury High for a TV documentary in 2002, she revealed that she couldn't believe how blasé she was about ending an important part of her life: 'I remember the last day, when I finished school completely. I just kinda walked out and it didn't really faze me. But coming back has made me a tiny bit emotional because you don't enjoy it at the time when you're in high school. You think, I can't be bothered to do study.'

Keisha's mum, Beverley, made an effort to make sure she stayed in touch with her school friends and in between studio sessions regularly hosted sleepovers at their flat. Keisha said, 'My mum helped to make things fun for me and would let me have my friends over to stay.'

With school out of the way, Sugababes had more time to spend in the studio to concentrate on recording *One Touch*. At the same time, they had to be self-disciplined to study with their private tutors. While the girls were happy to be away from school, they desperately missed the social aspects. In February 2000 – six months before they would become 'proper pop stars' with the release of their first single – Keisha and Mutya got in touch with an old school teacher to ask if they could join their friends at the Valentine's Dance. Keisha said, 'One of the teachers said we couldn't go back to school for it. I just thought we could have gone back for one last time. There were times when our friends would call us up to tell us there was a party going on and we felt really frustrated because we couldn't go – sometimes it did feel like we were under house arrest. We used to moan and groan about it all the time. But we had to balance that against the fact that we were in the studio recording our first album and in rehearsals with our own band.'

While Mutya and Keisha were lamenting the loss of their social lives, Siobhan was attempting to balance studio duties with revising for her GCSEs, which took place in May and June that year – just three months before the Sugababes' debut single 'Overload' was released. For Siobhan, the fact that she was older than the other girls and was also studying for something as serious as GCSEs further isolated her from the band.

Keisha admitted she struggled with tutoring and didn't learn as much as she could have. She had a variety of tutors for her various subjects and claimed one of them used to give an option to study or to hang out and eat sweets. As a 15-year-old girl, Keisha would opt for fun. One afternoon, she was on her way home from a study session when she had a terrifying encounter with a male stranger. Young Keisha was walking through Kingsbury when she started to sense someone was following her. Despite feeling comfortable in her neighbourhood, she felt uneasy in the man's presence. Soon enough, he confronted Keisha and told her he had a knife. She recalled, 'He came up to me and, indicating he had a knife, said, "You'll only see it if I have to use it." He told me to give him my mobile phone and to pay for his train home. The guy wanted me to come back to his hotel but it wasn't a hotel, it was a block of flats. He said if I wanted my mobile back I had to go with him but I didn't care about the phone. It was really scary. We were together from one o'clock in the afternoon until eight o'clock at night. Eventually I got away.'

Keisha regrets that police never caught the man in question, but through local gossip she believes he was deported to his country of origin. But the incident left her fearful for years afterwards: 'It really shook me up and I had panic attacks for a year or two after.'

CHAPTER 7

Getting in (One) Touch with the Charts

WHEN THE RECORD executives at London listened to *One Touch*, they initially thought that 'One Foot In' should be the first release. While the track was a funky, R&B number that would appeal to the young music-buying public, it soon became clear that it was too pop. Instead, 'Overload' had to be the first single because it would set the group apart from current acts. Despite this, Mutya's favourite song on the album was 'One Foot In' because of 'the heavy bass lines'.

The charts of summer 2000 had been dominated by saccharine pop artists such as Ronan Keating, A1 and 5ive. Kylie Minogue made her chart comeback in *those* hot pants with 'Spinning Around'. Rock was nowhere to be seen (or heard) and Robbie Williams was the British music industry's biggest name. In terms of girl bands, the Spice Girls were on the verge of splitting and were preparing to release their last single 'Holler', while differences between members of the All Saints were bringing the group to breaking point. Heidi's old band Atomic Kitten were only in the early stages of their chart career, and had achieved a Number Six position with their second release 'See Ya' in April of that year. Meanwhile, Irish foursome B*Witched released 'Jump Down' in the same month – unbeknownst to them their last ever UK single – before going Stateside in a bid to break America. London bosses knew the time was right to introduce Sugababes' cool pop and had high hopes the trio would fill the space the All Saints would imminently be leaving.

Sixteen-year-old Siobhan and 15-year-olds Keisha and Mutya entered a London film studio just weeks before their debut single was due for release. The teenagers were excited and nervous; after all those years in the studio, they were finally getting the chance to star in a glamorous video shoot. Director Phil Poynter had a simplistic treatment for the video that complemented the record executives' wish for the focus to be on the music. The trio were each given a pile of clothes to wear in the video – Siobhan appeared to have the most costume changes with eight different tops. Over the course of several days, the girls mouthed the words to their song as they walked past the video camera. Poynter split the screen time between the girls singing their verses as individuals with the chorus sung by the trio sitting shoulder-to-shoulder while appearing to spin around on a turntable.

Keisha's excitement at starring in a pop video was obvious – the cute 15-year-old grinned more than her bandmates in the video and flashed the gap in her teeth several times. Mutya's serious face in the video was the starting-off point for her sulky, moody media persona, which the British press continued to perpetrate until her departure in December 2005. The 'Overload' video presented the girls with three personalities – Siobhan was the pretty one with her long, flowing red hair, giggly Keisha was the cute one and kohl-eyed Mutya the mysterious, moody one. When the video was shipped out to the terrestrial and cable channels, London Records and the girls waited in anticipation for the response.

The opening shot of the video introduced the song's infectious bass line over shadowed images of the girls' legs and torsos. Their age was not apparent until Siobhan stepped out of the shadows to sing the first verse. The video was well received by serious music fans and critics alike, with Scotland's *Sunday Herald* dubbing the promo 'a kind of subdued Gap advert, with a soupçon of United Colours of Benetton'. When the song was released to magazines and newspapers, London Records and the group were delighted by the critics' reviews, who hailed the song as 'teen pop it was cool to like'. But the biggest shock came when rock weekly *NME* named 'Overload' as single of the week. The *NME*'s critic April Long hailed the song as 'an irrepressible R&B/Pop crossover that bristles with class … the hauntingly infectious quality of this tune – its looped beats and soulful vocals unlike anything in recent memory'. *NME*, whose loathing for pop groups such as Steps, S Club 7 and Spice Girls is well documented, decided Sugababes were talented and credible, which gave their album selling power with 20-something serious music connoisseurs.

In September 2000, the single entered at Number Six,

quite a feat considering there hadn't been an influx of noisy promotion unlike so many other girl bands before them. The song remained in the charts for several months and sold over 138,000 copies – just 20,000 less than All Saints' debut 'I Know Where It's At'. In December 2000, the *Independent* named 'Overload' their top single of the year, beating Eminem's 'Stan' and Sugababes' label-mates All Saints' 'Black Coffee'. Besides their native Britain, the song was released in Europe, Japan and Australasia to varying degrees of success. New Zealand, Austria and Germany loved the song even more than the UK and sales brought 'Overload' to Numbers Two, Three and Three in each country's respective chart.

When the trio made their first appearance on BBC's seminal show *Top Of The Pops*, the too-cool-for-school, moody persona of the band appeared to continue. The girls' static stage performance and lack of dance moves were soon pointed out by the media, who were used to the hyperactive back flips and general jumping around by the Spice Girls, B*witched, S Club 7, Steps and similar acts. Their *TOTP* performance initially comprised of Mutya, Siobhan and Keisha seated on three high stools, with their video playing as a backdrop. The Sugababes would move their heads to the floor or the left, occasionally accompanied by crossing their legs. During the guitar instrumental towards the end of the song, the girls jumped off their stools and shook their hips in time to the drum beat.

Despite their brief dance, it was clear the girls were unused to performing in front of a TV audience. During Mutya's verses, she nervously fiddled with her hair and avoided looking into the camera. In truth, she was acting more in disbelief than anything else; since she was a little girl, she had dreamed about being on *TOTP* and she couldn't believe she was actually in BBC Television Centre's studio in Shepherd's Bush, west London. 'I grew up watching the programme,' she said. 'Ever since I was a baby, I wanted to go on it, and remember saying to my mum that I'm gonna make it on there one day. So the first time we did it was amazing. From watching it on the TV, you expect it to be a big stadium with different stages where the bands perform. It's actually really very small, but it's a comfortable place to be. When we go on *Top Of The Pops*, it makes us realise how lucky we are, that we've really arrived.'

Keisha remembers their performance vividly and cringes at the memory: 'I don't understand why we didn't smile. I remember being happy; we must have been really nervous or something – it was murder on the dance floor … horrible!'

While Mutya and Siobhan were happy to just sing, Keisha was dying to 'shake her booty' on stage. She admitted, 'They don't like dancing. I am actually quite different; I would love to do the whole Jennifer Lopez dance routine; that is my personality. But Siobhan and Mutya are more vocal based and don't like the whole dance-routine thing. I like doing that. So we just try to work out routines we can all do.'

Before she left the band, Siobhan admitted they still had a way to go with their stage confidence and presence: 'In the past, we have been concentrating on what our musical director has been telling us to do without being focused on what it looks like. Our record company say that the shows should be more visual, and they are probably right. It is not that we don't want to do dance routines and things – we make them up and then forget them or get them wrong.'

After the good response to their debut single, London released the album *One Touch* on 27 November 2000. The group was thrilled when the disc followed in the footsteps of 'Overload' and again wowed the critics. The *Guardian*'s Betty Clarke praised the music, but urged the moody teenagers to lighten up: 'Sugababes should really cheer up, though, because *One Touch* is a fantastic album that encapsulates the sound of young America with enough style, attitude and originality to mesmerise us all. The kids are all right.'

The *Sunday Mirror*'s Ian Hyland gave the album 9/10, declaring, 'All Saints can go off and have their babies. The future of funky British R&B is safe.'

The *Independent*'s Tim Perry wrote, 'It's about time a half-decent pure-pop album got released, and over a dozen songs that jump playfully between upbeat R&B, poppy soul and groove-laden ballads, these three London schoolgirls have achieved it. What's more, they can actually sing.'

And their musical superiority to the Spice Girls was cemented in print when *Sunday Times* critic Mark Edwards proclaimed, 'Keisha, Mutya and Siobhan already possess a maturity and musical proficiency that the (relatively ancient) Spice Girls have yet to attain.'

When the album was released in the United States eight months later, music bible *Rolling Stone* journalist Aidin Vaziri wrote, 'The music on *One Touch* still remains vital and raw; like a downtown version of TLC or All Saints without the gargantuan studio budget. Lead-off track "Overload" is a pulsating, cool-headed R&B concoction, while the title track sounds more deep, down and dirty than anything that has appeared on pop radio in recent memory.'

Much to their chagrin, Sugababes were being compared to a whole host of other girl groups. Mutya was desperate for the girls to be seen as a completely new and original act. She explained, 'We are getting compared with Spice Girls, All Saints, TLC ... They're all great, talented groups, but at the same time we would rather hear, "Here's the Sugababes", not "Here's the new All Saints". We don't mind being compared. The All Saints are very talented; they brought a lot of attention to British music. They weren't doing pop; they were doing a mixture of R&B, a bit of indie, a bit of Miami Bass, which I love. But All Saints and us are nothing alike. We worked with the same producers and we were in the same record company, that's all it was.'

Siobhan remained diplomatic about her label-mates, who were just on the verge of imploding in February 2001. She remarked, 'I think we're coming out with something different so there's an opening in the market for us. I think All Saints are great because they have a really wide audience. That's what we're trying to do, not go for one specific market. We want to be a credible band. Serious reviews do mean more than reviews in pop magazines because we don't just want to be performers; we want to be known as singers.'

It was clear that Mutya wasn't so impressed with the comparison to the Spice Girls, whose singing skills have long been questioned. In late 2001, she said, 'We've met every single one of the Spice Girls except for Mel C. They're really nice people. I didn't listen to them too much when I was younger because I wasn't into pop music; I loved R&B, soul singers. But they're really talented. I wasn't a proper fan, I didn't go out and buy their singles. My sisters did.'

Sugababes ended up sharing many a stage with Melanie 'Scary Spice' Brown and Emma 'Baby Spice' Bunton at summer festivals in 2001.

While critical reaction to the album was positive, and generally expressed amazement that such young girls had creatively contributed towards it, a frequent question was, 'What do these 16-year-olds know about love?' Despite the dominant love theme, many of the tracks made references to their ages, singing about cutting class and wanting to 'hang out' with their friends. 'Look At Me' was addressed to the girls' parents. The song was Keisha and Siobhan's favourite on the album because, according to Siobhan, 'it was the first thing that we wrote together', adding that the song was about 'dealing with parents smothering you a bit'. In defence of the relationship issues addressed on the album, Mutya said, 'If you're a teenager, you go through drama every single day, as much as an older person goes through in a year. So there's a lot to write about. Our main problems are falling out with each other, boys and going out too much with friends.'

Asked why they thought the album was so well received, Siobhan reasoned, 'The album is so diverse because, between the three of us, there are a lot of different musical ideas. We write about things people can relate to. "Overload" is about when life gets a bit mad and things get on top of you.'

When *One Touch* hit the record store shelves on 27 November it proved to be a slow seller, much to the record company's chagrin. On Sunday, 3 December, the Official Chart Company released the rundown and *One Touch* had missed out on the charts. Despite the good reviews by respected broadsheet critics and *NME*, it seemed the teen audience was the stronger force in the album market at that time and had barely heard of Sugababes. Hoping to gain publicity in a bid to boost album sales, the group's second single 'New Year' was pitted against Westlife's 'What Makes A Man', Bob The Builder's 'Can We Fix It' and *Big Brother* winner Craig Phillips's 'At This Time Of Year' for the coveted Christmas Number One spot. The Sugababes wrote the song with McVey, Matt Rowe, Jony 'Rockstar' Lipsey, Felix Howard and Paul Simm. Mutya, in particular, enjoyed her working relationship with former Spice Girls' songwriter Rowe, admitting, 'He's so lovely. He's really easy to work with and he knew what we liked.'

The video followed a similar premise to 'Overload' and featured the girls once again in a simplistic studio. Director Alex Hamming filmed the trio in black and white, but injected some colour with computer graphics of butterflies, snowflakes and letters. As with 'Overload' and their subsequent TV performances, the girls remained fairly static – either seated or standing. Much to Mutya's annoyance, all three were dressed as 20-somethings, with skinny jeans and high-heel stiletto boots. And, the following year, when the girls were dropped by London Records, they moaned about how much control the label had over their dress sense. When they signed with Universal's Island Records, a defiant

Mutya swore she would never wear pointed shoes again. In a 2002 interview, she said, 'In the beginning, clothing was pushed on to you. With the pointy shoes – I can't actually wear pointy shoes, before I hated them. I used to cry over it, I'd be shouting, "No, I don't want to wear it!" Because I was forced into it, I really disliked it, but now it's much better because it's our decision of what we wanna wear.'

The song was held up as a rare example of a good Christmas song, which avoided the expected cheesy lyrics. The *Independent*'s critic Tim Perry wrote, 'These teenage Londoners present another minor shock with a seasonal ballad that doesn't irritate. This largely acoustic and soulful number bears their hallmarks of tight production and three good voices (that's three more than the Spice Girls ever had).'

Bob The Builder went on to claim the top spot that Christmas, but 'New Year' entered the charts at Number 12 and sold 75,000 copies during its four-week run in the Top 40. In comparison, Bob The Builder sold 1.1 million copies – the girls didn't have a chance against the BBC merchandising machine. Mutya was stunned by the sales and, as a practising Christian, questioned why a non-Christmas song was at the top of the charts during the season. She said, 'We wrote New Year as a Christmas song, because there aren't many Christmas songs around any more. In England, Bob The Builder came out at the same time and it was Number One. It just proves England isn't very Christmassy any more. It also proves crap sells … whoever thought Bob The Builder would be Christmas Number One? We thought it could have done better.'

While 'New Year' failed to reach the Top 10, the

Christmas Number One competition spread word of Sugababes' existence and 'One Touch' finally entered the charts at Number 67 on 17 December. *Sunday Mirror* critic Ian Hyland gave the girls another boost by placing the album on his 'Hits Of The Year' recommendations, adding, 'All Saints are sweating already.'

On 15 January 2001, it was announced that 'Overload' had been nominated for Best British Single at the Brit Awards. While the Brit nomination was a boost for the band, the girls had stern competition against Coldplay's 'Yellow', Craig David's '7 Days', David Gray's 'Babylon', Moloko's 'The Time Is Now', Sonique's 'It Feels So Good', Spiller's 'Groovejet (If This Ain't Love)', All Saints' 'Pure Shores' and Robbie Williams' 'Rock DJ'. Even at the tender age of 16, realist Keisha knew their debut didn't stand a chance – the winner being decided by radio listeners. The three teenagers were more thrilled to find they would be sharing the red carpet with a host of A-list stars, including their idols Destiny's Child and Kelis. Keisha recalls, 'I wasn't that excited when we got nominated for a Brit Award; it was more that we were getting the chance to go to the Brit Awards. The worst thing was that I got chicken pox on the day, and the spots just kept spreading from my back to my arms during the night – by the end my face was covered in them.'

Despite Keisha's illness, the teenagers were ecstatic to be part of the biggest music event of the year. As they sat with their manager and London Records' executives, they watched in awe as Destiny's Child, Robbie Williams, Eminem, Coldplay, Westlife, Sonique and Craig David performed on stage. Former Spice Girl Geri Halliwell stunned the audience with her svelte yoga-toned body when she presented Williams – her then-rumoured lover – with the Best British Male Artist gong, while Eminem shocked everyone with an expletive-laden rendition of 'The Real Slim Shady' while brandishing a chainsaw. As Keisha predicted, the group lost out in the single category to Williams's 'Rock DJ' – one of three awards he won that February night. But the nod from Brit bosses was enough for Mutya: 'It was really nice to be nominated with the likes of Robbie Williams. We didn't win but we were in the same class, which was so exciting.'

While the group missed out on a trophy, it was clear that the nomination boosted sales of their album and 'One Touch' reached Number 26 on 11 February – just two weeks before the awards ceremony. Just days after the Brit nominations were released, the British Phonographic Industry (BPI) confirmed the album had sold over 100,000 copies and the group were awarded a gold disc. The girls were elated and proudly took their gleaming discs to their parents to be hung on the walls at home with pride. The album went on to sell 216,000 copies.

Meanwhile, great changes were taking place at London Records' headquarters in west London. Previously an independent label, London merged with WEA Records on 16 February. While Sugababes kept the same A&R team, they soon found new faces in the marketing, promotional and press departments. Sugababes were now sharing a label with Cher, Enya, Catatonia and The Pretenders. WEA Records' managing director John Reid was now in charge of London as well. The label's parent company Warner Music

UK released a press statement heralding the union of WEA and London, but announced that regrettably there would be some job losses. London Records' chairperson Tracy Bennett said at the time, 'This is a fabulous opportunity for everyone involved.'

The same month, London Records' biggest act All Saints announced they were going 'on ice' after differences surfaced, with the Appleton sisters on one side, and Shaznay Lewis and Melanie Blatt on the other.

London knew they needed to step their publicity machine up a gear. Instead of trying to get the group into the newspapers, the press would come to the Sugababes. A special one-off gig was scheduled at the Notre Dame Hall, a small dance venue in 5 Leicester Place, just off Leicester Square in London. On 29 March, journalists from British newspapers and magazines joined Sugababe fan-club members and winners of an *NME* competition to watch the girls prove their vocals weren't just studio trickery. Because the gig was a private party, not a regular concert, it meant they could perform at Notre Dame Hall with no legal problems. The venue had a licensed bar and with the girls aged between 15 and 16 years old, they were still two years shy of legal drinking age, so the bar was closed for the night. Getting ready backstage, the Sugababes were incredibly nervous. They knew the press had been thrilled with their album and the Brit nomination had shown them they were obviously accepted by the music industry. While years in the studio had been relaxing and fun, the three would be up on stage with their four-piece band showcasing their vocal talents in just under an hour. If they messed up in the studio, they could simply go for another take, but the performances that night had to be spot-on. Not only were there critics from broadsheets such as the *Independent* and the *Guardian* in the audience, but the notoriously hard-to-please *NME* was also represented.

The group's stylist put the kibosh on any of the girls' wishes to flash the flesh – the awaiting media would be quick to accuse the record company of child exploitation if the Sugababes were presented with a sexy image. All three were given jeans to wear, while Siobhan wore a slinky grey top, and Keisha and Mutya were in black. As usual, the girls were given funky pointed stiletto boots again, despite Mutya's hatred of them.

Finally, the curtain rose and the girls strode on stage, singing 'Look At Me'. The song had been chosen for two reasons: the title of the track was exactly what Sugababes and their management wanted the media to do – look at them and take notice. But also the lyrics conveyed that the girls acknowledged their youth, but were making decisions on their own. Members of the audience quickly picked up on the girls' anxiety, which only began to subside when they performed 'Overload' – their most successful single to date and the one they had sung in public most often. The *Guardian*'s John Aizlewood commented the trio 'looked petrified … as they should', while the *Independent*'s Fiona Sturges wrote, 'During their first couple of songs, they exuded awkwardness and, at times, unadulterated fear.'

It appeared the group's choreography from their first *Top Of The Pops* performance remained the same and they repeated their stool routine for 'Overload'. Sturges noted the 'half-hearted choreography', but praised their 'pitch-perfect' harmonies. Aizlewood also noticed the group were 'not natural movers', but suggested Mutya had some body rhythm.

The *Observer*'s Akin Ojumu noted, 'On the evidence of tonight, Keisha is the most natural and confident performer and Siobhan is the most bashful.'

The media agreed the girls could sing and, much to the delight of London Records, put great emphasis on the fact that the trio contributed to the album's songwriting. Aizlewood told *Guardian* readers to give the girls a bit more time to gain stage confidence, declaring 'time is on their side', while Sturges said, 'They are a perfectly adequate band who need a few more years before they can be called a great band.'

Following the Notre Dame Hall gig, the record label scheduled further appearances in small venues around the UK in conjunction with *NME*.

While her bandmates liked listening to garage and R&B – music that was dominating the charts at the time – Siobhan was much more interested in rock and loved raiding her parents' record collection when she was back home in Ruislip. She said, 'We were very lucky that the tour was done in conjunction with *NME* and it meant that we were playing to an older audience. We never set out to appeal to under-10s. If we manage to incorporate even a hint of that in our own music, we should appeal to quite an adult audience.'

Despite their growing gig experience, the Sugababes' stage presence still failed to match their powerful vocals.

sugababes

Siobhan admitted they knew they needed to improve their performance techniques: 'We were all very nervous at all the gigs, but that was just because we were so worried about it going well. We would love a huge budget to go out on tour, but I don't think that necessarily means doing a big production show like S Club 7 or someone. We would just concentrate on what it sounds like, but it would be nice to have some cool lighting or something. I love doing intimate gigs and performing with a band. When we played Ronnie Scott's earlier this year, it just felt brilliant. If it's a really good performance you remember nothing of it – it feels like it last for three seconds.'

CHAPTER 8

Situation's Heavy

EVEN THOUGH LONDON Records was disappointed with UK sales of *One Touch*, across Europe the album was getting a good response. The disc reached Number Seven in the German charts, Six in Austria and Eight in Poland and Switzerland. The company decided to schedule a huge promotional tour of Europe in the spring, before bringing the girls to Australasia and Asia the summer after Mutya and Keisha had sat their GCSEs.

Although the Sugababes were pretty recognisable in Britain, they were stunned to find hordes of German fans waiting for them when they arrived in Berlin that April 2001. Much as she loved her German fans, Mutya admitted she found the attention a bit too much. She said, 'Everyone's quite mad over there. Hearing the German girls and boys singing our songs, even though they don't speak English, it's quite mad. You go to the airport in Germany and everyone's screaming. When we get back to London, no one cares, everyone's like, "It's the Sugababes – let's walk off."'

Keisha agreed, 'Our first ever album wasn't that successful in the UK – even though it was critically acclaimed – whereas in Germany our album was burning up, it was huge. So when we went over to Germany we'd be treated like stars – you know, screaming fans everywhere. Then when we came over to the UK, no one cared. People would just walk past us; no one knew who we were.'

While Keisha lapped up the attention, one of their German gigs was steadily going down in Siobhan's personal history as her worst ever concert. She said, 'When you are on stage you don't hear or see that much of the audience and it is sometimes difficult to tell whether anyone is enjoying it or not. If people don't like it, I find it really dispiriting and heartbreaking. There was one show in Germany where we were playing to this seated audience in an amphitheatre-like situation, and there seemed to be absolutely no reaction at all. Then when we finished the show everyone told us how great it was – that felt like the worst gig, though.'

Out of all the girls, Mutya loved travelling the most. She had seen a lot of Europe during her childhood performances with her dad and especially enjoyed Germany and Switzerland.

Siobhan, meanwhile, was slowly cultivating a love for Spain, which would play a crucial part in her solo career two years later. In a 2001 interview, she said, 'We've recently been to Spain and I really enjoyed it. I was learning Spanish at school and I definitely want to learn it fluently. It's very interesting to see me going to Spain and *trying* to speak Spanish.'

The girls' age was also hindering their chance of huge success – Mutya didn't turn 16 until May 2001, which meant that legally she couldn't work more than 72 days a year. While the girls didn't realise the pressure the record company was under to deliver huge sales, they were enjoying living the pop-star lifestyle on a part-time basis. At the time, 16-year-old Keisha said, 'We get weekends off and everything else – we only work twice a week. And if there is a showbiz party at a bar, we can't go because it is over 18. We think, Oh, no one's going to know, but they do, so we just can't risk it.'

At the tender age of 16, Keisha was starting to feel insecure about her body. She still had a bit of puppy fat and wasn't as slim as Siobhan and Mutya. For two weeks, she attempted a crash diet, without her mother's, her manager's or her tutors' knowledge, until her body reacted in a painful way. She recalled, 'I didn't eat hardly anything for about two weeks. I had a slice of bread a day, and that was it. I was getting private tuition. My teacher had left the house and I felt a sharp pain in my stomach. I was in pain for eight hours. I had to wait for my mum to come back. I tried to call an ambulance and reached for the phone but it dropped on the floor and I couldn't move from the spot. I was screaming the house down, it was horrible. I thought I was going to die. I don't know why I was doing it – I wanted a flat stomach or something like that.'

Distinctly unimpressed, Keisha's mother sternly told her she was beautiful and she had no reason to diet, but the pain she had experienced was enough the put her off dieting for life.

Having started to study A-levels with her private tutors following the release of 'Overload', Siobhan decided to drop her education in early 2001. Besides finding the travelling and performing quite tiring, the pretty 16-year-old had also found love for the first time with Ted May – nine years her senior and a producer who worked at London Records' parent company Warner. Though the controversial relationship was kept secret from the media, Siobhan openly discussed May when she launched her solo career two years later. She admits news of their coupling was not well received by executives at the record label, smirking, 'We met when I was a Sugababe. He got into a lot of trouble for shagging the artist.'

Despite her joy at being paid to sing and falling in love, Siobhan was beginning to doubt her talent. 'I felt like I had no talent. I thought I couldn't sing and that I was in this band because I'd never be able to make it on my own.' She also began to grow further apart from Mutya and Keisha – their age gap seemed huge because they were still studying for their GCSEs while she had ended her education and was in her first adult relationship. In a 2003 interview with the *Observer*, she said, 'We didn't have a laugh, we didn't go out together as a band. I was trying to enjoy myself, but everyone else made it so complicated. Being one of three sisters, I'm used to two ganging up on one. But at home I always knew the dynamic would change, it was never the same two. In Sugababes, it was always those two and then me. I was bewildered. Why couldn't we all just get on? Travelling the world, why couldn't it have been fun?'

The promotional tours of Europe were exhausting and homebody Siobhan desperately missed her family. 'I suppose it's all come as a bit of a shock because being in the studio is quite chilled out,' she said. 'You're just hanging around, writing songs and singing, and you're alone there. You've got no idea about the TV or all the publicity, and all the travelling around and really the work bit of it. Being in the studio wasn't really work, it was more like fun.'

But, whenever she did return home to Ruislip, Siobhan was stunned to find a negative response from some of her old school friends. She said, 'I have got three best mates from school who I've known since I was four, who don't see what we are doing as a big deal – they treat me no different. But there are some people who I went to school with, who recognise me and stuff, and can be really mean. There's this one person who calls me the "Sugabitch". Other people became jealous and were bitchy. They said we would never make it and called us names. But the way I look at it, they were never true friends in the first place if that's how they act now. I suppose you could say we have grown up a lot and very quickly because of what we have been through. We have had to.' Despite the bad reaction from some old pals, Siobhan's closest friends Zoë, Amy, Shona and Bell treated her as usual. During her rare time off, Siobhan would rush home to Ruislip to drink in local pubs with her girlfriends.

After spending three years away from school, Keisha was also feeling abandoned by her friends. She too was stunned by the negative reception she received when she met up with her old school gang back in Kingsbury: 'I don't think people knew how to relate to us. Friends would say, "Why am I not being mentioned in all your interviews?" And I would say "hi" and "bye" to them. Without wishing to sound snobby, I more or less only know 22- or 23-year-olds now. Because we left school and got private tuition, we completed our education, but we didn't get to develop with the rest of our friends. You make sacrifices. We left school at 14 and had private tuition, so we've lost our teenage years. I used to be really popular at school 'cause I had a big mouth and I'm really bossy. But I haven't got any friends now 'cause they all became really jealous of me. I don't keep best friends – isn't that really sad?'

On the album sleeve of *One Touch*, Keisha wrote, 'To all the haters … nothing.' She explained, 'After I left school, people were kind of like that with the success of the Sugababes; they would say to me that I would never make it and I never would amount to anything. So that was not a new message to them, but just a message to people in general that have anything negative to say about me or the group.'

While Keisha became estranged from her school friends, Mutya managed to keep hold of her childhood relationships – even though they shared mutual friends. Mutya said, 'In the beginning of the Sugababes, my friends were like, "You're lying. Why aren't you in school?" Everyone was like, "Come back to school, nothing's going on." Then a few months later, "Overload" came out and everyone was really supportive, everyone stuck by me. So I haven't lost anyone. You find out who your friends are. But everyone I know has always stuck by me and bought the singles and the albums.'

But Keisha was also feeling emotionally low. She was struggling to adapt to growing up in the public eye and the lack of support from her friends made her feel lonely. While Mutya had a huge family and circle of friends to rely on, Keisha was feeling increasingly isolated. She started to sink into a depression, which would last for nine months. Despite travelling all over Europe to perform in front of thousands, she was crying almost all the time. She couldn't put her finger on it; she had fantasised about being a singer since she was a little girl and now she was living the dream and she wasn't happy.

In July 2004, Keisha went public about her battle with the blues in an interview with the *Mail On Sunday*. She explained, 'It was probably going on from when I was about 16 and lasted for about nine months. I just kept crying all the time but I felt I couldn't say anything about it, and bottling it up only made things worse. When you are taken away from certain things, from normal life, when you are younger, it does something to you. I think we were much too young. My friends weren't speaking to me any more because they couldn't accept what I was doing. Me and Mutya never really told anyone that we were in a group, and when we got on TV, that's when everyone saw us and said, "You aren't going to make it, you aren't gonna be anything." The relationship between Mutya and I was changing too. Obviously when you grow up you turn into different people, but I wanted everything to stay the same. By the time I was 17 years old I was very depressed, suicidal, if I'm honest. There were moments when I would think stupid things to myself. I would think, "If I just put this pillow over my head or sleep with it over my head what would happen, what if?"'

Despite her sadness, Keisha put on a professional face during the group's gigs and TV appearances, leaving her bandmates, management and record label ignorant of her problems.

After the jump in album sales in January 2001, London Records decided to release the single 'Run For Cover' in April. The trio were given the chance to show off their urban side in the dark, gritty video, which clearly had a bigger budget than previous promos. Following the formula from earlier videos, Mutya, Keisha and Siobhan spend most of the video apart, singing their verses in the back seat of a cab, a London subway or on a sofa at a house party. Unlike previous tracks, in this song Siobhan does not have a solo section. When the girls performed the song on *Top Of The Pops* and *T4*, it was clear they were growing more confident with performing. They danced throughout the song, with Keisha showing extra enthusiasm during her solos. Halfway through, Keisha and Mutya drop to their knees for Keisha's second solo in the track, leaving Mutya to ad lib in between verses. Siobhan is left to awkwardly dance by herself – an early sign to onlookers that all was not well in camp Sugababes.

The same month 'Run For Cover' was released, Sugababes won their first award. Listeners of London radio station Capital 95.8FM voted them Pop's Best Kept Secret on 11 April. After they accepted their glass trophy, the girls were ushered into the pressroom to pose for photos.

Dropping their usual sullen glares, Sugababes couldn't stop smiling with glee as they tightly clutched their gong. The question was: who was going to go home with it? After their win, the teenagers socialised with fellow stars Craig David (who picked up two awards that night), Ronan Keating, Westlife, The Corrs, The Bee Gees and Dido.

Following the ceremony, Keisha and Mutya took time out to revise for their GCSEs. Siobhan, who had seriously begun to question why she was in the band, welcomed the break from them. While Keisha and Mutya crammed, she was able to relax with her friends and boyfriend Ted, and do the occasional interview for radio stations or press. Siobhan barely saw the girls except for the odd photo shoot, but they spent the day together on 25 May when they recorded the video for their fourth single 'Soul Sound' – which would be Siobhan's last single with the band. The group were booked to perform at a string of festivals over the summer so it was up to Siobhan to fulfil the group's press duties. In an interview with Scotland's *Sunday Herald*, she said, 'It's been fairly quiet recently, but it usually is between singles. The other two have been doing their exams, and I have been doing some interviews for newspapers and magazines abroad. Apart from the video for "Soul Sound", we have not been doing too much together.' Without giving away too much detail of how unhappy she really was, she hinted at the strain between bandmembers to the *Sunday Herald*, saying, 'We all have other interests as well. I'm really into photography, Mutya is interested in make-up and styling, and Keisha is interested in cinematography. But I think we are much

77

closer now as a group because we spend so much time together. Of course we have arguments, but it is usually when we are tired and ratty and never about anything important. We are more like sisters now than friends.'

'Soul Sound' was a real change in pace from the other songs on the album. The vocals were more dominant than the instruments and, after taking a back seat in 'Run For Cover,' Siobhan was given the chance to show off her skills. The song was written and produced by Ron Tom, who had discovered Siobhan five years earlier.

Max & Dania were enlisted to direct the video by the group's record label. The promo was set in a funky apartment, with the girls' 'souls' drifting out of their bodies as they listen to the music. Now she was 17, Siobhan's 'pretty girl' image was taken up a gear and she spent the video perched on a cabinet in a tiny mini-skirt and high heels, swinging her legs in time with the music. Mutya lay on a comfy brown sofa as she listened intently to the music in her headphones, while Keisha relaxed on a beanbag on the floor. Gradually the music spills out of the apartment on to the floor below and suddenly everyone on the street below is dancing to the 'Soul Sound'.

But the Sugababes' festival run in 2001 started off badly. The girls were booked to share the stage with Westlife, Blue, Hear'Say, 5ive, Damage and Atomic Kitten, at the 'Irn-Bru Live 'n' Loud' festival at Bellahouston Park in Glasgow, Scotland on 17 June. Just two days before, the organisers were forced to cancel the event because heavy rain had left the venue waterlogged. A week later, Sugababes joined Wyclef Jean, Outkast, Usher, Mis-teeq,

Muse and Emma Bunton at the BBC Radio 1 'One Big Sunday' event at Manchester's Heaton Park. It was the first time the girls had performed to such a large audience – there were thousands of screaming teenagers in the audience. In the press tent before the gig, the three posed for the throngs of paparazzi. It was clear that Siobhan felt segregated from her bandmates. Photos taken that day show Mutya and Keisha cuddled together, just as you would expect from old school friends, while Siobhan is further away from the camera, tucked behind the other two and looking unhappy.

Over the year, the girls had slowly been getting used to meeting celebrities, but this time they were sharing the stage with their idols – they all loved Jean and his former band The Fugees, while Siobhan enjoyed the rockier sounds of Muse. Towards the end of the free event, the group performed 'Overload' and 'Soul Sound' and it seemed to go down well with the audience. Reports at the time claimed a man was arrested following the sound of a gunshot towards the end of the gig, but no follow-up information was released to confirm this.

The following weekend, Sugababes cemented the beginning of a beautiful friendship with their gay fans and performed at the Mardi Gras in Finsbury Park, north London, which took place after the annual Gay Pride March through central London. But the group were unsure how they would be received at a high-profile gig, where the majority of the crowd would be waiting for Steps and Belinda Carlisle. Much to their delight, everyone loved Sugababes even more than their chart rivals Atomic Kitten.

Yahoo! Launch critic Jamie Gill approved: 'They are stupidly young, but their music has a sultry maturity that their rivals can only dream of. "Run For Cover" is a dreamy, dubby wonder and the crowd screams appreciation.'

On 7 July, Sugababes made their most high-profile performance to date. The girls had secured a slot on the star-studded bill at Party In The Park for The Prince's Trust in London's Hyde Park, where they would sing in front of Prince Charles. They sang in front of a 100,000-strong audience, as well as millions of TV viewers, on the same stage as Ricky Martin, Shaggy, Destiny's Child, Usher, Wyclef Jean, Sisqo, Craig David, Eddy Grant, Geri Halliwell, A1 and Atomic Kitten, among others. But it was Geri Halliwell and Atomic Kitten who managed to attract the big press. The former Spice Girl's svelte frame in her tiny black leotard and onstage cavorting with her sexy female dancers guaranteed Halliwell the front pages, while Atomic Kitten member Jenny Frost caused a furore when she forced an 'I love AK' T-shirt on to Prince Charles's chest.

When 'Soul Sound' was released on 16 July, the re-energised and refocused Sugababes were ready to really put everything into the group. Keisha and Mutya had finished their education for good, while Mutya finally turned 16 in May, meaning Sugababes could work full-time.

Keisha admitted her GCSEs had been quite a struggle: 'It was pretty tough to find time to go over our notes but we came up with a quick and easy way. Me and Mutya had small reminder cards with our notes scribbled on them. We carried them everywhere and looked at them whenever we had a spare few minutes. We had study leave but it was difficult because we were knackered from travelling or doing photo shoots. Siobhan tested us when she could. I took six GCSEs and Mutya five. They went OK but I'm glad they're over.'

The pair were delighted when their management told them they had planned a tour of Australia, New Zealand and Japan for August, which meant they would be thousands of miles away from home – and their parents – when the GCSE results arrived. Before receiving her results, confident Mutya said, 'If the results are bad, at least we're away. But we think we've done OK.'

Behind closed doors, Siobhan was battling with her feelings, unsure if she should stay or go. While she was getting the chance to travel to countries she had never been to before, her closest friends were planning their first package holiday without adults and she felt she was missing out. Her friends were also preparing for their final year of A-levels and planning what universities they were going to apply to. After the release of 'Soul Sound' and their Asia-Pacific promotional tour, there were plans for Sugababes to go to New York, and to start work on their second album in the New Year. But Siobhan managed to keep up the charade of planning for the future and enthused about what the group would be doing next to the world's press. 'We will be going over to Australia, New Zealand and Japan; we will be travelling and playing on the radio circuit,' she revealed. 'After that, we will be going after America – we really think we've got what it takes to succeed where others have failed.'

When the single was released, the cover image was

telling of the relationships in the band. Keisha and Mutya sat on a bench together, facing one another and smiling, while Siobhan was isolated from her bandmates on a higher seat, without eye contact.

The song entered the UK singles chart at Number 30 on 22 July, but the record company was not happy: after spending £2 million on Sugababes and the festival dates over the summer, 'Soul Sound' had performed way below expectations. Then, the following week, it slipped down to 52 and then out of the charts altogether by the beginning of August. For a whole year, the group had been in the public eye but, despite the impressive reviews, Sugababes were yet to taste true success.

A year later, Keisha claimed the group attempted to discourage the label from releasing 'Soul Sound' as a single: 'We didn't want to release our final single from *One Touch* because we knew it wasn't what the kids wanted to hear. It wasn't upbeat, it was too mature. The record company were trying too hard to keep us cool and we looked too moody. They just went ahead and released it. Then it flopped.'

CHAPTER 9

Sayonara, Siobhan

ONE TOUCH WAS quietly released in the United States in July 2001 on London's sister label London-Sire and went on to sell only 1,000 copies. To break the States, British artists need to be prepared to travel the length and breadth of the country, talking to regional radio stations and newspapers, as well as nationwide magazines. It's a long and gruelling task, but, if successful, the large financial benefits are clear to see.

Although many British pop stars would love to break America – Sugababes being no exception – they need to neglect their fans at home and abroad while they attempt to conquer the huge market. To achieve success in America, Craig David spent nearly two years away from the UK. Some have blamed his time away for the lacklustre sales of his second album *Slicker Than Your Average*, which sold 520,000 copies in Britain, compared to the 1.8 million sales of his debut *Born To Do It*. For Irish group B*witched, their trip Stateside coincided with the end of their success in the UK and Ireland. After two years in the European charts, they went to America in 2000 and devoted nearly two years to cracking the market there. Their albums *B*witched* and *Awake And Breathe* went platinum and gold respectively in the US, but they never had another success back home.

In summer 2001, Sugababes had plans to go to America at the end of the year. This seemed optimistic because London Records were coming to terms with the sales performance of *One Touch*, for which they had high hopes. Despite the promotion and good reviews in the UK, *One Touch* had failed to sell – could the label afford to make the same losses in such a tough territory as the States?

In August, the girls flew Down Under to formally introduce themselves to the Australian and New Zealand market. The countries had responded fairly well to the Sugababes' album and singles, considering the lack of promotion until their visit. 'Overload' reached Number Two in New Zealand – its highest chart position in the world – and Number 27 in Australia. New Zealand music fans were so enamoured with the song that it remained in the charts for an amazing 17 weeks, while Australians kept buying it for 12 weeks. 'New Year' failed to chart in both countries, while 'Soul Sound' was not released in New Zealand at all. When the girls arrived in Sydney, their most recent release – 'Run For Cover' – was given a boost by their presence and climbed to Number 36.

The Sugababes had never before been so far away from home and would have loved to explore Sydney and the surrounding country, but, in the few days they had before flying on to Auckland, it was work, work, work. Mutya enthused, 'We didn't know how far "Overload" was gonna go and we didn't realise it was going to go all the way around the world. Coming to Australia is really good because we get to see the world, get to see the countries and get to meet the people and the fans. We've been to New York, all around Europe. Getting the chance to come to Australia and do all this promotion is really cool.'

By this point, Siobhan's isolation from the band was at its worst. The constant interviews and promotion were not what she had dreamed about as a young girl. Siobhan wanted to be a singer and, despite her stage fright, she loved performing and recording in the studio. She found the promotional side boring and was feeling the pressure from the label over their album sales. But, in interviews, the girls were defensive of finding fame at such a young age and reassured the media they could cope with the pressure. Mutya said, 'It is hard work, but, if you have a strong mind, things seem to go faster and you don't get as much pressure as some people think you have. I love singing; this is my job.'

Next stop Auckland, New Zealand's biggest city. After experiencing the relatively warm temperatures of Sydney – 17 degrees Celsius mid-winter, they expected New Zealand to be just as warm. In preparation for the hot and humid conditions of Tokyo the following week, the girls had packed summer clothes. Arriving in New Zealand, they were quick to complain about the 10-degrees Celsius weather and delighted in telling reporters that it was on a par with England. Keisha told the *New Zealand Herald*, 'It's freezing here. You talk about English winters but we're not going outside – it's popsicle weather.'

The girls spent two days holed up in their hotel room talking to journalists and radio presenters about their album and plans for the future, instead of enjoying Auckland's tourist sights, such as the Sky Tower or a boat trip to Waiheke Island.

After enduring negative press in their native UK over their alleged refusal to smile, Keisha and Mutya were friendly and happy during their interviews in a bid to avoid attracting the same media stereotype Down Under. But, throughout the tour, Siobhan's cool image continued – she was so unhappy at this point that she declined to grin for the cameras. In 2003, she explained that her sullen expression had nothing to do with her trying to be cool, it was a true representation of her feelings: 'You know all those photos of us refusing to smile? I was just really unhappy and I couldn't be arsed.'

Years later, on reflection, Keisha analysed their poses: 'We were three teenagers with attitude and we didn't like our teeth.'

Local press attention boosted sales of their albums and *One Touch* entered the charts just a week before they arrived in Auckland and two weeks later climbed to Number 16.

Despite her imminent departure, Siobhan kept up the pretence to the media that she was in Sugababes for the long haul and believed they would outlive their current chart contemporaries, such as Atomic Kitten, Steps and Blue. While she was right regarding Sugababes – they

Above left: Siobhan performing at Party In The Park in London in July 2001. This was one of the group's last festival performances before they left for their fateful Asia-Pacific trip, where Siobhan quit the group.

© *WENN*

Above right: A new star is born. This was Heidi Range's first ever Brit Awards, in 2002 – she had only been in the group for about six months at this point.

© *WENN*

Below: A few years on and the girls had developed a young and funky sense of style. They are pictured here leaving the studio of London's LBC radio.

© *WENN/Brian Mackness*

Above: Heidi and Keisha sing 'Round Round' at the 2003 TMF Awards in Rotterdam, The Netherlands. Mutya lost her voice on the group's UK tour so couldn't attend the TMF Awards, leaving her bandmates to perform and (*below left*) accept an award alone.   © *WENN*

Below right: Mutya leaves Justin Timberlake's party at the Rex Cinema in May 2003. Mutya is pictured here at the height of her partying, while the group were recording their *Three* album.

© *WENN/ Z. Tomaszewski*

Keisha Buchanan enjoying a night out in Ayia Napa during the Sugababes'
well-earned break from recording, August 2003. © *WENN/Habib*

Above left: Mutya performing 'In The Middle' at the 2004 TMF Awards in Rotterdam. © *WENN/Mmp*

Above right: Keisha and her brother Shane at the UK première of *Be Cool*. © *WENN/Z. Tomaszewski*

Below: The gorgeous girls enjoy a night on the town at Kabaret's Prophecy Club, London. © *WENN/Daniel Deme*

After some time out during Mutya's pregnancy, Sugababes reunited on the Brit Awards' red carpet for what was Mutya's last public appearance before she gave birth.

© WENN

Inset: Heidi arrives at the Capital FM Awards ceremony, with a balloon to celebrate the birth of Mutya's baby girl.

© WENN/ Brian Mackness

Mutya, Heidi and Keisha at a photoshoot in Amsterdam – one of the last
photoshoots of this Sugababes line-up, November 2005.

Above: At the 2005 MTV European Music Awards. In what was one of Mutya's final public appearances as a member of the band, Sugababes wowed the crowd with their stunning looks and stylish sophistication.

© WENN/ Rui M Leal

Below: In December, Mutya announced that she no longer wanted to sing with the band and Heidi and Keisha performed as a duo at the NEC Clothes Show Live.

© WENN/ Pn News

Enough was enough, Mutya wanted out.

would outlast all of those groups – she would not be a part of the band in the future. Keisha echoed Siobhan's comments and boasted of their extremely close relationship, which Siobhan would later disparage. Keisha told the *Herald*, 'The only thing I've ever wanted to be was a singer. It's the same with the others – we're sisters living the dream.'

When the Sugababes arrived in Tokyo, on the final stop of their Asia-Pacific tour, Siobhan was about to reach breaking point. Just as they had done in Australia and New Zealand, the girls were booked for a string of TV, radio and press interviews, where they would have to repeat the same answers over and over. Again, they told the story of their meeting, aged 13, at a garage party, which Siobhan later contradicted when she left the band as she explained how Ron Tom teamed her up with 12-year-old Mutya.

All summer, she was beginning to think what she was missing out on back home. Even though she had been given the chance to travel all over the world, she was doing so with people she didn't feel comfortable with. Her beloved grandmother had died just a couple of weeks after 'Overload' had been released and her passing had really upset Siobhan's close-knit Irish family. While she was in Japan, her family were marking the one-year anniversary in Omagh, County Tyrone, in Northern Ireland, where her granddad, aunts and uncles lived – a stone's throw away from the village of Beragh where Siobhan's father Charles grew up. She was also exhausted and needed some time out. As she explained, 'Our schedule was round-the-clock and I felt totally drained. There were no breaks in my routine so I plodded on. After all, I was living thousands of girls' dreams. Things didn't slow down and I started to question my life. I'd often worry about my voice and if I was good enough. I didn't tell Mutya or Keisha – I sensed three was a crowd.'

During the first few days in Tokyo, Siobhan had a disagreement with Mutya and Keisha, and claimed they 'froze her out'. The days leading up to her shock departure were very tense between the bandmembers and further fuelled the redhead's resolve to leave.

After several interviews on that fateful late-August day, in between press engagements Siobhan took management aside and told them she was leaving. She had begun to detest the music industry and couldn't stand spending so much time with girls she had nothing in common with. Instead, she wanted to be with her real friends back home in Middlesex, doing things that normal 17-year-olds were doing. Her parents and sisters were in Omagh spending quality time with her grandfather and huge family, while she was in Japan, talking about the album she had made over a year ago.

After conducting her last interview as a Sugababe, Siobhan excused herself from the room, leaving Mutya and Keisha blissfully unaware of the trouble that was about to erupt. Having talked to the managers, who were understandably unhappy about her decision, she packed her bags and was left at Tokyo Airport to find her way home. In 2003, she told *The Face* magazine, 'We had another interview in five minutes and I just left the room. Something clicked in my head that I couldn't be arsed to do it any more. For their sakes, if we don't get on, what the fuck is the point?'

Left in Tokyo's Narita International Airport, the gravity of what Siobhan had just done hit her hard. Though she didn't realise it at the time, she was sinking into depression. She had never felt so alone in her life and couldn't stop weeping. As she wandered aimlessly around the airport, she tried to find out where the check-in and the departure gates were located. She had never travelled alone before and was used to relying on an adult to organise her. 'I didn't know where I was going, I just followed numbers on the wall – it was the most bizarre experience of my life,' she recalled. 'It was four days before the end of the trip, and I made a decision and that was it. I thought, I'm not doing four more days – I'm not doing one more minute. I had to put my health and happiness first. I cried the whole way home on the plane. That was the last time I heard or saw of anyone I had worked with for three and a half years.'

After two years of silence following her dramatic exit, Siobhan started to open up about the group tensions when she was promoting her solo career. She said, 'I was so depressed when I left. The rest of the band was so ambitious. They wanted to be Destiny's Child and I was doing it for a bit of a laugh. But that doesn't mean I did not work hard. It got really bad at one stage. The other two girls did not speak to me. But what hurt me was that some of the people around the group, who I had become very close friends with, cut me off. I thought they were my best friends. We did have a falling out in Japan, me and Keisha. But it was just never good. Right from the start, we just didn't get on. We ignored each other and went about our business. It was very much a working relationship and we couldn't even work at that.'

Meanwhile, back at the hotel, Mutya and Keisha were given the news that Siobhan had left the band. Although they knew that they hadn't been getting on as well as usual during the past few weeks, they had no idea Siobhan was planning to leave. Despite the shock, they had to go and perform that evening as a twosome, singing Siobhan's parts from 'Overload' and 'New Year'. The news didn't take long to reach the UK and the *Daily Star* was the first to break the news of Siobhan's departure on 6 September 2001. In the immediate aftermath, the story was denied. A spokeswoman for London Records released a statement, saying, 'She came home three days early because she thought she had a kidney infection. She is better now but she is still resting.'

However, an unnamed friend told the *Star*, 'She is glad to be out of it. She didn't like the way things had been going for a while.'

While the media furore was only just beginning, Siobhan was at home alone in Eastcote. She said, 'The day I came back from Japan it was the first anniversary of the death of my nan and I wasn't in Ireland so I was thinking, Christ, where are my priorities? I missed that, which was crap. So I came home to an empty house and just sat there. I can't imagine being any lower – I wouldn't know how else to describe it other than as a breakdown.' Even though she had left the group, something she had wanted to do for months, she was shocked to find she didn't feel elated. In

Japan, she had thought that, if only she removed herself from the Sugababes – what she saw as the cause of her unhappiness – then she would be happy. Unfortunately, things weren't that simple – she was clinically depressed; she just didn't know it yet.

When Mutya and Keisha returned to London five days later, a media storm was waiting. The pair and their management realised Siobhan's departure hadn't been on a whim and it was permanent – it was time for the Sugababes to sink or swim. 'Insiders' had come out of nowhere and were talking to all the newspapers, claiming the girls had been bullying Siobhan for months. Mutya's cool urban image was beginning to backfire on her, because the media were blaming her for Siobhan's departure. In hindsight, Siobhan claimed relations between her and Mutya were never that bad and her problems mainly involved Keisha. Both girls denied bullying, however, and Siobhan did explain that there were many reasons for her departure.

The Sugababes had to do some damage control – and fast. First, they went on BBC Radio 1 to fight allegations they had thrown Siobhan out of the band. Keisha said, 'First of all, we'd like to say we didn't kick her out. We have spoken to her since, but we haven't seen her. I think it's going to be hard not seeing her, having been with her for four years.'

Press reports claimed Siobhan had left because she wanted to pursue a career in fashion or photography. Mutya and Keisha claimed Siobhan had stood up during an interview in Japan and told them she was 'going to the toilet', never to return.

Although Siobhan insists the group's publicists made up the bathroom angle, it's clear that Keisha and Mutya were hurt by their old bandmate's decision to leave without telling them face to face. In a 2003 interview, Mutya said, 'From what we know, Siobhan wasn't happy. When she left she didn't actually speak to us … we all went back to our hotel room in Japan and we were told, "Siobhan has left, she's on her way home." So we were obviously shocked. We had four days left until we went back home, so Keisha and I stayed on for promotion. We thought she would have probably changed her mind by the time we got home. She didn't change her mind so we just went straight on with auditions.'

Already decided they had come too far to give up on their dreams, Mutya and Keisha were convinced they had a bright future in the charts.

CHAPTER 10

Hello, Heidi

EIGHTEEN-YEAR-OLD Heidi Range was fed-up and frustrated with her bar job when she received a phone call from her entertainment lawyer Sarah Stennett – who was also part of the Sugababes' management team – asking her to come to London for an audition for the band. Partly due to the fact that her time with the Automatic Kittens had not gone as she had hoped, Heidi was unsure if she wanted to join the group but decided to make the trip down to the capital anyway. She auditioned in front of the group's management and – unbeknownst to her – Keisha and Mutya, who were watching her from a hiding place. Heidi was one of just five girls asked to audition and her powerful vocals – plus reassurance for Heidi that she would have more creative control than she had been given in the Automatic Kittens – clinched the deal.

As Heidi's song came to an end, she saw two little heads poke around the door and it was then that she came face to face with Mutya and Keisha for the first time. The pair was speaking in their 'Ski' language, which had allegedly caused so much trouble with Siobhan. Heidi recalls, 'Keisha and Mutya weren't in the room when I was singing and then I saw these two little heads looking through the door. They've got this code which they speak in and I didn't know it then. They were talking in it in the auditions and I'd be sitting there thinking, What are they saying?'

Heidi was informed that it was highly likely the group would be dropped by London Records in the coming weeks, but another deal was guaranteed because other labels had already expressed interest.

The existing Sugababes admitted they were at first unsure when Stennett told them about Heidi's past with Atomic Kitten – their arch rivals – but they soon changed their minds when she sang. Keisha said, 'When Heidi first walked in, we were a bit off with her, we were thinking, OK, here we go. Blonde hair, blue eyes, used to be in Atomic Kitten … When she sang we knew that she was the one. Heidi presented the formula that we needed. What you see with her is what you get – she's a strong girl and honest, but she doesn't put up with any crap. We had some friends who were great singers who came along, but we had to think on a business level – what would make the Sugababes successful? It's not contrived at all. If she couldn't sing, she wouldn't be in the band, but it's good because it shows that all races can work together. She has stability, we can trust her and she isn't going to walk out.'

Mutya agreed: 'She gelled very quickly. When she walked into the studio, we saw a pretty-looking person. We had already watched three people at the auditions who looked right, but they didn't sound like what we wanted. As soon as we heard Heidi sing, we said, "Yeah, we're taking her."'

Heidi was on the train back from Euston to Liverpool Lime Street when she received a call from the Sugababes' management declaring she could be in the group if she wanted. While many girls would have jumped at the chance straight away, Heidi needed some time to think. Heidi, sister Hayley, mum Karen and her grandmother, Nanny V, were a tight family unit and she wanted to consult them before making such a life-changing decision. After wasting time recording songs as part of Automatic Kitten before eventually deciding to leave, she couldn't afford to choose another band in which she wouldn't feel comfortable. The band's imminent dropping by London Records concerned her slightly, but she believed the Sugababes were talented: 'I'd loved the first Sugababes album. Even without a deal it seemed like the best idea in the world,' Heidi said. 'I was travelling on the train back to Liverpool when I got a phone call saying they really wanted me in but I said I'd have to ask my mum. It was a bit of a shock because I was only told about the audition the day before.'

When she got back to Aintree, there were some big decisions to be made. Heidi had heard rumours of trouble between Siobhan and her future bandmates and she thought that if she did join it wouldn't be 'to make two best friends. It was a job and a career move for me.'

Supportive mum Karen decided to come back down to London the next day with Heidi, where they would talk things over with the management team.

sugababes

The next day on the train to London, the Sugababes' management phoned again, insisting they needed an answer straight away. Somehow the press had found out about Heidi's audition so they would need to release a statement as soon as possible. Flustered, Heidi thought for a second and said, '"Yes," and that was it. I didn't even get to go home. I had to stay in London, and my mum had to bring all my stuff down.'

Heidi had to phone her boss at the Pan American bar to tell them she wouldn't be returning – an elating feeling for the young singer. She was told she had to go to a photo shoot straight away with her new bandmates, who were total strangers to her. Heidi explained, 'I thought Mutya was very quiet and I was shocked at how young she was as well. I'd only ever seen the girls on telly so I thought they were quite high fashion. I got a shock when I saw the two of them because they've both really small, even though I am as well – I'm just five foot two. But Keisha was wearing a bandana and trainers, big massive pants and baggy jumpers. She just looked really different to what she looked like on telly and I thought it was really strange. Keisha and Mutya seemed like total strangers. I didn't know if they'd even like me or not; I'd only ever seen them in videos. When I met them, they were like little ghetto girls who spoke in this weird street slang. I didn't have a clue what they were talking about.'

Arriving at the photoshoot, Heidi was given a selection of clothes that had been unknowingly chosen for Siobhan. She recalled, 'I had to wear Siobhan's clothes and the jeans were really tight. Siobhan was tiny. I was quite skinny when I joined, but not as slim as her.'

Despite the fact that Sugababes were now a trio again, London Records dropped the group from their roster literally days after Heidi joined but the band had already seen it coming. The label had put £2 million into launching Sugababes and their album: by summer 2001 they had only made £1 million in return. The surviving Sugababes insisted they were unfazed at losing their record contract, having dealt with Siobhan's shock departure as a bigger blow, and were confident they would find another deal. Keisha said, 'Everyone knew we were going to get dropped so lots of people were actually waiting for us, wanting to sign us, so it wasn't like we were out of contract for ages. One of the offers was from Island. I said to our manager, "I've never heard of them before. Who've they got on their roster?" He said they had Bob Marley, and I was just like, "Yeah, have you got anyone who's still alive?"'

Mutya added, 'But then we discovered they had Shaggy. We love Shaggy.'

Keisha continued, 'When Island came in, we did one song and that was it, they really liked it.'

Island A&R manager Darcus Beese approached the girls' manager Mark Hargreaves, offering them an album deal. Beese, who went on to sign Amy Winehouse a year later, had been impressed with their work on *One Touch* at such a young age and saw great potential. In a 2003 interview with the *Observer*, he told of his confidence that the girls would be successful, because they sing 'thinking people's pop' and were not '25-year olds pretending to be teenagers, or vice versa'.

Months into their deal with Island, Mutya and Keisha

were able to share how unhappy they were with London Records. While they praised London for giving them the opportunity to contribute to songwriting, they remained unimpressed with their lack of freedom in other areas. Mutya said, 'With the old record company we were allowed to write our own songs but we didn't have much of a say other than that. We couldn't wear what we wanted. As the Sugababes, we know the look but the record company would tell us what our style should be. London Records wanted us to go down the same road as All Saints and wanted to market us the same way. They spent £2 million on us and got £1 million back but that wasn't the result they were looking for. People in the industry still told us London Records were stupid to drop us because that money could have been recouped in the future. Letting us have more say as artists goes a long way in this business, so we are much happier. We have respect with Universal [Island's parent company]. We were dropped, but we knew we had to carry on. We are starting afresh, but we aren't forgetting about the past. We are just so much happier in what we are doing now and we expect it to do well.'

Keisha, on the other hand, was glad they could act like teenagers and appeal to younger fans, something she claimed London had dissuaded them from. She explained, 'I don't know why we got dropped. I don't think we were what they wanted. They were cool people, but maybe the idea they had of the Sugababes and the idea we had were two different things. And we wanted to do a lot more teen magazines to let our fans know about us. We were disappointed about what happened to the first album because we feel it could have done so much better. That's why it was a good thing when we got dropped. They wanted to make us really pop but we wanted to be more R&B.'

Following her swift entrance into Sugababes, Heidi was put up at the Pembridge Court Hotel in Pembridge Gardens, Notting Hill, a stone's throw from Portobello Road Market. Little did the young singer know it at the time, but the 19th-century, 20-room hotel was to be her home for the next eight months. She was given a room named 'The Last Resort', because it was the smallest room in the hotel. Far away from her family and friends and in a strange city, Heidi immediately bonded with the hotel staff – manager Valerie, barman Joe and the hotel's cat Churchill. She explains, 'I moved straight to London the day after auditioning and was living on my own in a hotel. It sounds glamorous, but it was really lonely. I'd go to work with the girls, then be sitting on my own in a room the size of a sofa. It literally had a bed, TV and a shower.' After a long day in the studio, hungry and tired, she would to the hotel and join Joe in the quiet bar. Speaking in the 2006 documentary *Sugababes: Uncovered*, Heidi recalled her life in Pembridge Gardens: 'The hotel was really special. There were only a few members of staff that worked there and they became a little family to me. On a Thursday, I used to go down to the bar to see Joe and we used to watch *Cold Feet* together. He used to make me ham and cheese toasties.'

Her first few weeks in the band were difficult for everyone. Mutya and Keisha were still reeling from Siobhan's departure and didn't know how to act in front of a complete stranger. Sixteen-year-old Mutya decided to remain silent when Heidi was around, rather than force awkward conversation. While the difficult relationship between the original members and Heidi only lasted a few weeks, the story was leaked to the media and spun up into newspaper stories, claiming Keisha and Mutya were bullying Heidi, just as they had allegedly done to Siobhan before her.

In 2003, Mutya admitted she was initially annoyed by Heidi's Liverpudlian accent, which was vastly different from her London 'street' twang: 'The first time I met her, she was speaking in a high-pitched voice and I was like, "Oh, God, shut up!" because she's got that Liverpudlian accent. I found it very hard to adjust to the fact that Heidi was the new girl. She was from Liverpool and we were from London. They are two different cultures. It's a big difference to get used to. So I did find it hard, and I did give her the worst week of her life. She's a lovely girl and I never want anything to happen to her now. I was really the biggest bitch of the week. I didn't really speak to Heidi for the first week. I didn't like what was going on. I couldn't get into the same cars, I left interviews early, I really made a big deal of it, and then I thought, Mutya, you're a stupid little bitch, and I stopped it. I saw videos of some interviews we did and it was terrible. Every time she left the room, I would give her a dirty look or be constantly staring at her. But it's cool now ... I love her to bits. We're very, very close now. Everyone has their own opinion [of us], but we're in our little circle together. I was a bit cruel. I did like her – I just didn't show it.'

Some of the reports suggested Mutya was jealous of Heidi

because she was such a happy, conventional blonde pop star. Mutya found the rumours ridiculous, insisting, 'It wasn't because I was jealous of her, like everyone thinks. I just couldn't get over the fact that we had been working hard from the age of 11 to get where we are, then this girl comes from nowhere and she has it handed to her on a plate.'

During her early days with the band, Heidi's positive attitude and enthusiasm in interviews quickly established her as the friendliest Sugababe and, looking back, Keisha admits she made the band more accessible to their younger fans. Unlike Mutya and Keisha, Heidi had trained as a performer since the tender age of three and influenced the other two to smile more. Keisha explained, 'The moment Heidi joined the group, I know that's when we became Sugababes. We were just three awkward teens in the beginning. When we first started out, we'd not had any media training. If I look back at our early days, I get embarrassed. We'd do all these TV shows and forget to smile – smiling would have helped. But then we never came from stage school and I think that showed. Things improved a lot when Heidi joined because she is from Liverpool and people from the North are always more chirpy, aren't they?'

In November 2001, Heidi got her first chance to experience the pop-star lifestyle when the group travelled to Frankfurt, Germany, for the MTV Europe Music Awards. The trio had been nominated for Best UK & Ireland Act and were up against Artful Dodger, Feeder, S Club 7 and Heidi's idol Craig David. Despite a host of big US names being nominated at the awards, including

sugababes

Jennifer Lopez and Janet Jackson, a majority pulled out over fears of flying following the September 11 attacks in New York and Washington DC just two months earlier. On the morning of the awards, the girls boarded a plane from London to Frankfurt, which caused much distress to Heidi, who had a fear of flying. The recent terrorist attacks in America had made her even more scared, but she kept herself calm during the 90-minute flight by thinking of all the stars she would meet later that day at the Festhalle venue.

Keisha and Mutya couldn't contain their excitement in choosing what to wear for the ceremony after enduring fashion decisions being made for them during their days with London Records. Keisha had just turned 17, while Mutya was 16, and, like many girls their age, they were beginning to feel comfortable with their bodies and wanted to flash the flesh. Mutya chose a hot-pink bandeau top, while Keisha went into full-on sexy mode and wore a minuscule blue backless halter-top, which showed off her slim waist and cleavage. It was Heidi's first award appearance and one of her first public engagements as a Sugababe so she had to make sure she was noticed and looked fabulous too. She wowed the paparazzi in a multi-coloured off-the-shoulder crop top, which displayed her famously toned abs. Heidi's penchant for crop tops and flashing her stomach would soon become a trademark of the pretty blonde, with one UK gossip magazine even pleading with her to 'put it away!'.

On the red carpet, ecstatic Heidi told reporters she couldn't wait to meet man-of-the-moment Craig David:

'I'm really excited as I'm a huge fan of Craig – I think that he's gorgeous.'

Heidi's excitement at being at such a huge event escalated during the course of the evening when she helped herself to the free booze – which left her new bandmates unimpressed. She recalls, 'It was the drunkest I'd been in my life. Keisha hated me after that. Keisha just thought, What have we let ourselves in for? because I was in a bit of a mess. It was the excitement of joining the band.' Heidi couldn't believe she was partying in the same room as Mary J Blige, Limp Bizkit, Nelly Furtado, Shaggy, Kylie Minogue and Pink. Later that evening, the girls lost out on the award to Craig David, who also picked up Best R&B Act.

Even though Heidi and her bandmates were starting to become part of the showbiz social scene, the Liverpudlian was desperately lonely and yearned for her friends and family. London was such a big place and the only people she came into contact with were producers and executives at Island and her bandmates, who had lives and family in London. At her lowest point, she admits she had a list of people she could socialise with during rare moments off. She recalls, 'I had a Post-It note on my wall with the names of people I might be able to call for a coffee because I didn't know anyone in London.'

Having spent her early years in a tight family circle of females, Heidi was comfortable expressing her feelings and would often feel so homesick that she would be moved to tears. The outpouring of sadness would make Mutya and Keisha uncomfortable as they were typical London teenagers and didn't think it was cool to cry in public. Heidi elaborates, 'I used to get homesick when I first joined the band. I was always crying. It was hard to get used to because I've had to move from Liverpool to London. Northern and southern people are so different. They're a bit younger than me, too. Mutya and Keisha aren't girlie at all. They prefer a ghetto style, whereas me and my friends wear loads of flimsy little things.'

Heidi soon realised she and Mutya were very different people when it came to dealing with their emotions. Laidback Mutya retreats silently into her shell when upset or during an argument, while Heidi expresses any anger or sorrow she is feeling the moment it hits her. Over Mutya's five years as a Sugababe in the media, she was wrongly portrayed as the tough, moody band member because of her cool exterior. In her defence, Heidi explained, 'It's not that Mutya's bitchy, it's more that she has her own personality and deals with things in her own way. She shuts up. If I'm in a mood I cry and tell everyone about it.'

In a 2002 interview with *Top Of The Pops* magazine, Mutya admitted she doesn't like to get involved in arguments: 'Keisha and Heidi were arguing about what DVD to watch last week. I just kept out of it. I get days where I don't want to see Heidi or speak to Keisha. Sometimes, though, you just want your own space and not to have everyone know what you're doing.'

Keisha added, 'If Mutya's upset about something, she'll go silent, sit in a corner and sulk.'

CHAPTER 11

Becoming Number One 'Freaks'

AFTER THEIR TRIP to Frankfurt and a small promotional tour in Prague, the girls returned to London to work on their second album. With the wave of publicity the group had been getting following Siobhan's departure and Heidi's arrival, label bosses at Island were keen for them to release a single in early 2002. Originally, bosses thought of an old Sugababes track 'The Word', which had been recorded when Siobhan was in the band. However, when the girls went into the studio to re-record the track with Heidi's vocals, a producer told them about a great bootleg track he had heard in the capital's nightclubs.

In August 2001, songwriter/producer Richard 'Richard X' Phillips had created a mash-up, using the music of Gary Numan's Tubeway Army 1979 track 'Are Friends Electric' with the vocals of Adina Howard's 1995 debut hit single 'Freak Like Me' under the pseudonym Girls On Top. The track, entitled 'We Don't Give A Damn About Our Friends', was a huge hit in the clubs for months, but couldn't be released commercially because Howard refused to give permission for her vocals to be used. An executive at Island was convinced the track would be perfect to relaunch Sugababes. Not only did it sound like a guaranteed hit, it would also set the group apart from the schmaltzy, production-line pop that was dominating the charts.

Island approached Richard X, suggesting the Sugababes sing Howard's lyrics, which he agreed to, on condition that the 'raw' production values remain. He explained, 'The A&R people had heard one of my records and for some reason they thought, "Wow, that could be great!" I was very keen to do it as long as it remained what it was. It was raw, it was against the grain and it was still pop music. When we made the Sugababes thing, there was a loop, some hand claps, the Sugababes and a semi-broken synthesiser. You could probably forget about the synth and, as long as you had the Sugababes around at your house, you could recreate that record.'

Sugababes recorded various versions of the track and finally the winning formula was chosen. When they played back the version of the single that would be chosen for release, the Sugababes, their producers and their record label knew they had a hit on their hands. Keisha said, 'When we actually finished it and it had our vocals, people kept going on and on about how good it was. It's exactly the same as the bootleg version.'

She was thrilled to record a version of the song because she had been a huge fan of Howard in the mid-1990s, despite the fact that she was just 11 years old when her song came out. The media found it entertaining that the Sugababes were so young; they didn't know who Gary Numan was, or his former band Tubeway Army, although Keisha was vaguely aware of his 1979 hit 'Cars', which had been used in a Nissan Altima TV commercial. Keisha explained, 'We'd never heard any of his other stuff. My parents knew it. Actually, he's been on TV saying we did a better job than he did, which was nice. We all knew Adina Howard's "Freak Like Me". I was very young, but that's when I really got into heavy R&B, people like Jodeci and Bell Biv Devoe. I remember taping the video. Those kinds of records were how I practised my singing style. The lyrics in "Freak Like Me" are quite racy, I know. And I got the worst verse in the song. I remember I had to go to church after it was released and they were saying they loved the song and that my verse was really great. How embarrassing!'

The single had already been shipped out to the radio stations when the Sugababes attended the Brit Awards at Earls Court on 20 February 2002. The group had not been nominated for any awards, but Island wanted to keep them in the public eye in the run-up to their new single release and it gave the girls a good opportunity to mix with fellow artists. Their label-mate Shaggy was a performer on the night, entertaining the crowds with a rendition of 'Me Julie' – a duet with Sacha Baron Cohen's Ali G creation. Mutya and Keisha were huge UK garage fans and were thrilled to watch the So Solid Crew perform '21 Seconds' before collecting the award for Best Video. The pair's friendship with the So Solid Crew sparked reports that rappers Harvey and Romeo would be working on the Sugababes' next album, but they proved unfounded. The girls' new work colleague Sting was the big star of the night picking up the Outstanding Contribution Award. Only months earlier, they had asked his permission to use his vocals and lyrics of 'Shape Of My Heart', which they used on their album track 'Shape'. The song went on to become the fourth and final release from their second album.

A poignant moment for the band came when Keisha ran into one of her former executives at London Records, who she hadn't seen since the label dropped Sugababes six months earlier. She explains, 'We saw the man who dropped us. He was like, "Hi, I love your new track – it's great", and we said, "We know!" and walked off. But we don't want to rub anything in. Yeah, they dropped us and we got a Number One, but we've always had faith in ourselves. We knew we were good from the beginning. We kind of knew they were going to drop us. Normally there's a big fight to keep the band on the label, but we were actually hoping they'd drop us. They wanted us to go in a different direction and we had other ideas. They basically said, "We don't want you on the label any more" and we said, "OK."'

The day after the awards, the press concentrated on Kylie Minogue's performance of 'Can't Get You Out Of My Head', focusing on her tiny Dolce & Gabbana mini-dress and silver knickers. Minogue's bottom graced the front cover of many of the newspapers and was dubbed 'Britain's national obsession'. It didn't take long before the Sugababes were asked to weigh in on the issue. Keisha, who remains fervently proud of her curvy Caribbean physique, is baffled by the fascination with the Australian superstar's backside. She said, 'I'm not trying to be funny but to me, being black, it's not a big deal that she has a big butt because most black girls and Latinos have big butts.'

However, Heidi disagreed, declaring, 'I think she has a really good bum. She has a nice figure, especially for her age. I mean, she's 34 and she looks amazing.'

While it appeared to Heidi and Keisha that they were just answering a reporter's question, the quotes contributed to a building story that the Sugababes secretly hated each other, a rumour that continued to circle the group until Mutya's departure years later.

The video to 'Freak Like Me' had to complement the song's racy and strange theme, as well as introduce Heidi to Sugababes' fans. Island enlisted acclaimed music video directors Dawn Shadforth and Sophie Muller to create a visually stunning promo to accompany the track. Shadforth had directed videos for two of Kylie Minogue's most important tracks – the hotpants-wielding 'Spinning Around' and her biggest hit 'Can't Get You Out Of My Head'. Meanwhile, Muller had done a string of videos with No Doubt, Gwen Stefani, Coldplay and Eurythmics, winning an MTV Video Music Award for the video to Annie Lennox's solo track 'Why'. The video was set in a surreal grimy nightclub, created in a London film studio and was filmed the night after the Brits. While so many other stars wouldn't have been expected to wake up early after a hard night's partying at the industry event of the year, only Heidi was legally allowed to drink at that time.

In the beginning of the video, Keisha and Mutya are

obviously friends and do not like the 'new girl' in the club, Heidi, who is dancing and flirting with a group of men. A fight ensues between the girls and Heidi is knocked unconscious. When she wakes up, Heidi and one of the men leave the club, where she kisses him, before biting him hard – which alludes to the vampire-like suggestion of the song's lyrics 'I will be a freak until the day, until the dawn … it's all about the dark in me'. Keisha and Mutya are also seen to have supernatural powers. Arguing with their male companions outside, they are strong enough to throw them several feet in the air.

For Keisha, 'Freak Like Me' was the first video in which she was given the opportunity to act, having developed a fondness for plays at school. She suggested to Shadforth and Muller ideas for her scene with the mystery male, asking if she could be seen to tease him before throwing him. Keisha explained, 'People think it's sexual, but it's more about other kinds of freaks, the supernatural kinds. It was the first time we were able to put our ideas in. We're not babies any more – we want to see some action. We even got to design our clothes. We don't want to be covered from head to toe, but I don't think we've done anything really outrageous. I remember being up against the wall with a guy in the video and my mum's on set and I had to act all touchy-feely towards him, that was really embarrassing.'

After several weeks' radio airplay, the song was placed on BBC Radio 1's coveted A-List on 14 March, before being released earlier than planned on 22 April. The *Sunday Mirror*'s Ian Hyland gave the track 9/10, proclaiming the single 'the tune of the year'.

Dominic Mohan of the *Sun* also gave the song the thumbs-up in his 'Bizarre' column, declaring, 'Mutya, Keisha and new babe Heidi are set to take their record from the club dancefloors into the charts. This fantastic song is the first release from the band's forthcoming album.'

The girls started heavy promotion work, performing the song on *Top Of The Pops* and *CD:UK* and speaking to tabloid editors at the *Sun*, the *Daily Star* and the *Daily Mirror*. One subject that was unavoidable for Sugababes was the reasons behind Siobhan's shocking exit six months earlier. During a webchat with the *Sun* on the day the song was released, Keisha insisted there had been no rift with Siobhan: 'Siobhan left as she wasn't happy doing this. She was exhausted all the time. There weren't any arguments or anything, she wasn't that type to argue. She just didn't want to do it any more.'

Just days before the song was released, the Sugababes had dinner with their idol Mary J Blige at The Pharmacy restaurant in Notting Hill, having briefly met her at the MTV Europe Music Awards in Germany six months earlier. Ahead of the meeting, Mutya enthused, 'We met her at the MTV Awards, and she had her mood swings but then most performers do. We've been listening to her for so long now.'

Despite the good response from the media and fans, the even-younger S Club Junior's debut single 'One Step Closer' was also selling well. The Sugababes started panicking – maybe their 'surefire' Number One would miss out to a manufactured pop group with an average age of 12. Keisha remembers Sunday, 27 April very well: 'I was watching *Fresh Prince Of Bel Air* that day. It was really nerve-racking. You're supposed to know the chart positions by 11am on Sunday, but because it was a really close race that week I didn't know until 2pm, so I was really nervous, pacing up and down my house for hours.'

Meanwhile, Heidi was up in Aintree to share the moment – successful or not – with her family. In the early afternoon, her mum Karen picked up the phone and spoke to the group's manager Mark Hargreaves. It was official: 'Freak Like Me' had beaten 'One Step Closer' to Number One by 1,000 copies, knocking Oasis's 'The Hindu Times' off the top spot. Heidi looked nervously at Karen, who suddenly started screaming. Heidi knew her dream had come true. After all those years of dance and music lessons, the time in Automatic Kitten and her attempts at a solo career in America, she had finally made it. Only nine months earlier, she had been sitting outside the Pan-Am bar in Albert Dock, weeping because she wasn't getting anywhere with her music career. She enthused, 'I had a party back home in Liverpool. We opened a bottle of champagne and I just kept crying. I phoned Mutya and Keisha sobbing and they were like, "Oh, right, yeah." Later that week, when we were performing on TV and they announced us as Number One, I nearly started crying again. My eyes started filling up, and I thought, Nah, I'd better not, the girls will punch me if I start crying and make a fool of myself on live TV.'

Heidi made her TV performing debut on *CD:UK*, the Saturday-morning rival show to *Top Of The Pops*, where Keisha and Mutya had also made their own debuts 20 months earlier. Even though it was her first time on television, her stage-school training ensured she looked comfortable on stage, while Keisha's anxiety from the 'Overload' days had returned. She explained, 'When we did the first *CD:UK* after coming back, I was a tiny bit nervous and you could see that I was nervous. But Mutya was smiling and Heidi was smiling because they were happy to be on stage. I think we're too real. I don't know how that sounds, it might sound really cheesy, but we can't fake it. I think it's important for you to be yourself when you're on stage. We don't get told to smile, we don't get told not to smile, we do our own thing. But we really enjoy it. We're singers, so being on stage is what it's about. But Mutya and I are quite street-y, that's got a lot to do with the Sugababes having an edge. When you see So Solid Crew on stage, they don't have permanent grins because they're also street-y. We're just not stage-school beauties, we're just street, we're just raw.'

The same week, the girls returned to *Top Of The Pops*, Mutya's favourite TV show, and their performance was miles better than their debut. Despite having sung several times before on the show, going there with a Number One hit was extra special for Mutya: 'To have a Number One and appear on the show is special, and you know that all the kids are watching you.'

But it wasn't just the Sugababes and their record label who were happy when the song reached Number One – Gary Numan was suddenly back in the public eye and all the press wanted to talk to him. The singer was holidaying with his wife Gemma in Mexico when he found out that

'Freak Like Me' had got to Number One in the UK, which meant he could expect a tidy royalty cheque in the post. The *Sun* spoke to him on the phone the day it charted and he was stunned by the response: 'The Sugababes are very young. It's odd to think that when "Are Friends Electric?" was a hit, the girls weren't even a twinkle in their fathers' eyes. I spoke to someone who worked on their record and they knew absolutely nothing about me. But I don't know them either; I've certainly never met them. I first heard their track from a guy who does remixes, who had worked on it. I love what has been done with my song, I think it works. I wish the girls all the best. I'm flattered someone wants to use my music.' In a webchat the following month, Numan gave the girls a big boost, declaring, 'As for the Sugababes, I actually do prefer their vocal to my original. I've never thought I could sing very well and I think they do.'

'Freak Like Me' remained in the UK charts for an amazing 14 weeks and sold over 235,000 copies, making it the Sugababes' most successful song up until that point. And it wasn't just their homeland who loved the song; the track went to Number Two in neighbouring Ireland, and Four in Norway. Meanwhile, it charted in the Top 30 in Belgium, Switzerland, Denmark, Spain, Japan, Brazil, France, Austria, Germany, The Netherlands, New Zealand and The Philippines – much to the delight of Mutya and her family. The British Phonographic Industry (BPI) certified the single had sold over 200,000 and the trio were awarded a Silver disc. The single also entered the 'Babes into the history books for being the youngest girl group to achieve a Number One spot. When 'Freak Like

Me' entered the charts, Heidi was 18, Keisha was 17 and Mutya was just 16.

Following the Sugababes' Number One, Heidi packed her bags and moved out of the Pembridge Court Hotel into a rented flat in Kensington. During her first eight months in the capital, she had fallen for the Notting Hill/Kensington area. She loved shopping at the chain stores and boutiques in High Street Kensington and Kensington Church Street, as well as browsing through the stalls in Portobello Road Market; she also enjoyed taking walks in Holland Park and Kensington Gardens. On her rare days off, she would board a three-hour train from Euston to Liverpool Lime Street to spend even just a few hours with her mum Karen. She said, 'I'd get the train back to Liverpool if we had a day off. I'd have tea at home and then take the train back. I remember one time I went back and my mum was waiting for me at the station, and she said, "Your manager's phoned, you've got to go straight back." I was crying my eyes out.'

For Sugababes, life was busier than ever. Before and after 'Freak Like Me' was released, the girls spent seven months in the recording studio, completing their second release *Angels With Dirty Faces*. In all, they recorded over 40 songs and chose 13 tracks for the album. Some of the remaining tracks, such as 'Groove In Going On', were used as B-sides on their single releases. Throughout the summer in the run-up to the release of the album, they spoke to the press on a regular basis, promising a disc would contain 'a kind of hip-hop, R&B with some indie in there and a bit of techno as well.'

The group really got to know each other during their time in the studio. Like most teenagers, they enjoyed sleepovers at their parents' houses after particularly late recording sessions. A few months after their Number One, Keisha said, 'We didn't really force the friendship thing. We went into the studio for a couple of months and it just naturally happened. Sometimes we'll all sleep in Mutya's room and order a pizza in, or go stay at Heidi's house if we're working in Liverpool. Me and Mutya are always going to be very tight, like sisters, but we're all working together. I don't know, we've tried our best to make her feel welcome. It's hard for her, but only because she had to live away from home for the first time.'

When Heidi introduced her bandmates to her family for the first time, Mutya saw a different side to her new colleague and really began to warm to her: 'I met her mum and her Nanny V, and saw her with them. I realised that this girl was really nice. I thought, She only wants to do what I am doing, she just wants to sing. So I said to myself, "Mutya, get off your lazy behind and start talking to her!" It was hard at first, but now I would kill someone for her.'

'Round Round' was an obvious next release from the *Angels With Dirty Faces* album. The track was produced by Xenomania, a Kent-based company comprising Brian Higgins, Nick Coler, Miranda Cooper, Lisa Cowling and Tim Powell, who share writing credits with the three individual Sugababes. Higgins also co-wrote Cher's 1998 mega-hit 'Believe' and Xenomania are responsible for the majority of Girls Aloud's hit singles. Xenomania only work with artists that excite them, and, to the delight of the Sugababes, the team turned down their rivals Atomic Kitten, as well as *Pop Idol* runner-up Gareth Gates.

'Round Round' sampled 'Tangoforte', a percussion track by German DJ quartet Dublex. The drum pattern was infectious and, once the empowering lyrics were added, the catchy track was born. The song was written in a weekend, when Heidi, Mutya and Keisha went down to Xenomania's base in the rural Kent countryside. They also went on to co-write the album's title track 'Angels With Dirty Faces' with Higgins and another Xenomania producer Bob Bradley, released as a B-side to 'Stronger'. The partnership was the beginning of a beautiful friendship for the Sugababes and Xenomania, who to date have produced and written eight tracks for the band, including two Number Ones.

'Round Round' was a feisty girl-power song, lacking the contradictive 'feminist' shoutings of the Spice Girls in the late 1990s. The lyrics urged fans to kick their useless boyfriends to the side and go out for a dance with the girls. The girls were all single when they recorded the song and it would be another year and a half before they developed their first serious relationships.

The making of 'Round Round' was a huge collaborative effort. Heidi admits, 'The lyrics actually don't make much sense. We went away for the weekend to our producers' and recorded the chorus, and thought it sounded wicked so we tried out loads of different types of music and wrote lots of different verses. Then the producer picked out the best ones and then we put them all together. There are some different topics in every verse, but it seems to gel well. But basically it's about us girls sticking together against the guys.'

Working on the tracks for *Angels With Dirty Faces* was not only the start of a successful series of collaborations for

Higgins, but he also saw Mutya's potential as a solo singer. In a 2004 interview with the *Observer*, 17 months before she left the group, he said, 'I'll get on my soapbox here. Mutya's undoubtedly the finest female singer this country has produced in years – for me the closest comparison is Dusty Springfield.'

The video for 'Round Round' was dramatically different from 'Freak Like Me'. In the new promo, the Sugababes were dressed in clothes they might actually wear in real-life. For 'Round Round', the trio were dressed to reflect the song's rockier guitar and drum riff and they embraced their inner rock chick. After fairly static performances during their *One Touch* days, the Sugababes finally were beginning to embrace the importance of dance for aesthetic purposes and looked comfortable swinging their hips in time to the beat. Mutya, Heidi and Keisha were dressed in tight PVC and wearing dramatic make-up. Heidi was given a funky quiff hairstyle, while hair chameleon Mutya stood out with asymmetrical ponytails, covered in leather coils. The girls performed the song on a rotating platform, watched by an audience of rockers and punks. The 'Round Round' chorus is taken literally and the Sugababes were surrounded by a tornado, which manages to miss the group, but picks up accessories such as sunglasses and a ring from members of their audience, as well as the backing band. During Heidi's verses, the tornado comes to a standstill, which slows the tempo down rapidly before Dublex's drumbeat picks up the song again.

Sugababes started performing the song over the summer at festivals and it received a great response from audiences.

After playing at PopKomm in Germany and Party In The Park concerts in Cardiff and Swansea, Wales, the track was added to Radio 1's A-List on 25 July, just as 'Freak Like Me' earlier in the year. While the radio stations were buzzing about the song, pop svengali Pete Waterman, who masterminded the careers of Kylie Minogue, Jason Donovan and Bananarama, was unimpressed. He said, 'I don't like the Sugababes. Why would I? They're nothing special. I listened to their new single "Round Round" once and I'll admit it's nice and catchy, but it sounds like "Apache" by The Shadows. Then I heard 12 people had written the song and it made sense. They just threw everything in there – that's not enough to sustain a career.'

Meanwhile, the *Daily Mirror*'s Ian Hyland gave the 'Babes yet another good review and 8/10. He wrote, 'Sounds like "Wig Wam Bam". But it'll get you.'

The song was finally released in the UK on 12 August and Sugababes had tough competition from Daniel Bedingfield's 'James Dean (I Wanna Know)'; Romeo's 'Romeo Dunn' and Hear'Say's 'Lovin Is Easy'. The originality and drum riff of 'Round Round' beat the competition hands down and claimed the Number One spot on Sunday, 18 August, while the girls were performing at the V Festival in Chelmsford, Essex. The tabloids were quick to share the trio's joy at accomplishing their second Number One in four months. Heidi, 19, was photographed swilling champagne, enthusing, 'It's absolutely amazing to have got to Number One and we're all on cloud nine.'

To music critics, it was refreshing to see songwriting acts such as Sugababes land at Number One in a summer dominated by manufactured pop. 2002 had been a year for releases by a host of manufactured acts, including former Steps duo H & Claire, Hear'Say, Liberty X and former *Pop Idol* contestants Gareth Gates and Darius. Speaking to the *Sun*'s 'Bizarre' column in Chelmsford, Heidi boasted, 'I'm amazed we're at Number One. It's great because we've been working so hard. At least we wrote the song ourselves, unlike lots of manufactured bands.'

Despite selling just slightly less copies than 'Freak Like Me' in their homeland, 'Round Round' went on to be their biggest international hit so far, reaching the Top 10 in 12 countries, including the Number Two spot in Ireland, New Zealand and The Netherlands. The biggest shock for the group was the track reaching Number Seven on the US Billboard Dance Chart. In September, the single was certified Silver in Britain by the BPI after selling 225,000 copies. The song was also released as a ringtone, much to their teenage fans' delight, as well as the girls' own mothers. Both Heidi and Mutya admitted their mums Karen and Rose had 'Round Round' on their mobile phones, adding, 'How embarrassing!'

Sugababes were given a boost and their first taste of the movie world when they were approached for 'Round Round' to be used on the soundtrack to a new romantic comedy called *The Guru*, released in August 2002. The Working Title movie starred Heather Graham and former EastEnders' hunk Jimi Mistry as an American porn star and an Indian immigrant falling in love under difficult circumstances in New York City. At the UK première at London's Empire cinema, the Sugababes embraced the

Indian theme of the movie, much to the horror of the press. All of the girls wore transparent Indian-style chiffon tops and had jewels stuck to their foreheads. When they were shown a photo of their outfits three years later, they were understandably horrified. Keisha lamented, 'This look is absolutely dreadful! I just don't understand why everything is see-through.'

Heidi continued, 'I don't like my outfit in the slightest. I would never wear this again, I hate the whole thing.'

After attending the screening, the Sugababes joined Graham, Mistry, their co-star Marisa Tomei, Kelly Osbourne and Melinda Messenger at the after-party at Elysium on London's Regent Street.

Just two weeks after 'Round Round' was released, it was finally time for *Angels With Dirty Faces* to hit the shelves on 26 August. When the critics saw a song called 'Virgin Sexy' on the tracklist, the Sugababes were asked to explain themselves. Mutya, who was 17 at the time, said, 'The song is basically saying, "Hey, girls, you can still be sexy and a virgin. We want fans to understand that if you're a virgin that's fine, but, if you're not, that's OK, too.'

Of course, the tabloids were eager to know if the Sugababes themselves were virgins, a shocking question for three girls who had been brought up Catholics. Heidi remained coy, replying, 'We know we'll now get asked if we're virgins ourselves. We went on a promo tour to Germany and that was all people wanted to know. The song isn't about us. So we're not saying whether we are or not.'

Keisha added, 'At first we were embarrassed by the lyrics.

You don't even say the word "sex" in front of your parents, let alone sing it in a song, but it's OK now.'

Sugababes' marketing power was beginning to increase and, following their work on *The Guru* soundtrack, they were approached for permission to use 'Virgin Sexy' in the new Rimmel mascara advert, starring Croydon beauty Kate Moss. It was one of two links the Sugababes would have with Moss. The sleeve images and album cover for *Angels With Dirty Faces* were taken by acclaimed photographer Corinne Day, who is credited with starting the supermodel's career. Day launched Moss into the big time with her earthy photos of the then teenager in the park and used a similar setting for the Sugababes' album. She was renowned for her realistic, unembellished images and was chosen to give a visual depiction of the album's title.

The cover image portrayed the Sugababes dressed in smart/casual clothes hanging out around a lakeside at sunrise. Not only did the image match the song's story line, the sunny haze also added an angelic quality to the band. Within the album sleeve, close-up images of the individual Sugababes without make-up showed them as 'real' pop stars, reinforcing the fact the group were not manufactured puppets. In the album sleeve 'thank yous', Mutya made her peace with Heidi, saying, 'I'm really glad you joined us. You're very talented and have such a beautiful personality.'

As well as Xenomania and Richard X, Sugababes had teamed up with some of their production team from *One Touch*, such as Jony 'Rockstar' Lipsey and Felix Howard, as well as eighties pop star Howard Jones. Critical acclaim of their first album and the contacts of Darcus Beese at Island had brought in some big names to work with them. Surprisingly, big stars like Sting and Jones weren't offended when they realised they would be working with teenagers who didn't know of their existence.

Jones's biggest track 'What Is Love' was a hit in November 1983 – when Heidi was only six months old and Keisha and Mutya weren't even born. Heidi admitted she had to phone her mum Karen for advice when the label told her she would be working with him: 'We didn't know who Howard Jones was. I was in the studio one day and I called my mum and said, "I'm working with someone called Howard Jones today." She said, "*The* Howard Jones? Wow!" He keeps saying that he will show us his old videos one day. We want to see them as we don't know who he is!'

Together, Jones and the Sugababes wrote 'Blue', a feisty revenge anthem, telling an ex-boyfriend who was attempting to gain a place in their lives to return to the rock he crawled out from.

The album gave the girls an opportunity to look to the decade in which they were born for inspiration and further open their mind to different music genres. Mutya enthused, 'Howard Jones is an eighties legend. I'm glad Gary Numan liked our song and that Howard Jones likes what we do. It's cool to have that eighties cred. We're really proud to present these eighties stars to people who weren't born when they were around. Because it's a shame, they made some really good music and the sound today isn't as good musically or even vocally.'

Critics weren't so kind to the Sugababes when reviewing *Angels With Dirty Faces*, following the universal praise that

One Touch received two years earlier. The *Guardian*'s Alex Petridis was scathing, writing, 'The album frequently sounds as if the Sugababes were unprepared for "Freak Like Me"'s success and had no idea what to do next. It took 12 people to write the follow-up, "Round Round": that isn't songwriting so much as throwing ideas at the wall in the hope one of them will stick. "Acoustic Jam' is begging for the fast-forward button: "Breathe Easy" is no exception. "Shape" – collaboration with Sting – is a lumbering, mirthless AOR ballad, grown-up in the worst sense of the phrase. The rest of *Angels with Dirty Faces* is exactly what you would expect: one great single propping up a dull album, written by committee, devoid of emotion or spark.'

Graeme Virtue, critic for Scotland's *Sunday Herald*, had mixed feelings: 'Despite glacial-smooth production, *Angels With Dirty Faces* sadly doesn't sound quite as accomplished as that debut, but there are still some terrific moments.'

The *Independent*'s Simon Price was kinder, but dubbed Heidi a 'Scouse Atomic Kitten reject', although he declared, the disc was 'still very much the teen pop act it's more than OK to like'.

The *Observer*'s Akin Ojumu accused the girls of pandering to the US market, claiming, 'Unfortunately, the overall effect is more Britney Spears than Mary J Blige. The Sugababes don't cut it as R&B divas … the album suffers from the fact that it is obviously designed to break them in the States.'

Despite Sugababes' move towards the pop market with their second album, *NME* remained fans of the band. Their critic Alex Needham praised a lot of the album tracks, but singled out 'Shape' as a 'massive faux-pas', but predicted the album would 'keep them in slap and snakeskin boots' through healthy sales. And of course, the group could rely on the *Daily Mirror* critic Ian Hyland, who had steadfastly approved of all the Sugababes' moves up until then. He gave the album 9/10, adding the dreadful pun, 'Scouse Heidi hasn't affected their range.'

In December that year, Hyland added *Angels With Dirty Faces* to his 'Top Albums of 2002' list.

A week after its release, *Angels With Dirty Faces* entered the charts at Number Two and kept a chart presence for an impressive 40 weeks. Both the group and their label were delighted. The response to the album was a dramatic difference from *One Touch*, which had been released for nearly four months before climaxing at Number 26 in the UK charts. The BPI certified the album 3x Platinum after it sold over 900,000 copies, making it the Sugababes' most successful album ever. Compared to other girl groups of the millennium, the Sugababes lead in album sales. Mis-teeq's highest album sales were Platinum, while arch-rivals Atomic Kitten managed 2x Platinum with their second album *Feels So Good*, which was released two weeks after 'Angels'.

In the immediate weeks following the release of their album, the Sugababes were so busy they didn't have time to acknowledge how successful it had been, until months later when the BPI presented them with their Platinum discs. Heidi gushed, 'When we got the discs, that's when it sank in. We don't compete against other bands, but I was reading *Music Week*, and it was surprising to find out that we'd actually sold quite a lot compared to some really successful pop bands.'

sugababes

In the early years of Sugababes, Keisha adorned the walls of her Kingsbury home with the Gold and Platinum discs for their singles and albums. However, as Sugababes became a long-term part of her life, she has chosen to switch off her pop-star persona, preferring to be herself at home. In the 2006 documentary *Sugababes: Uncovered*, she admitted, 'I haven't got them up. They're in my attic. When I get home, I like to forget about everything because you're constantly a part of Sugababes, which is good. When you switch on the TV, you're there; when you go out, someone reminds who you are. I just like to see walls and regular pictures at home.'

The same day they discovered their album charting, Sugababes were announced as nominees at the Music Of Black Origin (MOBO) Awards in the UK Act Of The Year category. The group were in a particularly tough category being up against So Solid Crew, Beverley Knight, Daniel Bedingfield, Mis-teeq and woman-of-the-moment Ms Dynamite. The Sugababes considered themselves in the same vein as the rapper/singer; they were both minorities in the charts because they wrote their own music and performed live. Keisha said, 'I love Ms Dynamite, she's the UK Lauryn Hill. She tackles very touchy subjects. She's only 17, but to me that's really powerful – and I want more.'

Following their MOBO nomination, the Sugababes received their first ever award since Heidi joined the group. The trio were named Best Music Star at the *Elle* Style Awards, which took place on 16 September 2002 at London's Natural History Museum. The recognition was a boost to the Sugababes, who were now making their own fashion decisions, with help from their stylist Cynthia Lawrence John. While other pop groups were wearing matching lycra outfits, the Sugababes were experimenting with different looks and designers.

Lawrence John praised the girls' open attitude to fashion and their willingness to try quirky designs. In an interview with the *Observer*, she said, 'They're very vocal with what they want but they tend to get slagged off a lot in the press because they don't play the pop-tart game. They're really young girls, but they're very open-minded. Even if they don't know who the designer is, they're willing to give it a try. There's a little bit of me in them. Sometimes I'll take in the odd piece of Alexander McQueen or Ann Demeulemeester and they'll be like, "What the hell is that?" Sometimes they need a bit of coaxing to try something new. I remember one instance where I showed them a pair of McQueen trousers which they were a bit hesitant about at first. A few months later, all their friends were wearing the high-street rip-off version.'

The group also benefited from a business partnership with Adidas, who were gaining publicity by sending the girls free clothes. At the festivals all summer long, Mutya and Heidi in particular showed a penchant for the sports giant, with Mutya even opting to wear Adidas in the video for 'Stronger' and during her MOBO performance.

Following the album reviews, it was obvious to Island that 'Stronger' should be the next single. The powerful ballad, about inner strength and overcoming the odds, also showcased one of the many musical genres Sugababes can tackle, following the upbeat tempo of 'Round Round' and

'Freak Like Me'. The song was written by three songwriters – together with the Sugababes – and it holds a special place for Heidi because she contributed a lot of lyrics. Her words were inspired by her heartbreak at the hands of a mystery male model that she met shortly after joining the band. She explained, 'I've just had my heart broken by one – he was a model. On the album I was going through heartbreak so I had a lot to say. "Stronger" is all about what I was going through just before I joined the band, being away from home and not having family and friends around. We always write about what we know. I always need to experience something to write a song about it, so, to be honest, I'm trying to cram a bit of life in between work at the minute so as I have something to write about for the next album.'

Following the completion of the girls' fourth studio album in 2005, Heidi maintained the track was still one of her favourites: '"Stronger" was one of the first songs I properly wrote. I still love performing the song.' Strength appears to be an important motto for Heidi and her female family members. She says, 'My mum always said, "Never depend on anyone but yourself." It's harsh, but one day you might be on your own, and you've got to be strong enough.' On the *Angels* album sleeve, she pays tribute to mum Karen: 'the strongest woman I will ever know'.

Just as 'Stronger' was chosen as a single, Sugababes were approached by Warner Bros for another soundtrack opportunity. 'Angels' was deemed the perfect song to accompany kids' animation *The Powerpuff Girls* movie, which hit UK cinema screens in October 2002. The Sugababes were thrilled; life just kept getting better. Not only were they a success in their home country, but they were also being approached by film companies, which would further launch their music on the global stage, and in particular, the tricky US market. Island decided to release 'Angels' as a double A-side with 'Stronger'. The thought of doing two videos would have been exhausting for the Sugababes, who were already working every day promoting their album. Fortunately, the animation studios offered to turn the Sugababes into Powerpuff-style cartoon characters, with Heidi, Mutya and Keisha taking on the characteristics of Powerpuff Girls Bubbles, Blossom and Buttercup respectively.

Keisha encouraged their marketing prowess and was happy with her animated persona: 'It was so funny seeing us like that and the *Powerpuff Girls* cartoon itself. The video so much resembled our personalities with these three characters so it was very funny to watch.' The association with the movie meant the Sugababes were now accessible to all ages, including young kids. Keisha enthused, 'Ever since Heidi joined, we've had loads of younger fans. Before it was teenagers and older, but we've been meeting all these kids and they're really, really sweet.'

While the girls didn't have to worry about the *Angels* video, they had to make another promo for 'Stronger'. After the previous two videos were made in the studio, it was time to bring the girls outside for a change of pace. The majority of the video was shot at Park Road Lido in Hornsey, north London, and featured the Sugababes hanging out with locals. Two of the crowd included Keisha's big brother Shane and Mutya's young niece Jade, who briefly featured in a group shot at the end of the promo.

In the video the 'Babes individual story lines see the girls discover their inner strength to overcome a problem or find the courage to leave a bad situation. A scantily dressed Mutya leaves her unappreciative gangster boyfriend, while Keisha comes to terms with a romantic loss at a 'Heartbroken Anonymous' meeting. Heidi continued to sex up the Sugababes, playing a stripper who decides to leave the job she hates. The modest Liverpudlian admitted she felt incredibly bashful having to stand on stage for her verses dressed in knickers and a bra. She said, 'It wasn't exactly glam filming the scenes. Being part-naked in front of the camera was weird, and very invasive. I wasn't comfortable at all – I don't like to reveal too much.'

Shooting the poolside scenes in the video took all day and night on a chilly October day. Ironically, the Sugababes had to summon up real-life strength to stand under the pool's running shower in their clothes and sing at the same time. As they stood, freezing and soaked, the girls knew the temporary pain would be worth it. The finished product would be titillating for male fans and further establish them as adults, not young teenagers. After being covered up during their *One Touch* days, Keisha and Mutya were becoming young women and wanted to be seen as sex symbols. Mutya sported vampy hotpants, bra and leather jacket combo for her verse, while Keisha looked sleek and sophisticated during her verses wearing a strapless black top and poker-straight hair.

The girls later looked back on the 'Stronger' video with regret, insisting it didn't match up to their other efforts – even Heidi, who wrote much of the song, hated the massive frizzy wig she wore for her stripper scene. She said, 'I refuse to watch it. It looks like it's on fire. We'd sat for hours waiting for them to do it. I was ready to scream by that point.'

Keisha agrees, 'Some of our videos have been dodgy, like "Stronger". I had a moustache and a beard. They said it was a shadow, but a shadow can't be in every scene. Heidi had a thing about her hair.'

In late September, Mutya's family hit the headlines when it was reported her eldest brother Charlie was unwittingly caught up in a dramatic shooting incident in Colindale – just east of the Buena family's home in Kingsbury. The *News of the World* reported the 24-year-old was visiting friends in the area when he heard two gun shots. Fortunately, Charlie escaped unscathed, but one of the bullets hit his Ford Scorpion car. A police spokesman told the Sunday paper, 'There is a strong feeling that he got caught in the crossfire between Triads and Yardies.'

Before 'Stronger' was released, the girls were given their biggest gig yet – performing at the MOBOs at the London Arena on 2 October. While it may have seemed like just another awards ceremony to the Sugababes, they were unaware that the night would turn out to be dramatic. As their limousine pulled up at the venue, a small group of gay campaigners from Outrage! were protesting against the presence of reggae acts Elephant Man, TOK and Capleton, claiming their lyrics were homophobic. Protests aside, the pop trio attracted their own press on the red carpet by wearing £1 million worth of diamonds from Jade Jagger's Garrard range. When they were told they were going to wear the pricey jewels, the 'Babes abandoned their usual red-carpet look and turned glam for the night. The girls were accompanied by bodyguards to watch over the jewels, which had to be placed with security when they changed into their performance outfits.

Sugababes' management decided it would be inappropriate at a huge event like the MOBOs to showcase the new single 'Stronger' and decided to bring out the urban side of the group. Sugababes performed a dancehall version of 'Round Round' with a team of dancers and accompanying DJ. Keisha embraced her heritage by wearing a leather Jamaican flag ensemble – a noughties version of Geri Halliwell's Union Jack dress at the Brit Awards five years earlier. However, during their performance, disaster struck when a crazed member of the audience jumped on stage and headbutted one of the Sugababes' dancers. Keisha lamented, 'Suddenly this guy was on stage shouting, "This is my time!" Nobody knew what he was up to or what security was meant to be doing. The next thing we knew he had headbutted one of our dancers.'

Mutya remained professional and carried on singing: 'We'd seen him at the back of the stage before we went on and he looked over and smiled at me. The next thing he was up on stage but I just tried to ignore him.'

The stage invader was one of many violent acts to taint the night. After Sugababes lost out on UK Act of the Year, they retreated to the Sunborn Yacht Hotel, moored at the nearby Royal Victoria Docks for BMG Records' afterparty. Despite a strict 450 guestlist, a mob of 200 attempted to storm the ship and created chaos outside. The next day, police confirmed there had been overcrowding on the vessel and a young woman had told police she was raped in the toilets, though she decided not to take the matter further and no action was brought. Fortunately for the Sugababes, they were safely in the VIP room with Ja Rule, Ashanti and Blue singer Simon Webbe when the chaos erupted. However, MOBO winner Ms Dynamite and TV presenter Dani Behr were caught in the fracas. Behr told the *Sun*, 'Everyone was pushing and shoving … I was getting very claustrophobic – people were starting to panic as this mob of around 200 people, most of them wannabe gangsters, were trying to get in.'

The 'Babes spokesman confirmed they weren't in danger during the chaos, saying, 'The girls thoroughly enjoyed the night. All they told us was that when they left they saw a few police.'

During the afterparty, Keisha met her idol and celebrity crush LL Cool J, who had hosted the awards with Mis-teeq MC Alesha Dixon. Confident Keisha, who had just turned 18, admitted, 'I went up to him and I don't normally do this, but I said, "I just have to tell you that I think you're so sexy." He was just holding on to my hand and can I just say – I know he wanted me.'

Despite a tricky start to the month, Sugababes went on to triumph at two awards ceremonies later on. The girls had been nominated for Best Single at the Q Awards, a ceremony dominated by mature rock acts. The media and A-list guests were stunned when 'Freak Like Me' was chosen as the top song of the year, over The Hives' 'Hate To Say I Told You So', Nickelback's 'How You Remind Me',

Oasis' 'Hindu Times' and Red Hot Chili Peppers' 'By the Way'. The Sugababes were amazed to be presented with their gong by Gary Numan, who they had not met since sampling his 'Are Friends Electric' hit earlier in the year. Heidi was thrilled: 'He said he really liked what we'd done with the track and said that he'd like to do other stuff with us in the future. It's strange that we only met him nine months after recording the track.'

At the after-party, Heidi caught the attention of Fun Lovin' Criminals frontman Huey Morgan, renowned for being a celebrity lothario, thanks to alleged dalliances with Andrea Corr and Cat Deeley. Gossip columnists reported Morgan attempted to persuade the 19-year-old singer to join him for a drink at the bar, to which she replied, 'I'm all right here, thanks.'

A friend of Heidi's told the *Mirror*, 'They did eventually meet. Heidi is fully aware of his reputation with pretty girls. She chatted happily to him, but was a little wary. She's a fan of his music and loves his style, but simply isn't interested in him in that way.'

After the busy festival season that summer, the Sugababes continued their travels up and down the UK on the Smash Hits Tour. The group joined fellow chart acts, including Busted, Blue, Gareth Gates, S Club Juniors, Romeo, Abs, Liberty X, Harvey and Blazin' Squad, at concerts in Sheffield, Manchester, Glasgow, Newcastle, Dublin and Birmingham. Due to their Manchester Arena gig, they missed out on the inaugural National Music Awards back in London, where the group won Best Song From A Movie for 'Round Round'. The gigs provided an opportunity for the girls to promote 'Stronger/Angels With Dirty Faces', which was being released a week after the tour ended. They also got to know their fellow stars better after spending long hours on tour buses and in hotels with them.

The Sugababes struck up a close friendship with boy band Blue, which backfired slightly when they were forced to deny rumours Mutya was having a relationship with Antony Costa. Soon the girls also became the victims of the pop quartet's practical jokes. When the two groups were forced to share a dressing room backstage at Glasgow's Clyde Auditorium ahead of their Hallowe'en gig, Blue decided to play trick or treat on the Sugababes when they were on stage. Heidi moaned, 'The boys had written in graffiti all over my hat in permanent black marker. They'd also put a bread roll and knives and forks in Mutya's bag. I went to put on my trainers the next day and found a beefburger in one of them. I also saw a fly hovering round my bag and, when I had a look, I found a beefburger in the bottom. It was cold and greasy, and all over my designer bag.'

The crafty girls plotted their revenge and hours before the next concert at the Newcastle Telewest Arena, they caused havoc in the Blue boys' dressing room.

Backstage, during an interview with a local newspaper, Mutya boasted of her battle with the band, declaring, 'We love Blue, they're like our big brothers, but this is war.' The two groups came to a truce and promised to replace the Sugababes' damaged accessories. Mutya explained, 'They were in Asia and I got a phone call saying, "What kind of bag do you want?"'

As well as playing tricks with Blue, Heidi had an

embarrassing conversation with Gareth Gates, with whom she had shared a stage during one of her pre-Sugababes' performances. She was stunned when the stuttering *Pop Idol* runner-up reminded her that she had beaten him at a talent contest on holiday many years before. She recalled, 'I went to a Haven Holiday Park when I was younger. I'd go with my dance school and we'd enter the talent contest. I entered as a singer and actually knocked out Gareth, who was also there on his hols. He came up to me and reminded me – that's my real claim to fame!'

In between concerts on the Smash Hits tour, the Sugababes were involved in a terrifying motorway accident. The group were travelling in a people carrier from Sheffield to Manchester, where they were performing at the city's Arena that night. Debris in the road caused the vehicle's tyre to burst and their driver struggled to keep control of the car. While the passengers and driver were left with just minor injuries, in the heat of the moment everyone feared for their lives. Religious Heidi and Keisha admit they prayed. News of the drama soon reached the press, who were eager to hear of the girls' brush with death. Keisha said, 'We ran over something sharp and a few miles later the tyre burst. Suddenly it was like we were a snake, slithering all over the road at high speed. I lost the skin off my knees after scraping them on the seat in front. But I wasn't scared because I knew, if I died, I was on my way to heaven.'

Heidi added, 'It was really scary and my life kinda flashed before my eyes. It's amazing the motorway seemed to be clear while it was all happening. I don't know how. I guess God was looking over us.'

After the tour ended, the Sugababes were packed off on press duty to promote their double A-side single, which was released in the UK on 11 November. Through their experience with releasing singles from *Overload*, Mutya and Keisha expected their new release not to chart so high. The album had been out for nearly three months already, so established Sugababes' fans would have the tracks. However, the label knew the slow balladry of 'Stronger' would appeal to a different type of music buyer than the fast-paced funkiness of 'Freak Like Me' and 'Round Round'. The tie-in with *The Powerpuff Girls* movie would also bring the group to a young 'tween' audience.

The day the single was released, the Sugababes played a one-off exclusive gig at The Scala nightclub in London's Kings Cross. They sang a selection of hits from their first album, as well as their Number Ones. Critics singled out Heidi as the most professional performer of the trio and having the greatest charisma – her stage-school upbringing shining through. The *Guardian*'s Betty Clarke praised the vocal abilities of Mutya and Keisha, but appealed for them to lighten up. She wrote, 'Both are tightly controlled ice queens, concentrating on the music, not the performance … Range has given the group a huge injection of charisma … Only Range looks happy and confident … The Sugababes make good, catchy, credible pop. Now they just need to be as much fun as they sound.'

The *Independent*'s Simon Price was harder to please. He wrote, 'Mutya is the one who's foxier than a warehouse full of unsold Basil Brush glove puppets. Oh, she can sing too, which helps. Keisha Buchanan is faintly Orville the Ducklike, but does a mean hi-speed rap and an immaculate soulful wail. In this world of *Pop Stars: The Rivals* and *Fame Academy*, Sugababes' untutored cool, natural insouciance and unfakeable chemistry makes them a national treasure.'

Six days later, the single entered at Number Seven, a satisfactory position for the group, and remained in the charts for 34 weeks.

Towards the end of the year, the 'Babes were exhausted. In the 15 months since Heidi joined, they had written, recorded and released an album, released three singles, performed up and down the UK at summer festivals and the Smash Hits tour, as well as touring Europe. A few days before 'Stronger' was released, they turned up late for a radio interview on Capital FM after falling asleep in their people carrier.

During their rare evenings off, the Sugababes took full advantage of their celebrity status and partied at all the top nightclubs in London, despite the fact Mutya was still 17. Keisha admitted she had been clubbing underage long before she turned 18 that September and claimed the venue bouncers didn't care about her age: 'It sounds bad, but they don't care about your age if you're famous.'

Heidi was determined to have a normal after-work life, despite the long hours: 'I make the time to go out, even if I finish work at 11 and I've got to get up at 5am. I'll still think it's important to make a bit of time to be normal and see your friends.'

Through their social life, the bandmembers were being romantically linked to members from So Solid Crew, Big Brovaz and Blue, as well as former 5ive singer Richard 'Abs'

Breen, although there was rarely any truth to the rumours. Heidi publicly admitted to having a huge crush on Coldplay frontman Chris Martin, but she knew she couldn't compete with Oscar-winning actress Gwyneth Paltrow, who started dating the rocker in October 2002. She gushed to the press, 'Chris Martin is gorgeous, just the best. I don't blame Gwyneth for being with him. I wish he was mine. But we're so busy we don't have time for boyfriends. I can't remember the last time I had a date.'

After their double A-side single was released, the Sugababes thought they could relax, but they still had plenty to do before the year was out. The awards season was kicking off, so their presence was required all over the UK, as well as Barcelona, Spain, for the MTV Europe Music Awards. The girls had been nominated as Best UK and Ireland Act for a second year running – but this time Heidi could attend, knowing she had contributed to their nomination. Yet again, they faced tough competition, this time from Coldplay, Ms Dynamite, Atomic Kitten and Underworld. The night before the ceremony, the trio were stunned when they were invited to rap mogul and awards host Sean 'Diddy' Combs' pre-awards party at a lavish villa in the hills above Barcelona. At the bash, the Sugababes started chatting to friendly R&B singer Kelis, who introduced them to their millionaire host. Over his few days in Barcelona, the Bad Boy Records boss attracted a string of bad press for his diva-like behaviour. The Sugababes backed up the rumours when Keisha told the British press: 'Puff Daddy's not very nice. Kelis introduced us and then he ignored us. You can't treat people like that.'

sugababes

Later that night, Combs was left red-faced when his party turned out to be a flop. During the night, three power cuts interrupted the champagne swilling and the annoyed rapper decided to leave his own party early to return to the Arts Hotel.

The next day, the Sugababes posed on the red carpet alongside Eminem, Kylie Minogue, Christina Aguilera, Nick Carter, Anastacia, Pierce Brosnan and Pamela Anderson. Like the previous year in Frankfurt, the group flashed the flesh again – especially 17-year-old Mutya, who grabbed the paparazzi's attention in a slashed-to-the-navel grey top. While Sugababes missed out on the award to Coldplay, they were honoured when the rock group's frontman Chris Martin paid tribute to them, saying, 'We didn't think we would win this because we are not as sexy as the Sugababes.'

Despite losing out on a trophy, the girls were more than happy to party with the A-list stars, following the poor turnout at the awards the previous year. The trio returned to Combs's rented villa for a second party, where they rubbed shoulders with Christina Aguilera, Jade Jagger and Italian designers Domenico Dolce and Stefano Gabbana. Although the 'Babes had been unimpressed with Combs's behaviour the previous night, they knew his party would be the hottest spot in town.

Following their dice with death on the motorway, a few weeks later there was more drama. The girls' all-work and too-much-play lifestyle began catching up with them. After taping a pre-recorded performance for *Later With Jools Holland*, Sugababes were invited to a special Orange-sponsored gig by Ms Dynamite, who shared the same parent label Universal. It was a long day for Heidi, but she was a fan of the female rapper and wanted to see the gig. Heidi joined Liberty X, *EastEnders'* actor Gary Beadle and 'Abs' – with whom she had been romantically linked – at the CC Club in London's Coventry Street for the exclusive concert. But she hadn't eaten properly all day and, once she was in the hot, sweaty club, Heidi was overcome by a sick feeling. She staggered outside with one of her record label aides, where onlookers claimed she fainted for 15 seconds, before being roused by one of her friends.

When news of the incident reached the press, it was blown out of proportion. One 'witness' told the *Sun* that Heidi had been 'foaming at the mouth'. The band's spokesman was keen to stress that Heidi wasn't ill and released a statement: 'The girls have had an amazingly busy year. Their schedule has been intense. Last week alone they flew to Barcelona for the MTV Awards on Thursday, then performed for Children In Need on Friday night in Middlesbrough. Then it was down to London on Saturday morning for the *Saturday Show*. That started at 5am, so you can imagine how tired they must be. On Wednesday, Heidi hadn't had a square meal all day and was feeling very faint. But she is now feeling OK and after the morning off on Thursday the girls are working again.'

The *Liverpool Echo* newspaper quickly got on the phone to her mum Karen, who reiterated Heidi needed to make sure she was eating properly. She said, 'Heidi's fine. It was packed and before she got out she fainted. She phoned me afterwards and was a bit upset about it and the first thing I said to her was: "Have you eaten?" She had been racing around all day and hadn't eaten enough and the doctor told her her blood sugar levels were too low and she was exhausted. He told her to make sure she eats if she is working that hard.'

Heidi's mum wasn't the only parent worried by the group's busy schedule. Mutya's mother Rose was astounded at her daughter's energy and pleaded with her to get more sleep. Despite the Sugababes' busy schedule, Mutya was out to all hours with her friends, then retreated to her Kingsbury home for a few hours' sleep before she was back to band duties. She admitted, 'My mum's complaining 'cause I work all day, go home, eat something, get dressed and go back out. So my mum's like, "You're gonna collapse. You're gonna really seriously damage yourself." And I'm like, "Yeah, yeah, whatever," and in the mornings, when I know I have to get up, I'm feeling the pain and know I should have listened to her and should have gone to bed early.'

Besides working long hours, in interviews it soon appeared to be the case that Heidi wasn't eating as well as she could and was insecure about her weight. She complained her younger bandmates could eat whatever they liked and not gain weight. Keisha boasted to reporters that she loved eating fast food: 'Everyone knows I eat like a pig – say four packets of crisps at a time. I love KFC in the morning and McDonald's for lunch, and then I'll go to a Caribbean shop for my dinner.'

Despite appearing to be the most confident on stage, it seemed Heidi was less confident in real life. She thought she looked 'fat' on television and told Q *magazine* she was on a diet to 'make me feel better'. She moaned, 'The other girls are so lucky. I'm on a diet. I'm always starving. I live on tuna and I like baked potatoes. I have to watch what I eat, I'm the only one. These two eat and eat, and don't put any weight on.'

Just four days after Heidi's collapse, the group performed at the Smash Hits Poll Winners Party at the London Arena, the same venue at which they sang for the MOBOs just six weeks earlier. The Sugababes were desperate to meet Justin Timberlake, who was scheduled to host the star-studded ceremony, but he pulled out at the last minute after breaking his foot. After winning the Best Album for *Angels With Dirty Faces*, the Sugababes carried on their quest for the Party Animals of the Year award by joining their chart contemporaries at the Click nightspot in Wardour Street, Soho. They barely had time to think before attending rival awards ceremony *Top Of The Pop* Awards at the Manchester M.E.N. Arena a few days later. Despite being nominated in a handful of categories, the group went home empty handed. The *TOTP* Awards finally brought an end to their UK promotional duties for the moment and the 'Babes were whisked off to sunny Australia to film the new video for 'Shape' and to perform on the Rumba tour Down Under.

During their trips to Europe over the past year, Mutya and Keisha had become used to Heidi's fear of flying but they were dreading the 24-hour flight to Australia. Fortunately, because Heidi and the band had been so busy in the run-up to their Antipodean adventure, she had little time to think about the journey ahead before boarding the plane. She was excited about visiting the country – she hadn't been a member of Sugababes when Keisha and Heidi visited Australia just 16 months earlier with former bandmate Siobhan. The brief stopover in Los Angeles meant Mutya and Keisha would have to hear her running commentary of the plane starting up and taking off twice, much to their annoyance. Keisha explained, 'The plane will move a bit, and she'll be giving us a running commentary: "That's the wheels, that's the engine."'

Heidi admits she drives her band and management team insane with her in-flight behaviour, but she can't seem to get past it. She says, 'I'm petrified of flying so by the time we arrive in a country I feel like I am destroyed before we even start doing any work. I have to go through the whole traumatising experience of flying and I just hate it. I cry and grab hold of Keisha. I cry and shout obscene words across the plane. Flying is the one thing I hate about my job. I'm not scared of heights, I just don't think I should be in the middle of the sky.'

First stop on the Rumba tour was Perth, Western Australia. The girls shared the stage with label-mate Shaggy, Pink, Natalie Imbruglia and Liberty X, along with other homegrown stars. Keisha and Mutya were especially glad to have been given the opportunity to perform in Australia. Their first trip in August 2001 was mainly promotional and they spent their few days Down Under talking to newspapers, radio and TV stations instead of singing. Their Australian album and singles sales had been adequate, but the group and their label knew they could sell much more. Their highest-charting song there had been 'Round Round' at Number 13 earlier that year. During the five-date tour, the Sugababes visited all the major cities in Australia, including Adelaide, Melbourne, Brisbane and Sydney. In between sets, they hung out backstage with Pink, who soon started telling the media that she was a fan of the English pop trio. Pink, real name Alecia Moore, chatted backstage to Heidi about their respective families and found they were worlds apart. While Heidi had spent most of her teenage years living with her mum following her parents' divorce, Pink remained closer to her father, a Vietnam War veteran, after her parents' split. Pink said, 'I was on tour with the Sugababes in Australia and one of them was like: "I really miss my mum." I was like: "Oh, wow! I've never said that before, are you OK with it? Do you need some therapy?"'

In between dates on the Rumba tour, the Sugababes were summoned to Fox Studios in Sydney to record the big-budget video for 'Shape', their fourth release from the *Angels'* album. The group's producer Craig Dodd dreamed up the idea for Sugababes to sample Sting's song 'Shape Of My Heart' from his 1993 *Ten Summoner's Tale* album. Initially, the girls were happy to sample the track if they received permission, but were amazed when the superstar offered to re-record his vocals. Keisha enthused, 'We sampled the guitar and the chorus and it had already been written for us. We went in there and we basically put our flavour on it, sung it, did a few free-styles and that was it. Sting got back to us and told us that not only could we use the sample, but he was also a big fan! That was great to hear.'

Ahead of the song's release, Heidi embarrassingly admitted she didn't know much of Sting's music and only knew of his work because Diddy had sampled The Police's 'Every Breath You Take' on one of his biggest songs. She explained, 'I was very familiar with "I'll Be Missing You" with Puff Daddy. I don't think he has gone by his sell-by date. He is cool and hip. My mum was a big fan of his. But it's not what I grew up listening to.'

The Sugababes invited Sting to join them in Australia to film the video, but he was too busy. The group had landed a huge coup by enrolling the team behind Baz Luhrmann's visual masterpiece *Moulin Rouge!* to direct the promo for 'Shape'. In the video the girls are turned into fairy-like creatures at a masked ball, wearing moving butterfly outfits. In reality, the Sugababes spent hours in nude suits, so the butterflies could be added digitally later on. After attracting the attention of handsome males at the ball, the Sugababes flee the party as their butterfly outfits disintegrate, before they leap in the air and land in a pool below. The *Sun* newspaper claimed the video was originally sent back to the studio for re-editing, because too much of the Sugababes' flesh was on show in the first copy. Heidi revealed, 'There was just one butterfly covering each nipple. We've got the copies and they're being kept away from fans. My dad would shoot me if he saw the original. There was practically nothing to cover me – you could see the whole of my bottom!'

Returning from Sydney, the girls were stunned to bump into ex-member Siobhan in the London nightclub Propaganda. Siobhan had signed to London Records and was recording her debut solo album, which was scheduled for release the following year. She was having a night out with her friends when she noticed Mutya. At first she couldn't believe her eyes. She realised it was inevitable they would run into each other at some point because they socialised in the same nightclubs, but when she saw Mutya in the flesh she panicked. But she needn't have worried: a few months earlier, Mutya offered an olive branch in an interview with Scotland's *Daily Record*. She said, 'We haven't spoken to Siobhan since she left. It was a difficult time, but we haven't fallen out – we want her to have good luck in whatever she is going to do.'

Speaking to *The Face* magazine in 2003, Siobhan recalled, 'I saw Mutya – I walked straight past her at first because I didn't notice her. I hadn't seen her in a year and a half and I was saying, "Fuck, what do I do?" I went up and spoke to her and it was like, "Whatever shit happened…" Keisha came down later and we spoke as well, and it was … polite. I met Heidi and she's very nice, a nice girl. I really hope they get on.'

A few weeks later, Keisha declared they had made their peace: 'She said she didn't get in touch because she didn't know how me and Mutya would react to the fact she had left without giving an explanation. But she said it was nice now we've got things sorted. We just didn't know, because she said she'd be back one minute and the next, she never came. But now I've spoken to her, we're fine with it. We had no idea why she left the group. We still don't. We chose not to ask because that was then and this is now.' Despite being somewhat perturbed that Siobhan had managed to secure a contract with the label that had dumped them, the Sugababes still wished her luck with her solo career.

CHAPTER 12

Three's A Crowd?

AFTER THE SUGABABES' return from Australia just in time for Christmas, it was another three months before 'Shape' was released in the UK. This gap gave the group time to start working on their next album. They started off the year on a good note when the BPI confirmed 'Freak Like Me' and 'Round Round' were two of the best-selling singles of 2002, at 28 and 31, respectively. By January 2003, the girls were bored of performing songs from the *Angels* disc following an incredibly long touring schedule the previous year. Exhausted, the Sugababes were ready to sign off *Angels*, but were given a huge lift when the Brit Award nominations were released on 13 January. They were told they should attend the nominations party press launch at Abbey Road Studios and were astounded to learn they had received nominations in the Best British Album, Best British Group and Best Dance Act categories, and had also been invited to sing 'Freak Like Me' at the ceremony.

sugababes

Despite having been nominated for a Brit Award before, to be mentioned in so many categories made the band feel truly successful. Heidi gushed, 'It's been an incredible year with two Number Ones and a Platinum album. Now we've got three Brit nominations. It doesn't get better than this!'

Just days before the Brits, Heidi's fear of flying appeared to have 'infected' Mutya and Keisha when a terrorist alert hit the UK. British and American Intelligence claimed there was a threat to aircraft security and Prime Minister Tony Blair authorised the presence of soldiers at London's Heathrow Airport. The group were scheduled to fly to Denmark for a promotional trip, but, after seeing tanks and soldiers marching around the airport on the news, they were terrified. Mutya explained, 'I think there are certain places you can travel to, but I think if it's just to do another TV show – I know it's bad to say – but, if it's one TV show, then I don't think you should risk your life for it.'

While the threats were real at the time, Heidi decided to make an attempt to tackle her fear and contacted celebrity hypnotist Paul McKenna. She knew she would be flying all over Europe for the next two months promoting 'Shape' and it was unfair to expect the 'Babes and her label colleagues to continue to tolerate her behaviour on planes. After undergoing several sessions with McKenna, he gave her a CD to play during her flights. Heidi enthused, 'I was really bringing Mutya down. Paul gave me a CD to play as well so, when we're flying, we sit there like a pair of nutters listening to it. We're really happy with the way everything has gone for us but the downside is we do spend a lot of time travelling.' Heidi briefly conquered her fear, but later claimed that she was scared of flying again.

Fortunately for the Sugababes, they didn't have to leave the country for the Brit Awards. In fact, Heidi only lived a stone's throw from the Earls Court venue. Even though she had attended the Brits the previous year, 2003 was extra special because the group had been nominated in so many categories, so Heidi invited her mum Karen down from Liverpool to share the night with her.

That night the red carpet became the battle of the babes, with Mis-teeq and Liberty X dressing up just as sexily as the Sugababes. Instead of going for all-out glamour, the girls decided to experiment with their looks and reach for the hair dye. Keisha mixed up a crimper style with red streaks, Mutya piled her hair on her head and had dyed most of it pink, while Heidi's hair was braided in green extensions. The pretty Liverpudlian attracted a lot of media attention on the night because of her slashed-to-the-navel green outfit. The crop top and matching skirt left little to the imagination and the sleazier tabloids zoomed into her chest the following day, much to Heidi's embarrassment.

Unlike previous years, the girls were disappointed to find normal concert seating instead of tables, meaning they were too far apart from their record-label colleagues. They barely had time to think about their nominations because they were too nervous about their set. Having got through a successful performance, they were finally able to relax and were completely caught off guard when they were announced as winners of the Best Dance Act. When they went on stage to accept the award, an ecstatic Heidi grabbed the microphone and admitted they 'really hadn't expected to win' and thanked her mother. Mutya was stunned they were even nominated in the category, let alone that they had beaten established dance acts The Chemical Brothers, Groove Armada, Jamiroquai and Kosheen. After her 'awful' acceptance speech, Heidi brought her mum Karen to the after-party, but found all the adrenalin of the day had exhausted her. She said, 'I went to the party but I left really early – I was knackered. Everyone's probably shattered and don't want to talk to everybody. Mum didn't cramp my style at all. In fact, it was one of the best nights of my life.'

Party animal Keisha was disappointed because she expected to see raucous behaviour when the stars had had a few drinks. She complained, 'I preferred the tables at the Brits though, it was a bit like a conference this year. It was like being at a cinema, it was really restricting. Justin [Timberlake] – he kept himself to himself at the Brits.'

The following night, it was another awards ceremony for the Sugababes. They sang in front of 400 people, including Sir Michael Caine and Brenda Blethyn, at the Variety Club Showbusiness Awards at London's Dorchester Hotel. Their high from winning the Brit the previous night was given another boost when the Variety Club named them Recording Artists of 2002.

Three months after making the video, 'Shape' was finally released in the UK on 10 March. Normally, the group wouldn't have such high expectations for a fourth release, but the song's chances of success were boosted by the expensive video and the live performance of 'Freak Like

Me' from the Brits was included as a B-side. As expected, the *Mirror*'s Ian Hyland praised the single, giving it 8/10 and declaring it 'could make Sting hip again … maybe'.

Legendary singer Sir Elton John gave the group extra kudos by admitting he enjoyed their music. He told America's *Interview* magazine, 'Some of the music those kinds of pop bands make – Sugababes and Mis-Teeq, for example – isn't bad at all.'

Ahead of the single's release, Keisha correctly predicted the song would miss the Top 10: 'I doubt it will be Number One because it's the fourth single off the album. We'll be lucky to scrape the Top 10.'

Heidi explained the release was just to boost album sales: 'People don't understand that the record companies are more interested in album sales and you put singles out to promote the album. It's sold nearly a million now so most of our fans probably have the single already.'

The Sugababes' buzz about the single dimmed somewhat when they discovered Craig David had also sampled the same Sting song on 'Rise And Fall', which had begun to hit radio playlists just before 'Shape' was released. Just as he had done with Sugababes, Sting re-recorded his vocals for David, but was able to share studio time with the Southampton R&B singer. In retrospect, it appeared Sting preferred the David version: '[I'm very proud] because the thing that you created evolves into something different … particularly with Craig. He made a fantastic song. Then he invited me to sing on his record, in a style that matched his, so I had to learn. And you know, he's a young lad and he directed me, very confidently.' Even though David's single entered the charts two months after 'Shape', it was at Number Two compared to the girls' Number 11.

As the Sugababes began the first headline tour of the UK, in the press rumours spread like wildfire that Keisha and Mutya were bullying Heidi. Some newspapers claimed they were on the verge of splitting, despite the group's and Island Records' insistence that the girls were recording a third album. The British press expected the trio to socialise together, even though Keisha and Mutya had mutual friends from their schooldays and a different taste in music to Heidi. While all the girls shared an interest in R&B, Heidi loved neo-soul such as Alicia Keys and India.Arie, while Mutya and Keisha were into UK garage and drum'n'bass. Heidi didn't understand garage at all, admitting, 'You don't get a lot of garage in Liverpool.'

When she was spotted partying in plush nightclub Brown's without her bandmates, and then Keisha and Mutya were seen together at Funky Buddha the following night, the gossip columns claimed there was a huge rift in the band. The *Mirror*'s 3am girls commented, 'It seems the only time the girls are together these days is when they are on stage.'

Rumours were further fuelled when the Londoners were photographed leaving a nightclub hours before Heidi. Keisha protested, 'When we go out, so what if one of us gets tired before the others and goes home?' Heidi insisted she got on well with the group, declaring, 'I know the truth. I wouldn't stay somewhere I was unhappy. I was in Atomic Kitten and I wasn't happy being part of that, so I left.'

Heidi's domination of the Sugababes' acceptance speech

at the Brit Awards a month earlier didn't help dampen the rumours either. An 'insider' was quoted in the *Daily Star* saying, 'The other two feel like they are the founding members and Heidi's just the new girl. Keisha got really annoyed when they got up and collected their Brit Award. She had several people she wanted to thank, but before she got a chance Heidi grabbed the microphone and just screamed down it.'

Out of all the girls, Keisha was growing the most frustrated with the bad press. After being cast out by her friends when she first became a Sugababe, she was sensitive to other people's opinions and hated being portrayed as a 'bitch'. In a 2006 interview with the *Daily Mail*, she admitted, 'I can be the most paranoid person in the world. When Heidi joined, if anyone spoke to me, I was automatically on the defensive. From the beginning, people have tried to knock us. We were portrayed in a certain way that wasn't always fair. Heidi was the innocent one, Mutya was the bitch, I was the boring one – that's how I saw it.'

Keisha's attempts to stem the negative rumours were made harder when Siobhan announced she had a solo deal with London Records – the same label that had dropped the group two years earlier – and started opening up about her time in the band. Siobhan's description of her unhappy life with the group singled Keisha out as the main problem, not 'moody' Mutya as the media had previously assumed. Keisha was devastated at being portrayed in such a way. She said, 'We have definitely been tarred with a bit of a ruthless image and I think that has been blown out of proportion. We have been called bitches, back-stabbers, everything under the sun. It's hard to shake an image like that and I think it all stems from when Siobhan left the band. We get on fine with Heidi and there has been far too much made of any disputes we have had with her. We all fight and argue sometimes, especially when we are on the road for a long time. But the bottom line is that we all get on well. It would be impossible to have any success if we were always falling out with each other.'

The girls' tour was kick-started at the Manchester Academy on 26 March before going to Heidi's hometown. Proud Heidi invited her whole family down to the city's Royal Court. After months away from Liverpool, she was thrilled to be able to visit home in a working capacity and make her mum and her Nanny V proud. Ahead of the gig, she said, 'I am really looking forward to the Liverpool gig because I'll get to see my family and friends, and relax and have a nice time hopefully. I want it to be a really great night for my mum as well.'

Following the Liverpool concert, there were more dates in Glasgow, York, Cambridge, Southampton, Bristol and London. All went off without a hitch, until they returned to Keisha and Mutya's home turf. The second gig of their two-night stint at the Shepherd's Bush Empire in London was interrupted when Mutya was struck down with a painful throat infection. Over the past two weeks, the girls had spent hours on an air-conditioned coach so it was no surprise when one of them fell ill. Mutya had just finished singing a solo number at the Empire when her voice cracked. After fleeing the stage, Keisha and Heidi were forced to continue the concert as a twosome, while Mutya went home to bed. The group's spokesman released a statement: 'Mutya caught a bug from the tour bus driver. She was feeling unwell before the gig but decided to go on anyway. In hindsight, it probably wasn't the best idea.'

Even though Mutya's illness had fortunately arrived on the last night of their tour instead of the beginning, Island Records had arranged studio time immediately afterwards for their third album, so that would have to be delayed a few weeks. Sugababes were also booked to sing at the TMF (The Music Factory) Awards in Rotterdam, Netherlands, but were forced to attend as a duo, leaving Mutya at home in London. Keisha and Heidi performed 'Round Round' as a twosome, but failed to wow the crowd. At the beginning, Keisha sang Mutya's verse, but, during the chorus, it was clear that the song required three voices. Keisha lamented to the press, 'It all came as a total shock. Poor Mutya is not allowed to speak but she'd better recover soon because we start recording our new album. All she can do is lie there, feeling miserable. She's become a text maniac.'

Mutya managed to get better in time to attend the Capital FM Awards at London's Lancaster Hotel. Despite the Sugababes being nominated in several categories, the ceremony was dominated by manufactured acts, with Westlife, Will Young and Atomic Kitten all winning awards. The group were thrilled when they beat Ms Dynamite and Coldplay to the coveted Best Album trophy for *Angels With Dirty Faces* – a last laugh to all those critics who had lambasted the disc.

Despite making friends in the celebrity world, Heidi was still lonely and missed her family, so she was thrilled when older sister Hayley offered to move down to London. Now sharing a flat in Kensington, the siblings thought they would spend lots of time together. Despite the change in pace from the previous year, it still wasn't as relaxed as Heidi hoped and she spent all day holed up in the studios writing and recording songs for *Three*. Her mum Karen said, 'They might have a chat before bed but Heidi is so worn out she just collapses into bed. Now the band are recording their next album there's no let-up. She starts work at 6am and gets back all hours.'

Despite her busy schedule, Heidi apparently had enough time to record a duet with Rod Stewart's stepson Ashley Hamilton – according to the press. Hamilton, ex-husband of *Beverly Hills, 90210* wild child Shannen Doherty, was attempting to get his pop career off the ground. After meeting Heidi in a London members' bar, the pair discussed a possible duet. Hamilton planned to record a cover of new-wave group Animotion's 1985 hit 'Obsession' with her. He said, 'Heidi has a great voice. She'll be perfect. We got chatting about music and I can't wait to work with her.'

In June 2003, Hamilton released his single 'Wimmin', which failed to make an impact on the charts. The alleged duet with Heidi never happened.

After contributing lyrics to the first two albums, the Sugababes wanted to get even more involved with the songwriting process and had been writing lyrics at home all year. Keisha had a love-hate relationship with TV talent shows such as *Pop Idol* and *Pop Stars: The Rivals* and was torn between whether the programmes were good at finding talent or cultivating a falseness in the music industry. The Sugababes prided themselves on being one of the few pop groups to sing live and write their own songs, giving them more in common with acts such as Coldplay and Busted. Keisha said, 'At the moment, pop's caught up in hype and image – people don't seem so bothered how you sound. *Pop Idol* brought that into the open. A lot of people didn't get through purely because of the way they looked. This doesn't seem to happen in America, where talent comes first. In England, being a pop star is starting to be something to be ashamed of, like being an undertaker. I don't have a problem with manufactured bands. Destiny's Child are manufactured, but they're one of the best bands around. The problem starts when bands are purely puppets. I find the S Club Juniors thing all a bit disturbing, although one of them told me they wanted to sing live, which is a good sign.'

After watching *Pop Stars: The Rivals* and being disgusted by one of the judge's comments, Keisha vented her fury lyrically by writing 'Whatever Makes You Happy'. Explaining the line about the definition of a pop star, she said, 'One of the judges said they couldn't choose between voices and looks. I can't understand how you can define someone's musical abilities by the way they look. They'd rather go with someone who looks good but can't sing. I think it's appalling that you have to look a certain way to be successful. It's not fair.'

Since the last album, Keisha had been romantically linked to a string of celebrity males, including Big Brovaz rapper J-Rock, More Fire Crew's Ozzie B and even Richard 'Abs' Breen – who had also been associated with Heidi. In

'Whatever Makes You Happy', Keisha accuses a mystery male of using her for media attention. Keisha used the man in question for inspiration in several of the tracks on the album that would become *Three*, including their hit song 'Hole In The Head'. She explained, 'That line was about someone I was dating who was in the music industry. This guy, well, some of his intentions were blatantly to get publicity off me. I haven't used his name, but we don't talk much anyway. But just before we stopped talking I told him lots of the songs on the album, like "Hole In The Head", were inspired by him because around that time I hated his guts. I'd never slag him off, I'd never use his name, but he did help me write some songs. I was going though heartbreak hotel [when we wrote the album], so, if there's any lyrics in any of those songs that are quite harsh, that would be coming from me. "Whatever Makes You Happy" describes how I am as a person and how that can mean I get judged for doing things I want, whether that's with people getting the wrong idea that I'm the flirty one in the group or whatever.'

'Whatever Makes You Happy' is the one song on the album in which she is the only Sugababe mentioned in the writing credits.

In between songwriting in England, the girls celebrated Mutya's 18th birthday at London's Funky Buddha. Even though she'd only hit legal drinking age in May, Mutya had been a regular guest at the capital's trendiest nightclubs all year. Now she was officially an adult, British tabloids let loose and began criticising the young singer. When she was photographed leaving her birthday party looking worse for wear, the gossip columns had a field day. The *Sun*'s 'Bizarre' column cruelly wrote, 'Some people have it – and some don't. Mutya Buena from the Sugababes really doesn't. To use a Jade Goody phrase, she is a bit of a minger.'

Mutya admitted later that she overdid the alcohol on her birthday: 'I felt so ill I was crawling on the floor and I puked on the stairs.'

The rumours of rifts within the band continued, but this time it appeared it was old school pals Keisha and Mutya with the problems. The *Daily Mirror*'s 3am girls claimed Heidi and Keisha were 'scared' of Mutya and had avoided her during her birthday party. A source was quoted: 'They stayed on opposite sides of the room – there was definitely an atmosphere between them.'

A few weeks later, the Sugababes were on a plane to Los Angeles to work with former 4 Non Blondes singer Linda Perry, who had written Number Ones for Pink ('Get The Party Started') and Christina Aguilera ('Beautiful'). The girls were huge fans of both Aguilera and Pink, and had started a friendship with Pink on the Rumba tour in Australia the previous year. When they entered Perry's lavish Hollywood mansion, they were nervous about working with such a huge producer. Their concerns were soon cast aside, however, when they met Perry, who was clutching a bottle of tequila. Heidi recalled, 'She's like, "Girls, we can't get started, we can't write anything, until you have a bit of liquor." We had a tequila bowl and were taking tequila shots. She basically had us on the floor and sat us down on beanbags and mics on the floor and just sing whatever we wanted to sing.'

sugababes

Keisha insists she has the best memory of the night, because she sat back and watched her bandmates get blind drunk on the Mexican tipple. She said, 'She [Perry] wanted us to be honest when we recorded, so she kept giving us tequila. She got Heidi and Mutya over-the-top drunk one night, and they made a rock song. Heidi was so drunk she thought she could play drums. They recorded this song that lasted for ten minutes and they couldn't even remember what it was about. We've got it on a CD; it's the worst song you've ever heard. They were so embarrassed. I had nothing to do with that. I fell asleep and woke up the next day and they've recorded a whole song!'

The first song they came up with was called 'Jesus Ghetto', about a pastor involved in a sex scandal. However, after considering the risqué content and how the congregation of their churches back in England would react, they changed the lyrics. Keisha explained, 'We didn't really want to sing about that, so we changed it to being about meeting a guy who brings girls into his nasty ghetto.'

When discussing their work with Perry, the Sugababes refused to be drawn into the controversial argument that Perry had written a song with Christina Aguilera that sounded remarkably like 'Overload'. Perry and Aguilera had written 'Make Over' for the singer's 2002 *Stripped*. When the album was released, several music critics commented on the similarity between 'Make Over' and 'Overload'. Originally the song was listed with just Perry and Aguilera as the writers. However, in 2004, the American Society of Composers, Authors and Publishers (ASCAP) quietly added the team behind 'Overload' – Felix Howard, Jony Lipsey,

Cameron McVey and Paul Simm – to the credits of 'Make Over'. Asked if she spoke to Perry about 'Make Over', Keisha replied, 'I think it would have created too much tension to mention that when we were trying to write a song. At the end of the day it's flattering, but she doesn't seem to think there was any similarity between them ... I suppose "Make Over" is very similar to "Overload".'

While working with Perry, the girls were approached by Californian ballad writer Diane Warren. Warren had heard good things about the group and wanted to work with them. The 'Babes admitted they had never heard of her, but were stunned when they discovered she had written songs for Celine Dion, Mariah Carey, LeAnn Rimes, Tina Turner, Meat Loaf, Whitney Houston, Cher, Michael Bolton, En Vogue and Aaliyah – many of their idols. Keisha admitted, 'It was a shock when we heard that Diane Warren wanted to work with us. Initially, we didn't know who she was but then we heard that she'd worked with people like Whitney and Mariah. So when she said she had a song for us we were like, "Cool." When we heard the song we loved it.'

'Too Lost In You', a romantic ballad about feeling completely consumed by a relationship, was the only song on the *Three* album which wasn't written by the group. The Sugababes visited Warren's home and discovered the rumours about her superstitious behaviour were true. Warren writes all of her songs in a small room at the back of her house, which hasn't been cleaned for nearly two decades. Heidi explained, 'It was just after the earthquake in Los Angeles a while back, and the whole room fell about and she hasn't touched or moved anything in the room since because she's really superstitious. There's this thick layer of dust on everything. There's this tiny little keyboard in the corner of the room that she writes all of her songs on.'

After their brief time working in sunny California, the Sugababes returned to England for their biggest gig ever – playing at rock festival Glastonbury on 29 June. The trio were shocked when festival owners Michael and Emily Eavis approached them in May, because they were so different to the normal Glastonbury acts. When they were first announced as an act on the main stage, the Sugababes were forced to listen to negative comments from the media and fans on internet chatrooms. While inside they were terrified, they were determined to prove the rock audience wrong and to show off their live-performance skills.

The day Sugababes played at the Somerset festival, they shared the stage with Moby, Manic Street Preachers, Feeder, Macy Gray and Asian Dub Foundation. As they drove to the festival, they heard their names mentioned on the radio by a misinformed DJ, who claimed they'd pulled out. Heidi recalled, 'We hadn't; we were on our way there! It was a bit hairy for a sec but it was fine.'

When they arrived at the Worthy Farm venue, organisers warned them that they might face being pelted with sausages by a few disgruntled stalwarts. Toning down their pop backgrounds, the girls opted for jeans and black T-shirts for their set, in which they belted out 'Overload' and 'Stronger'. Their fears subsided when they realised the crowd loved them – bar a small minority who obviously had too much meat on their hands.

Mutya enthused, 'Glastonbury was wicked. It was

definitely different from how we thought it was going to be. We were actually really nervous 'cause you know you hear certain stuff, us being … well, not "poppy" but the "poppiest" band on the stage it was like "Will they accept us?" But they did.'

Despite Mutya's enthusiasm, Keisha admitted her bandmate had ended up stepping in the pork: 'I was trying to give signs to Mutya but she would not read the signs. I was like, "Mutya, sausage, sausage!" and Mutya was like, "OK" … squash! Stepped right in the sausage. Me and Heidi were fine, though! It was one of the best shows we've ever done. We got a really good reaction though, and proved a lot of people wrong and proved to ourselves we could do it.'

After Glastonbury, it was back to Linford Studios in Milton Keynes to continue work on *Three*. The girls were reunited with Jony 'Rockstar' Lipsey, Stuart Crichton and Craigie Dodds, with whom they had worked on the *Angels* album. They also formed new working relationships with Karen Poole and Guy Sigsworth, who had worked with Madonna and Björk. Keisha, Heidi and Mutya continued their writing pattern of working separately and spending time alone with producers that enabled the girls to expand their production and songwriting skills. Keisha explained, 'I'd be with one producer doing some writing and the girls would be in another studio with someone else, and we all swapped rooms during the day. So there's not just one person writing each song, it's like there'll be one song where Mutya has written all of it with a producer, some together with all of us.'

Keisha ended up getting more involved with the album

than her bandmates, who she claimed were out partying a lot more than she was. She explained, 'I wrote quite a few songs on the *Three* album and that wasn't because I'm probably the best writer, it was only because sometimes Mutya couldn't come in because she had a hangover, and sometimes Heidi was ill, and vice versa. That's what the group's about – pulling together. If one can't make it, the other two will. Usually, we are together but obviously when mishaps happen, when you go out the night before or whatever, the show must go on.'

Heidi confirmed that Keisha wasn't such a party animal: 'Keisha doesn't really drink, so has two sips of wine and she's drunk. Mutya can get a bit lairy.'

Since the last album was released, tragedy had hit Mutya's family. In 2002, her youngest sister Maya died unexpectedly and the whole family was devastated. Defiant, Mutya put on a brave face and continued to fulfil her performing and publicity commitments. She was very private about her family and refused to discuss the circumstances surrounding the tot's death. It was only when *Three* was released in the UK in October 2003 that fans found out about the sad event. Mutya, who already had a 'Buena' tattoo on her arm, had returned to the tattoo parlour to honour her late sister with a permanent etching on her hip. Together with Craigie Dodds, she wrote the majority of 'Maya' in honour of her sister in the early hours of the morning. She explained, 'Maya's no longer obviously with us but it was just a song that both me and one of the producers that we work with quite a lot came up with. He's a Buddhist, and so he's very into the whole life and, you know, that kind of stuff, and so he was, you know, wanting to find out more about my sister and so we ended up just writing a track about her.'

The following morning, her bandmates returned to the studio and were stunned by Mutya's beautiful song.

Mutya was still sleeping after her late-night recording session, so Heidi and Keisha listened to it without her. Heidi said, 'I thought, I can't wait to give her a hug. That's a really personal song to Mutya.'

After writing the song, Mutya wrestled with her conscience whether or not to include it on the album because it was so personal to her and her family. She invited her mum Rose to the studio to hear the song, and she was understandably moved to tears. Mutya said, 'It made my mum sob a lot.' After discussing the song over with her producers and family, Mutya decided to put the track on the album as a public tribute to her little sister. She explained, 'I didn't really want it on the album mainly because of the fact that obviously it's personal and it was more of a fun thing to see what we could come up with, and we ended up really liking it. And so we just decided to, you know, put it on. But it was just something that, you know, was never really mentioned too much ... But it was nice doing it.'

After the success of 'Round Round' in 2002, the group returned to Xenomania's studios in Kent to write more tracks for *Three*. This time the girls wrote four tracks with Brian Higgins and his team, including two future singles: 'Hole In The Head' and 'In The Middle'. When the 'Babes arrived at Higgins' bolthole, he had already come up with the music and chorus for 'Hole In The Head'. The girls couldn't believe he had touched on the subject of annoying ex-boyfriends – something very close to their hearts at the time. Due to their recent romantic dalliances and mishaps, the bandmembers had plenty of inspiration and wrote their individual verses. Keisha explained, 'The meaning of the song is basically about a girl or a guy being in a relationship with someone and then breaking up. At first you were sulking and upset and then after a couple of hours you go, "You know what ... I'm going to go and get my hair done, and get myself ready, because I'd rather sell my arse than think of you again!" That's basically it. Normally, when we go in, we listen to the backing track and vibe off and write what we're feeling that day.'

Like 'Round Round', the band admitted one of their follow-up Xenomania tracks 'In The Middle' didn't make much sense. Higgins and his writing team – Miranda Cooper, Niara Scarlett, Shawn Lee and Lisa Cowling – had composed the music and written the chorus, leaving the Sugababes free to write their verses. Asked to explain the meaning of the song, chatty Keisha was unusually lost for words: 'To be honest with you, that song makes no sense to us whatsoever. When we heard it, we were like "OK, this reminds us of 'Round Round." Because, when we heard "Round Round", we didn't know what the heck it was all about. So, with this one, we basically just went off into different parts of the room and wrote what we thought it was all about. With my verse, it's just about me going out with my girls to an underground rave and getting dirty with it on the dancefloor, that's basically it. But I can't tell you what Mutya and Heidi are talking about, and I've never really asked them and I don't really want to know.'

Sugababes revisited the parental theme they first tackled in 'Look At Me' on the *Overload* album, in 'Situation's Heavy'. Even though Keisha and Mutya were 18, their parents were still very protective of them and fearful their daughters had lost the ability to be young and carefree. The song's lyrics appeal to their parents to let them make their own mistakes. Keisha explained, 'I was just thinking about growing up, because my mum still sees me as a baby, even now, she's very overprotective. All our mums are a bit like that.'

Heidi found *Three* an enjoyable process and an easier album to make compared to *Angels*. When she started work on the previous album in 2001, she had only known the girls a few weeks and they were studio veterans, having spent years recording *Overload*. In *Angels*, Heidi had contributed more lyrically to slower songs, such as her favourite 'Stronger', because of her recent heartbreak. Despite preferring to write ballads, she admitted her lack of a lovelife since joining the band had made it difficult for her to write slushy lyrics. She said, 'I haven't been heartbroken for two years now so it's been quite hard to write sad songs. Now I just think, God knows how we did the last album together. Because we didn't know each other really, knowing how well we know each other now, and how close we are. We thought we knew each other but we didn't really. So I think this is a lot more comfortable.'

Heidi did manage to recall her heartbreak for 'Buster', however, which was a song addressed to 'players'.

CHAPTER 13

Time Out, Please?

OVER THE SUMMER, while the girls were travelling around the country working on their album and performing at festivals, former Sugababe Siobhan released her debut solo single 'Overrated'. Almost inevitably, while promoting the single and her forthcoming album *Revolution In Me*, she was asked about her time in Sugababes and her response was mostly negative. While Keisha and Mutya thought they'd made peace with Siobhan, they were devastated when she went on to spill the beans about her time in the band. Mutya was amazed by what she read: 'We don't know what to believe because we saw Siobhan at Christmas and it was all hugs and kisses. Then we turn around and read all that. We forgive her but we can't trust her.'

Keisha added, 'We saw her before Christmas and she was cool. Then, all of a sudden, her single came out and she was saying that. I think it was her record company pushing her to say stuff.'

sugababes

The Sugababes' lifestyle was really getting on top of them. When they weren't in the studio recording *Three*, they were on planes or tour buses travelling to festivals or TV studios. During the few hours they had off in the evening, being normal 18-year-olds, they hit the nightclubs in London. Heidi's homesickness remained, even though she had lived in London for nearly two years. Her schedule had been so hectic; she was beginning to forget what her friends in Liverpool looked like. After the group's high-profile set at Capital FM's Party In The Park in London's Hyde Park, the following weekend was a manic jaunt across three countries! Heidi was thrilled to return home to Merseyside for the Summer Pops festival. Her family all got tickets to see her in action at the city's Kings Dock, and were upset when she was only allowed an hour to spend with them before flying to Ireland for a festival performance the following day. The next afternoon, Sugababes were one of the main acts alongside Coldplay and Badly Drawn Boy at the Witnness Festival at Punchestown Racecourse, just outside Dublin. On Saturday night, it was another flight to Scotland to sing at the T In The Park Festival in the Balado Airfield in Kinross. By Sunday evening, the group were completely exhausted. Not only had Heidi spent only an hour with her family, she had endured three plane rides, two across the notoriously choppy Irish Sea.

In late July 2003, Heidi's mum Karen made a public plea for the girls to have some time off in an interview with the *Sunday Mirror*'s Emma Cox. While the story was incorrectly spun to claim Heidi was close to a nervous breakdown, her mum admitted her daughter was homesick and exhausted. Referring to the Summer Pops concert two weeks earlier, Karen said, 'They only let her spend an hour with us backstage after the show before she had to go to a gig in Dublin. Heidi was heartbroken. She's only 20 and has to be so grown up and strong in her job – but sometimes she just needs her mum to give her a cuddle. She gets homesick and feels really down when she can't see her friends in Liverpool. The other girls are from London so it's not as hard for them.' Despite the tabloids' insistence there was a huge rift in the band, Karen maintained relations between the girls were good and it was the workload that was the problem: 'It's not the girls she has to worry about, it's the work and being away from home. They are all really close.'

A month later, the Sugababes were the subject of a string of bad press, claiming they were on the verge of splitting because of their heavy workload or rifts between bandmembers. While Heidi, Mutya and Keisha had no intentions of quitting the band, it was clear they needed a holiday. After a series of meetings, the management decided to cancel the Sugababes' November tour, so the group could concentrate on finishing the *Three* album ahead of its scheduled October release date. A spokesman said, 'The girls need more time to record their album so the tour had to be put back. We apologise to fans who have bought tickets but they will be valid for the dates in March.'

The group were thrilled when they were given two weeks off in August and booked holidays in Europe and the Caribbean. Heidi took her mum, Nanny V and sister Hayley with her to Mexico. Besides getting the time off, she was also glad she was able to treat her family for supporting her through her first two years in Sugababes. Despite the tourist sights on offer, Heidi and her family were happy just to chill out on the beach for a fortnight. She said, 'We just sunbathed and partied. My nan likes a good dance.'

But, while being able to switch off from her Sugababes duties, it appeared she couldn't completely stop being a Sugababe. Early in the holiday a paparazzo recognised Heidi and, despite her slim figure, she covered up in a sarong over fears she would be photographed in her bikini bottoms. She explained, 'I wouldn't walk around without my sarong on in case they caught a dodgy picture of my arse. I'm just the same as anyone else, I don't love my figure or anything, so it's not nice when the press pick up on things.'

While Heidi was swilling margaritas with her family in Mexico, Keisha was dancing in Cyprus party capital Ayia Napa with her girlfriends Emily, Kat and Jo. She had such a good time on her first 'adult' holiday without her family that she actually thanked her friends for the holiday on the album sleeve of *Three*, boasting, 'We definitely had it up over there.'

Mutya also booked a holiday to Europe with one of her female friends, but was dismayed when she lost her passport. After searching her house, she didn't find it, so decided to holiday in London. She explained, 'Luckily it was the hottest two weeks in years so I felt like I was abroad anyway.'

The Sugababes had been getting used to bad press, but couldn't believe the rumours that had been swirling during their two weeks off. Following the girls' performance at the Capital FM Party In The Park gig, the press speculated that

Mutya's slightly rounded stomach meant she was pregnant – despite the fact that she was single. An insider was quoted in *Heat* magazine: 'I heard some dancers in the artists' area backstage talking about her being pregnant and saying it wasn't too clever of her to wear something that made it so obvious if she wanted to keep it quiet.'

The Sugababes' spokesperson laughed off the rumours, insisting, 'I don't know if it was her outfit or the way she was sitting or the camera angle, but I've had 20 calls in the past week asking this question. But she's definitely not pregnant.'

Little did the Sugababes know the story would come true a year later.

Mutya wasn't the only Sugababe at the centre of ludicrous press rumours – Keisha returned from Ayia Napa to learn that she had recorded 'a whole album with So Solid Crew apparently'.

The stories about Heidi's 'fragile' emotional state continued and even claimed she had been approached about a solo record deal. Heidi was bemused: 'I went to Mexico and sat on a beach with a drink in my hand every day. When I came back, it was all over the papers that I had had a breakdown. I thought, Well, if this is a breakdown, can I have one of them every few weeks then? [The story of the solo deal] is crazy. All I have ever wanted to do is sing and now they say that once the band have ceased to be popular they can see me having a solo career like Beyoncé.'

It was back to work on *Three* and the label decided 'Hole In The Head' would be a perfect first single. The fact that it was produced by Xenomania was a good omen, after the production house gave Sugababes their second Number

One with 'Round Round'. With the pop scene dying out and rock coming back into the charts, the Sugababes embraced their inner rock chick for the video. But the group were astounded when they realised the video's director Matthew Rolston had helmed promos for their idols, including TLC, Destiny's Child, Brandy, En Vogue, Mary J Blige, Madonna and Janet Jackson. The plotline of the video very closely reflected the song lyrics. Heidi, Mutya and Keisha played girlfriends of a rock band called Erased. Backstage at an Erased gig, the Sugababes find their boyfriends in compromising situations with some female groupies. Furious, the girls storm the stage during the concert, throw the band to the wings and trash their instruments. Heidi admitted she felt incredibly nervous the night before shooting at the SE1 nightclub in London's Tower Bridge and phoned night-owl Mutya for a chat. She said, 'We hadn't shot a video for nearly a year before that and I couldn't sleep the night before. I was doing my solo shots first thing and was really nervous. Mutya never sleeps so I phoned up Mutya at about two in the morning. I was going, "Mutya, I'm really nervous," and she was like, "You'll be fine," and I was like, "It's OK you saying it'll be fine, but if it would've been with the girls doing it I would have felt OK."'

Despite Heidi's fears, the shoot went as planned and both the Sugababes and the label were pleased with the results.

After the video was completed, the girls were on full-time publicity duties to promote the single, and the album *Three*, which would be coming out in the UK just two weeks later. Mutya attracted media attention when she attended the Voyage fashion party in a transparent skirt.

The *Mirror* claimed the 18-year-old had spent the whole night flirting with Romanian football ace Adrian Mutu, 24, who had signed for Chelsea a month earlier. Meanwhile, the *Sun*'s 'Bizarre' column continued its criticism of Mutya's appearance, declaring, 'Whoever said pop stars have to be beautiful to make it obviously hasn't met Mutya Buena from Sugababes.'

Meanwhile, Heidi's partying wasn't going as well as planned. On a night out with sister Hayley at nightspot Trap, a drunken reveller started to hurl abuse at the singer. The *Sun* newspaper claimed Hayley quickly silenced the drunk with a slap around the face.

In interviews with the press, Keisha told of her excitement about the album and how she was looking forward to closure of the *Angels* material for now. She said, 'Last year was just amazing; we were just winning so many awards. A few people did say *Angels* was a comeback record and they didn't know what we were going to do afterwards, so we're really proud of the new album. We did get sick of performing *Angels With Dirty Faces* so we can't wait to go back and do all our new songs.'

Meanwhile, Siobhan Donaghy's solo career was not going as smoothly as planned. It seemed her debut solo album was echoing *One Touch*. Like Sugababes' first album, her disc *Revolution In Me* received positive reviews, yet didn't sell well. After her first single 'Overrated' charted at 19, her follow-up track 'Twist of Fate' entered at a dismal 52. By the end of the year, London Records had dropped her and the original Sugababes surprised the media when they admitted they were sad to hear it. Mutya said, 'Siobhan has talent –

she is a really good singer and she has looks. We think Siobhan has brilliant material, and it's the record company, not her, that made it chart really low. She's very talented, but I don't think she's got the right people around her.'

In late September, Sugababes attended the MOBO Awards at London's Royal Albert Hall. While not performing that year, the trio had been nominated for UK Act of the Year. The 'Babes were beaten to the gong by south London collective Big Brovaz, whose member J Rock had been romantically linked to Keisha months earlier. It was just two weeks ahead of the release of 'Hole In The Head' so Heidi revisited the rock chick look but with disastrous results. She was dressed in thigh-high PVC boots and a ruffled skirt of the same material, while Keisha opted for a loud multi-coloured shift dress. Mutya stood out from the other two with a glamorous slashed-to-the-navel black dress and strappy heels. In retrospect, the Sugababes admit the outfits were their first fashion mistake ever. Keisha said, 'The 2003 MOBO Awards weren't good for us. We didn't discuss our wardrobes ahead of the night and it didn't work.'

Two days later, when Heidi appeared on the PopShots panel on *CD:UK*, she criticised MOBO organisers for making the ceremony too Americanised. The award categories had been dominated by US acts, including 50 Cent, who took home three gongs.

When 'Hole In The Head' was released to the critics, it generated a good response. The *Independent*'s Simon Price claimed the song was 'the finest chart-topper since Kylie Minogue's "Can't Get You Out Of My Head"', over three years earlier. Yet again, the *Mirror*'s Ian Hyland loved the track and gave it 8/10. Sugababes also came 14th in the *Guardian*'s list of the '40 Best Bands in Britain'. They were singled out because, 'Every generation produces a girl or boy act that even indie types grudgingly admire – and, at the moment, the teenage Sugababes are it.'

The group went on *MTV Total Request Live* on 13 October 2003 – the day the single was released – and it was then that sparks began to fly between Heidi and TRL host Dave Berry. Heidi had fancied the cheeky Londoner for months and, now he was single, he was free to ask her out. After the show, the pair went for a drink at Century bar in London's Shaftesbury Avenue and so their romance began.

The day after the single was released, Sugababes launched a new Nestlé product, Kit Kat Kubes, in London's Covent Garden. It was their first advertising campaign and the group were paid a reported £250,000 to endorse the product. At the launch, giant sexy images of Sugababes posing in cubes were unveiled to the huge crowd of press and fans. The advertising concept behind the campaign was to encourage employees to take breaks, which the Sugababes found ironic, given their hectic schedule. Heidi said, 'This is a hint towards our record company. We're saying that everyone needs lots of little breaks and that we need a break. We so badly need it. We're basically involved with the launch of Kit Kat Kubes to encourage people to have lots of little breaks, but we don't get any!'

Nestlé chose Sugababes over rivals Atomic Kitten, who were also in the running, because 'their image is wholesome and family orientated. They appeal to a wide variety of people.'

sugababes

The week the group released 'Hole In The Head', there was tough competition. The Black Eyed Peas' 'Where Is The Love?' had reigned on the UK charts for six weeks, but the girls were hoping the British public were sick of it and ready to move on. Sugababes were up against Soca singer Kevin Lyttle's dancehall anthem 'Turn Me On', 50 Cent's 'P.I.M.P.' and Sophie Ellis-Bextor's 'Mixed Up World'. Midweek sales showed it was a close call between Sugababes and Lyttle – they were selling just 2,000 copies more than the solo artist. On 19 October, Sugababes were confirmed as the Number One artists after selling 58,500 copies of their single. In terms of international chart positions, the track performed better than previous releases 'Freak Like Me' and 'Round Round', scoring ten Top 10s worldwide, including their first Number One in Denmark and Number Three in the European charts. The single was in the UK charts for 13 weeks altogether.

Two weeks later, the group released their third album *Three* – named to reflect the number of members in the group and the fact that it was their third album. Despite various festival interruptions, the group also claimed they wrote the album in a total of three months. The disc was originally set to be titled *Points Of View*, taken from a line on 'Situation's Heavy'. The album met with a lukewarm response from critics. The *Independent*'s Andy Gill wrote, 'What is acceptable, even enjoyable, in the limited dosage of occasional radio play becomes, after only four or five tracks, a grimly repetitive and spiritually corrosive experience. It's not just that the trio's vocal performances are virtually identical from song to song, whatever the supposed mood; nor that the music seeks to avoid any idiosyncratic distinction that might challenge their fans' perception of the group.'

The London *Evening Standard*'s John Aizlewood believed the girls should take a step back from co-writing, claiming, 'Their insistence on co-writing everything save [Diane] Warren's "Too Lost in You" is *Three*'s ball and chain. The songs are just not strong enough.'

Graeme Virtue, writing for Scotland's *Sunday Herald*, said, 'Their third album is similarly scrubbed-up, chirpy and irritatingly polite ... Almost all the songs take place on an unspecified dancefloor in a club somewhere – presumably that's what the girls are up to whilst their army of songwriters come up with these identi-hits.'

But the reviews weren't all negative – the *Guardian* and the *Mirror* were pleased with the album. Dorian Lynskey of the *Guardian* gave the album three out of five: 'Thanks to seasoned hired hands including Xenomania, Linda Perry and Diane Warren, there are some terrific songs, among them "Hole in the Head's" sling-yer-hook skank, the predatory "Nasty Ghetto" and the deep-pile swoon of "Caught In A Moment".'

Ian Hyland at the *Mirror* continued his praise: 'This has been filling that hole in my head all week. 9/10.'

Coincidentally, *Three* entered the charts at Number Three on 2 November 2003. Sugababes couldn't compete with REM's greatest hits album *In Time: Best of 1988–2003*. In just six weeks, REM's disc went triple Platinum, although Sugababes managed to shift an impressive 300,000 albums in *Three*'s first month. Early the next year, the album would be certified double Platinum. *Three* remained popular up to a year later, when it re-entered the album charts at 25 in August 2004.

Despite their success in the music industry, the media continued to barrage the girls with negative press. Mutya became the gossip columns' Enemy No. 1 and endured more nasty picture captions when she was photographed stumbling out of a nightclub in the early hours – doing things most normal 18-year-olds were doing. The *Sun*'s 'Bizarre' columnist Victoria Newton criticised her appearance as she left her favourite club 10 Rooms: 'She continually looks like a prize minger. The hair, the make-up, the clothes – it's just all wrong. There's only so many times you can tell a girl to sack her stylist before giving the game up.'

Meanwhile, the *Mirror*'s 3am girls claimed Mutya had had to calm down her alleged homophobic friends when they watched Sugababes perform at the G.A.Y. club night at the London Astoria: 'Two of Mutya's pals couldn't handle the fact that two men in the club were openly kissing. "It wasn't like they were having sex. It was just two blokes having a snog in a dark club," said a source. "You see much worse in straight clubs most nights. But a girl and a bloke turned round and started giving the two guys real grief. They said it was disgusting and they got quite menacing with them. They said that they [should] stop what they're doing pretty damn quickly or else."'

Unsurprisingly, Mutya developed a hatred for the 3am girls in particular, and once declared in an interview with the *Guardian* that the columnists 'should've been number two' in the 2003 poll of Worst Britons. She fumed, 'I would love to know what the 3am girls' problem is. When we first started out, I met them at a premiere and then, when I saw them later, I had changed my top. They wrote this big article saying I was a diva because I was wearing a different top. Now they go out of their way to be nasty and mumble stuff when I walk by.'

The Sugababes were delighted when they were approached by writer/director Richard Curtis to provide a song for his new film. Curtis was one of the most important men in the British film industry, thanks to his scripts for *Bridget Jones's Diary* (2001) and *Four Weddings And A Funeral* (1994). He was making his directing debut with *Love Actually* with a star-studded cast comprising Hugh Grant, Emma Thompson, Keira Knightley, Colin Firth, Rowan Atkinson, Liam Neeson, Bill Nighy and Alan Rickman, to name a few. Ahead of its release there was a huge buzz surrounding the film and the girls didn't think twice about donating a song to the soundtrack. Curtis explained, 'I think the Sugababes are such an interesting band. "Too Lost in You" is really woeful, a worrying love song.'

Heidi was especially happy, because she loved Curtis's work. She enthused, 'I love all of the Working Title movies anyway. One of my favourite films is *Bridget Jones*. I'm a big fan of Hugh Grant too.'

The single was sent to radio stations ahead of the film's release and, by 16 November 2003, it had been given the BBC seal of approval and added to the Radio 1 A-List. Island Records enlisted Andy Morahan to direct the video for the song, which would need to be of especially high standard because of the *Love Actually* link. Morahan had been directing music videos since the early 1980s and had taken charge of promos for Michael Jackson, George Michael, Sir Elton John, Tina Turner, Ozzy Osbourne, Bananarama, among others. He had also directed Guns N' Roses' 1992 epic video for 'November Rain', listed as the ninth most expensive music video ever made on a reported budget of $1.5 million.

The video took two days to make and the Sugababes spent time in a film studio, as well as London's Stansted Airport. Because it forms such an important part of the climax of the film, an airport theme was chosen. A lot of the video takes place in the airport with the girls singing as they walk down a platform. They catch the eye of sexy male strangers and their imaginations run wild. Keisha explains, 'We imagine ourselves doing the ultimate fantasy with them.'

Each Sugababe acts out her fantasy with their desires – Keisha performs a lapdance for a man chained to a chair; Heidi throws an ice bucket over her hunk before feeding ice cubes to him, while Mutya teases her boy with a sword. Keisha's mum Beverley was on set during the day and the singer admitted she felt mortified to be acting sexy for the camera in front of her: 'It's really embarrassing because my mum was sitting there and I thought, I just can't do this in front of her. It's wrong! The crew were like, "Run your fingers over his skin," and I just thought, For crying out loud …'

Once the video was completed, the editor added clips from *Love Actually*.

A month before the single was released, the Sugababes were given a credibility boost by respected music magazine

Q, whose experts placed 'Overload' at 90 in a list of the 1,001 Best Songs Ever. The track was placed above Britney Spears's mega-hit 'Oops! ... I Did It Again' and just below Kylie Minogue's 'Spinning Around', which came out just months before. Meanwhile, tabloid gossips claimed the makers of the James Bond movies had been impressed with the Sugababes' contribution to the *Love Actually* soundtrack and had approached them to sing for the next movie. However, following 2002's *Die Another Day*, it was another four years before another 007 movie would be made.

Three years after their last race for the Christmas Number One, Sugababes returned to the yuletide competition by releasing 'Too Lost In You' on 15 December 2003. *Love Actually* had been a huge box-office success and remained at Number One in the UK for four weeks. The soundtrack album sold 60,000 copies in its first week and Sugababes were optimistic the song would chart well. On 21 December, the song just scraped into the Top 10, while the 'Babes fellow *Love Actually* soundtrack single 'Christmas Is All Around' by actor Bill Nighy entered at 26. Christmas 2003's Number One was the unusually sad 'Mad World' by Michael Andrews featuring Gary Jules. Sugababes' rivals Atomic Kitten managed slightly higher than them at Number Eight with 'Ladies Night'. In mainland Europe and Asia, the song fared better, however, reaching Four and Seven in Taiwan and Norway, while hitting Eight in China, Switzerland and The Netherlands.

Towards the end of the year, Sugababes were finally starting to see royalties coming in. Mutya wanted to reward her parents for their support over the years and bought a house in Kingsbury for her parents and younger siblings to live in. She enthused, 'I didn't move my parents to get away from the estate, but my mum's always wanted to live in a house, so it was nice to be able to do that for her. We're still just two minutes from the estate and we visit all the time because our friends and family are there. On a hot day everyone will be outside – the children playing and the mums chatting away.'

She also bought her own flat, but, after years of sharing a house with so many siblings, clearly she wasn't quite ready to live by herself: 'I think I've seen a ghost. I don't know if I was seeing things. I have just got this place and the bathroom light keeps switching on for absolutely no reason, which is really scary. Last time I moved out it only lasted six days because I was scared every time I heard a noise.'

Meanwhile, Keisha was growing concerned over the behaviour of one fan. A 19-year-old Liverpudlian began boasting of his 'romance' with her on Sugababes' fansites. The devotee was sending gifts and letters by the score to Keisha, c/o Island Records, leaving the singer worried about his alleged obsession. The report first appeared in the *Daily Star* and was confirmed by the band's spokesman: 'He's just constantly been bombarding her with teddies, gifts and letters. He's not a stalker, but it's getting that way.'

Getting into the holiday spirit, Sugababes performed at Capital FM's Christmas Live Concert in aid of the Help A London Child appeal at London's Earls Court in early December. In an attempt to finally quieten rumours about rifts within the band, the trio were incredibly tactile with each other on stage and boasted of their close friendship to the attending press. Mutya explained, 'As far as we're concerned, I say, if you want to kiss a girl, kiss a girl. Me and Heidi snog all the time. It's whatever floats your boat, it's no big thing. Tongues are too far, but lip on lip is cool. I'm always kissing my girlfriends.'

Despite Mutya's 'no tongues' insistence, the following day, the *Mirror*'s 3am girls quoted an onlooker who claimed to have witnessed Keisha and Mutya enjoying 'a real raunchy snog'.

CHAPTER 14

Year of the Cat ... Fight

2004 STARTED OFF well for Sugababes. All three of the girls had been dating new boyfriends for a few months and things were going smoothly. They'd had some time off over Christmas and the New Year to relax at home with their families and now they had a busy year ahead. That spring would be their first ten-date headlining tour of the UK and they had also been invited to perform at the MTV Asia Awards in Singapore in February. On 12 January, Sugababes found out they had been nominated for Best British Group at the Brit Awards the following month. They knew it was a tough category and this time they were up against rockier acts The Coral, The Darkness, Radiohead and Busted.

But, before they began the awards season, Sugababes had to record a video for their next single 'In The Middle'. To contrast with the smooth balladry of their last release the group had gone for the fast-paced Xenomania-produced track. After working with Matthew Rolston on 'Hole In The Head' five months earlier, Sugababes and Island Records asked him to direct another promo. When the American director phoned Keisha, asking her to explain the song lyrics, she admitted she had no idea what the track was about, but it involved chaos and confusion. After some brainstorming, Rolston came up with a video that would be their sexiest promo yet. Keisha said, 'Matthew was like, "Can you tell me what the song is all about so I can get a treatment?" We just said we don't really know, we just want a lot of attitude. I think whenever we do upbeat songs they are the poppiest things we do – like "Round Round", "Hole In The Head" and "In The Middle" now – and we always try and make the videos have an urban flavour to them – sexy, street, very stylish and fashionable.'

The futuristic promo featured the girls dressed as different types of adult entertainers – Mutya was a poledancer, Keisha a table dancer and Heidi appeared to be a sexy cabaret artiste. Before shooting the video, Mutya embarked on a series of poledancing classes so that she could perform the moves properly. Keisha appeared to be the bravest Sugababe and performed throughout the video in silver hotpants and a matching bra. Meanwhile, Heidi was the most covered up in a black suit, with the jacket revealing a hot-pink bra to match the hot-pink room she was dancing in. The girls' relationships appeared to have boosted their confidence in their sexuality and they showed off their raunchiest dance moves yet. Keisha boasted, 'I definitely think this is one of, if not *the* best, video to date. We just shot it and it looks amazing.'

After shooting the video, it was off to Singapore to perform 'Too Lost In You' at the MTV Asia Awards at the city state's Indoor Stadium. The ceremony and after-party turned out to be something of a reunion for Sugababes with their celebrity friends from the 2002 Smash Hits tour – Blue, Liberty X and Gareth Gates were all in attendance. The girls were also introduced to The Black Eyed Peas, who they would come to see regularly over 2004 during the summer festival circuit. The awards took place on Valentine's Day, which meant Keisha and Mutya were away from their boyfriends on the romantic day, but conveniently Heidi's boyfriend Dave Berry was covering the awards for his employers MTV so they got to spend the day together.

After socialising in Singapore, Sugababes dashed back to London to prepare for the Brit Awards. Following their fashion mistakes of previous years, the trio opted for sexy and sophisticated looks. Inspired by 'Hole In The Head' for her MOBOs outfit six months earlier, Heidi now turned to her sexy suit ensemble from 'In The Middle'. She stunned red-carpet photographers when she wore a white suit with black underwear, having undone the top button of her trousers to expose part of her knickers – a female twist on Mark Wahlberg's 1990s Calvin Klein look. Her male fans loved it, and the fashion industry was bemused.

Like many of the other celebrities in attendance on the night, Sugababes were glad to see the tables and the alcohol had returned. Despite losing out to glam rockers The Darkness on the night, Keisha was stunned when her idols 50 Cent and Pharrell Williams began flirting with her. She said, '[Pharrell] was like, "You are so beautiful!" and I was like, "Thank you", and he said, "What was your name?" And I was like, "Keisha", and he said, "Wow!" I felt really rough, but that put me in a really good mood. I had a smile on my face the whole night. I don't even think it was me, I think it was the dress ... [50 Cent] pulled me on to his lap and wouldn't let me get up. I didn't mind either; I just couldn't believe it – that's the fifth time I've met him.'

In the weeks running up to the release of 'In The Middle', Sugababes had a mini-tour of Ireland and Northern Ireland. After performing at the Meteor Ireland Music Awards at the Point Theatre in Dublin, they travelled north for a concert in Belfast and then to County Kerry in the Republic, before returning to Dublin. Hours before they were due on stage at Killarney, they were reportedly embroiled in an argument but managed to resolve their issues before performing successfully. The trio were then scheduled for two gigs at the Irish capital's Olympia. Before the first concert on Saturday, 6 March, the group were scheduled to have an interview with the *Telegraph*'s Thomas H Green and a German TV show and they had a meet-and-greet with fans.

At lunchtime, disaster struck. Britney Spears had just released her comeback single 'Toxic' the previous Monday and it was expected to chart at Number One the following day (which it inevitably did). During lunch, Keisha and Heidi began discussing the track at some point and it is clear they had very different opinions of the song. Both Sugababes have admitted to having a 'physical' fight, involving 'Britney Spears's "Toxic" and a plate of chips', but refuse to elaborate further. It's difficult to pinpoint which band member was defending the song, because both have said negative things about Spears.

A few months later, Heidi remarked, 'I think Britney Spears is a brilliant entertainer. I wouldn't call her a singer like I would call Alicia Keys a singer. She's not a vocal artist, she's never performed live.'

After the alleged fight, Heidi and Keisha were reported to have booked the next available flights to London, leaving worried management to arrive on the scene. Green, who was staying in the same hotel as Sugababes, claimed he witnessed some of the aftermath and his interview with the group was cancelled. He wrote, 'It's now nearly 4.15 ... Word arrives that the Sugababes' manager has flown in to "deal with a business matter that involves two of the girls". Everything is being delayed ... The clock reads 6.15pm ... The managerial talking-to, involving Buchanan and Range, is going on and on. ... By 8.45pm I've given up hope. The two Dublin gigs have been cancelled, and it's clear that no one will be seeing the Sugababes, neither the *Telegraph* nor the teens who flock round the Olympia.'

The management were forced to cancel the concert, giving the 1,300-strong audience just ten minutes' warning that the gig would not be starting. A statement was read out: 'Two of the girls have acute laryngitis so the shows were cancelled. They'll be rescheduled and tickets will still be valid. We will also offer full refunds. The rest of the UK tour is going ahead.'

Despite the official stance, rumours were rife that Heidi and Keisha had had a huge argument, although nothing was ever proven. For months afterwards, Sugababes denied the reports. All the Irish and British newspapers carried the story of the pair's alleged battle. The *Mirror* alleged a tour insider claimed, 'Two of the girls had a blazing row. It was chaos. They got on the first flights back to London which is where they are now and they are still not speaking. The problem is they spend so much time working together – and that causes friction.'

In an interview with Scotland's *Daily Record* three months later, Heidi denied the fight had ever taken place: 'There was no row. Our voices had gone. A footballer can't go on and play a game if he's got a broken ankle. We do a live show; we don't mime. So, if you can't sing properly, then you can't go on. It would have been cheating the fans.'

While denying the gig was cancelled because of any alleged fight, back in London, Heidi and Keisha were given a stern talking to by their record label. They were just two weeks away from their next single release and they had a whole UK tour to complete. Although barely out of their teens – Keisha was 19 and Heidi was 20 – they were told it was time to act like adults. The girls made up, but it was clear they needed some time away from each other. Universal's spokesperson said, 'They've had their meeting and they're now friends again.'

Just two days after the argument, the group appeared happy on Heidi's boyfriend Dave's show *MTV TRL* as they promoted 'In The Middle'. Sugababes were scheduled to appear on Channel 4's *Richard & Judy* show just six days after their argument when Keisha rang in sick with laryngitis. Her illness was called into question when the

Daily Star newspaper claimed she had been seen drinking and dancing until the early hours at club 10 Rooms the night before.

Three days before the single was released, the girls opened their first headlining tour at the Brighton Centre. Their small promotional gigs aside, this was the first time a whole audience was solely in attendance to see Sugababes. As much as they enjoyed performing at festivals and on the Smash Hits tour, this time they would be singing in front of a crowd who loved everything the group did. Before stepping on stage that night, the trio were incredibly nervous. Not only were they carrying the show alone, but they also knew the media would scrutinise their performance for signs of a rift.

Despite a technical hitch involving their guitarist Dave, the gig went smoothly. Keisha, Heidi and Mutya each successfully tackled a solo number – Ashanti's 'I Found Lovin'', Annie Lennox's 'Wonderful' and Monica's 'U Shoulda Known Better' respectively. After closing the show with 'Hole In The Head', Heidi reassured fans that the group were not splitting up. She shouted, 'We are not breaking up! Don't believe the papers – it's all rubbish!'

'In The Middle' finally went on sale. The tune was a catchy dance track with a strong bassline, but British single buyers were now turning towards more urban sounds. Sugababes had to compete against Usher's 'Yeah', Blue's 'Breathe Easy', Kanye West's 'Through The Wire', Outkast's 'The Way You Move' and Anastacia's 'Left Outside Alone'. On 28 March, they found out they had got to Number Eight, higher than their previous effort. As time went on, it seemed Sugababes' fast-paced, dance tracks sold better than their ballads. The song wasn't half as successful as 'Hole In The Head' and charted in the Top 20 across mainland Europe.

But the girls were too busy touring to spend much time lamenting over their chart position and later insisted charting isn't important to them. Keisha explained, 'As long as people recognise us for our music, we don't really care if we get to Number One or just in the Top 30. What's most important is whether you've got a good record or not.'

On the last night of the tour, Sugababes performed in London's Carling Apollo, Hammersmith. From the outset, the gig went very well but Heidi was frustrated with the bad press they had been receiving and decided to speak out about it on stage. She shouted, 'I want you to know that Mutya and Keisha aren't bitches and don't bully me!'

Journalists in attendance were shocked by her statement and remained unconvinced. The *Evening Standard*'s Chris Ewell-Sutton wrote, 'This would have been more convincing had it been delivered by all three, arm in arm, rather than just by Heidi, standing at a safe distance and wearing an expression that suggested she might have been relieved of her lunch money during the sound check. This bizarre outburst would fail to convince even the most loyal bunny-ear-clad fan that the Sugababes are best pals.'

Five days later, rumours were fuelled yet again when Mutya failed to attend the Capital FM Awards at the Royal Lancaster Hotel. Sugababes were nominated in four categories and won the Studio 7 gong for their live performances. A spokesperson for the band said Mutya was suffering from laryngitis – the same illness blamed for the cancellation of the Dublin concerts and Sugababes' non-appearance on *Richard & Judy*. A representative stressed, 'there are no big arguments' involved, and Mutya needed to rest her voice ahead of the group's European promotional tour. Whatever the truth behind Mutya's no-show, it was obvious Keisha and Heidi had put their feud behind them and they spent the whole ceremony chatting and laughing together.

Throughout April, Sugababes embarked on a tour of Europe, including gigs in Iceland, Germany and at the TMF Awards in Rotterdam, The Netherlands. Fortunately Mutya's voice was in fine form for a performance of 'In The Middle' that night, before the girls were awarded Best International Pop Group. Later that month, they were honoured to be nominated for a prestigious Ivor Novello award for Most Performed Work for 'Hole In The Head'. Unfortunately, they lost out to their friend Jamelia's 'Superstar'.

Meanwhile, in America, Sugababes were beginning to make an impact – albeit a small one. They had signed to Interscope Records, who were owned by Island's parent group Universal, for representation Stateside and released 'Hole In The Head' in April 2004. In the nightclubs the track had gone down a storm and went straight to the top of the US Billboard Dance Chart through its extensive popularity with American DJs. The following month it entered the Billboard 100 at 96 – the only Sugababes' single to do so. Interscope planned to release a special edition of *Three* in June, adding 'Freak Like Me', 'Stronger' and 'Round Round' from the *Angels* album. A new simplistic front cover replaced the original version, with just 'Sugababes' and 'Three' written in blue and purple type over a black background. *Rolling Stone* magazine reviewed the album, giving it three out of five stars. Critic Pat Blashill wrote, 'As synthetic international superstars go, the sprightly teens known as Sugababes may never be as big as the Spice Girls, but they're jiggier than Roxette and even more gangsta' than All Saints.'

The girls were hopeful of breaking America and knew it would take a lot of hard work and time. In between European gigs, they were booked to perform at a huge radio station event in Kansas in June. Often Sugababes had been criticised by the UK press for trying to make American-sounding music so they hoped they wouldn't have to try too hard to break the States. Mutya said, 'If we go to America I think it'll be good for us, because we're different. America's all about hip-hop and R&B, but we're not just that and it wouldn't make sense to change our sound. So hopefully we'll get to go there and see some funky people. I just want this album to do even better than we've ever done. It's a new campaign, new styling, new everything. We're hoping that our music will cross over and people will get what we're doing, and hopefully enjoying it, just seeing how it goes. We're not under any illusion that we're going to break America easily; we just have been given the opportunity and are going to have a go.'

Despite their plans, it soon became clear there wasn't enough time in Sugababes' schedule to devote months to breaking the US. Their summer 2004 festival season started early with a set at the PinkPop Festival in Landgraaf, The Netherlands. The festival was generally considered a rock

A new Sugababe is unveiled at the Meteor Irish Music Awards 2006.

Above: The sassy Sugababes at Berlin Fashion week, January 2006.

© *WENN/ Stefan Krempl*

Below left: The girls show off the new line-up.

Below right: Dave Berry, *CD: UK* co-presenter, steals a kiss from his girlfriend Heidi as they leave G.A.Y in London after Sugababes' performance.

© WENN/ Harsha Gopal

The sultry singers performing live. © WENN/ R Lawrence, © WENN/ Daniel Deme

Mutya moves on. She is pictured here with her good friend Shola Ama and her sister Sadie, at the 2006 MOBO Awards.

© WENN/ Z. Tomaszewski

bove left: Mutya with George Michael's boyfriend Kenny Goss at a arty in London. © WENN

bove right: Another ex-Sugababe is spotted out on the town. © WENN

elow: Keisha, Amelle and Heidi wow the paparazzi as they arrive at the orld première of *Casino Royale*. © WENN/ Z. Tomaszewski

The smiling, sassy Sugababes seem to cause a stir wherever they go.
© WENN/Z. Tomaszewski, © Daniel Deme, © Daniel A D'amato, © WENN

omic Relief 2007.

bove: Keisha, Amelle and Heidi line up for a photocall with Kimberley Walsh, Sarah Harding and Nicola Roberts from Girls Aloud. The two bands initially came together to record a cover of Aerosmith and Run DMC's Walk This Way' to benefit the annual fundraising event.

elow left: Keisha at the same event.   © *WENN/ Daniel Deme*

elow right: Amelle poses for a photo with a fan as she leaves a London studio.

© *WENN*

The stunning Sugababes looking simply spectacular at the 2006 MTV European
Music Awards.   © WENN/ Daniel Der·

event and the addition of Sugababes on the South Stage alongside The Black Eyed Peas, Muse, N*E*R*D and Lenny Kravitz was called into question by critics. In a backstage radio interview, Heidi defended the group's right to be at a rock festival, saying, 'We've been playing festivals for three years. We love playing with the live band. A journalist told us people were concerned because it's a rock festival, but, in my opinion, I don't think Black Eyed Peas are rock or N*E*R*D.' Sugababes silenced their critics with a good performance. They were given an unusual welcome on stage by local Dutch DJ Giel Beelen, who was naked as he introduced them!

In June, the group was added to the line-up of the six-day music extravaganza Rock In Rio, taking place that year in Bela Vista Park in Lisbon, Portugal. Yet again Sugababes were sharing the stage with The Black Eyed Peas and Britney Spears. The world's press decided to pit Spears up against Sugababes – even though they were unaware at the time that the American star's single 'Toxic' had caused the infamous fight two months earlier. Backstage, the Sugababes briefly chatted to Britney, who had met the trio at the London premiere of her film *Crossroads* two years earlier. Keisha wasn't impressed by Britney's then-boyfriend Kevin Federline, who she became engaged to just weeks after the Rock In Rio event. In a 2006 interview, Keisha said, 'Britney was a disappointment. She was doing this fake smile but at the same time saying, "It's so nice to meet you." Kevin gave me a *look*, and Britney just grabbed his arm and pulled him in close to her. You know when someone is trying hard to be something they're not. I don't think she's naturally very happy.'

Critical Mutya respected Britney as a person, but saw her as musically inferior to Sugababes: 'She's a beautiful girl … she strips and shows a lot of her body. She is making it because of how she dresses but it doesn't make her sound any good.'

Mutya was chuffed when the press praised Sugababes' performance over Britney's. While Sugababes' stage choreography failed to impress, their vocal gymnastics wowed the crowd, who were unimpressed with Britney's obvious miming. Mutya was horrified by the pop princess's performance, in which she writhed around on a bed with a sexy male dancer: 'It was full on. She just came across as desperate. There is a difference between wanting attention and *really* wanting it.'

Heidi said, 'I don't understand the whole Britney Spears thing. Britney Spears has always done playback. She's been going for about five, six years now and she's never really performed live and she's always sung to playback.'

In between festival sets in the UK, Sugababes travelled to Kansas City, Missouri, to perform at the KMXV's Red, White and Boom #9 event at the city's Verizon Wireless Amphitheater alongside Ashlee Simpson, Maroon 5 and JC Chasez. While their appearance went down well with the crowd, Interscope made the decision not to release the special edition of *Three* and so any American fans they acquired would have to import the album from the UK. No sooner had they performed to their new fans than they were rushed back to London to perform at the Big Gay Out festival at London's Finsbury Park on 3 July, where Mutya was photographed cuddling her 15-month-old nephew Enriquez. A week later, Sugababes performed at two huge festivals – the BRMB and Capital FM Party In The Park in Birmingham and London respectively. Backstage at the London concert in Hyde Park, the *Mirror* newspaper claimed Heidi and Mutya stormed off when a journalist questioned them about the Dublin fight. A backstage source told the paper, 'Someone asked them about all the in-fighting. Heidi and Mutya said, "Fuck this!" and stormed off, leaving Keisha alone to continue the interview.'

The negative press continued when it was revealed the trio were struggling to sell all the tickets for a special one-off gig at Ragley Hall, a country estate in Warwickshire. While some critics claimed fans had grown tired of the Sugababes' alleged warring, it was more likely a lot of the group's fans didn't want to miss the Euro 2004 football final taking place on the same day. Concert organisers introduced a two-for-one deal on tickets in a bid to shift them faster and realised the gig would have to start earlier. After warm-ups by Big Brovaz and the then-unknown Paolo Nutini, Sugababes began their hour-long set at 4pm so the crowd could return to their TVs in time for the 7.45pm kick-off of the Greece vs Portugal match.

The group took time out from the festival circuit to film the video for their fourth and final release from *Three*: 'Caught In A Moment'. Howard Greenhalgh, famous for his videos for The Pet Shop Boys, Sir Elton John and Sting, was brought in to direct. Unlike recent promos, there was no storyline to the video: the treatment included simple, black-and-white shots of the bandmembers singing because the song was so strong, vocally and orchestrally. Sugababes and Island wanted the video to focus on the track. Heidi said, 'The single is one of our favourites from the album because it's a track where we get to show our vocals. It's basically about being totally in love and out of control. It was because no one's ever heard us sing a proper ballad. We've always done down-tempo songs, but this is probably the closest anyone has ever heard us get to a proper ballad. With any of our albums, we never plan the direction it's going to go in, we just see what happens.'

The video included the individual Sugababes being caressed by male hands and an outline of a naked couple together. But the couple's antics in the video aroused controversy among some of the British media, which Mutya quickly laughed off: 'That's only because it's got nipples in it! The amount of fuss that's been made over the outline of a nipple, you know, of a man and a woman caressing each other which happens every day. It's nothing new to anyone. I'm sure all children have walked in while their parents were doing it.'

Before the video was even finished, the *Daily Star* reported the trio had been ignoring each other on the west-London set. A source told the *Star*, 'They quite blatantly weren't talking to each other. None of the girls had a clue what either of the others were doing, or where they were throughout the day. Keisha would ask the director or anybody else at hand whether he liked Mutya or Heidi's scenes and what they were up to. They didn't speak to each other once.'

Simon Amstell, then host of Channel 4's *Popworld*, visited the girls on set and mocked their lack of involvement in the video, asking, 'Does no one sit with you in a meeting? I can't believe no one tells you – even Girls Aloud get a meeting!'

CHAPTER 15

Babes Growing Up

THE WEEKS RUNNING up to the release of 'Caught In A Moment' were frantic. While the girls had spent August the previous year relaxing on holiday, this year Sugababes were travelling up and down the country performing at festivals and making TV appearances. The press had been so negative already in 2004 that they knew the only thing they could do was to perform live as much as possible and let their talent shine above all the rumours. Their open-air gig in Delamere Forest, Cheshire, started an hour late following technical problems but fortunately the crowd were understanding and cheered every song. A few days before the single came out, Sugababes took advantage of their celebrity status and joined Kylie and Dannii Minogue, Stella McCartney, U2 and designer Matthew Williamson at the first London date of Madonna's Re-Invention tour.

The single was released on 23 August and received a

mixed response from critics. Serious publications were impressed with the 'Babes vocal ability on the track, while magazines aimed at younger readers claimed it was too slow. The *Mirror*'s critique predicted Sugababes would outlast their fellow girl bands – which would turn out to be true. Atomic Kitten had already faltered earlier that year, while Mis-teeq went their separate ways in early 2005. The *Mirror* wrote, 'The Jony Rockstar production shows the girls at their most sophisticated, it's eloquent and slow paced containing a careful balance between cheesy endearment and professional pining. If they keep taking their singing lessons the 'Babes may yet outlive disposable pop life expectancy.'

During performances of the song on *Top Of The Pops* and *CD:UK*, the group wowed audiences because they sang it completely live, complete with violinists.

The day the track was released, Sugababes appeared on ITV's morning show *GM.TV*, where the diamond ring Keisha had been wearing on her wedding finger for several days caught the attention of the presenters. Keisha admitted she had been dating her mystery man – later revealed to be basketball player Zayne Alliluyeva – for a year and was completely in love with him. She said, 'We have no plans to get married just yet. He makes me so happy. I love him to bits.'

The song reached Number Eight in the charts on 30 August, but was unable to knock Natasha Bedingfield's mega-hit 'These Words' off the top spot. Despite this, Sugababes were pleased with the result – for a fourth release from an album the position was admirable. Having successfully contributed 'Too Lost In You' to the *Love Actually* soundtrack, the trio were asked to provide a song for another Working Title film production, *Wimbledon* (2004), starring Paul Bettany and Kirsten Dunst. The girls provided not only 'Caught In A Moment', but also album track 'Sometimes'. Meanwhile, the *Sun* claimed Sugababes were also in talks with composer Trevor Horn to record a track for the *Bridget Jones's Diary* sequel *The Edge of Reason* (2004), but the song never came to fruition.

In September, the group started work on their fourth album with American music-maker Dallas Austin, who had written and produced for some of their idols, including Boyz II Men, Monica, Janet Jackson, Kelis and TLC. The girls flew to Atlanta, Georgia, a city Keisha quickly fell in love with. So keen were they to make the most of being Stateside with Austin, that the 'Babes cancelled an appearance at the Smash Hits Poll Winners Party back in London, skipping the chance to pick up the Best Single award for 'Hole In The Head' at the Disney Channel Kids Awards.

The girls were getting very excited about their new material. They had only recorded a few tracks, but Mutya was enjoying what they had made already. She said, 'It's sounding very different to what we did before, but it's exciting. It's like the first time you hear it, it's like "Woah!" Everyone's walking in and listening to it and just like, "Oh my gosh!" It's the first time I think we've all kind of felt that excited about our music. We've loved what we did in the past, but it's like, when we hear it, it's like, "Oh my gosh!" – it gives you chills.'

sugababes

In early October, Keisha and Heidi attended the Q Awards as a duo, which inevitably sparked off reports of more Sugababes' rifts. What the press didn't know, though, was that Mutya was nearly three months' pregnant and experiencing morning sickness. No doubt the early arrival time of the awards ceremony put her off attending. The British tabloids were full of reports claiming the girls were making a greatest hits album, were on the verge of splitting and were in talks to start solo careers. While the group insisted they remained a trio, they were honest about their plans to go it alone one day. Keisha explained, 'We've never said we don't want to do solo stuff in the future. You see bands saying they're going to be together forever. We don't lie to anyone – we all want to do solo stuff.'

When Mutya found out she was pregnant, she was devastated – she'd only been going out with her boyfriend Jay for a little under a year – and Sugababes were just starting work on their fourth album. Instead of discussing it with her parents, she kept it a secret as she wrestled with her conscience over whether or not to keep the baby. Mutya knew her parents wouldn't be impressed to hear she had got pregnant at the age of 19 and she couldn't decide whether or not to proceed with the pregnancy. She had always loved children and adored caring for her nieces Jade and Chyna and nephew Enriquez, and she knew she wanted to become a mother in her future. On the other hand, she was just 19, her career was going better than ever and she loved going out clubbing and drinking all night with her friends. While she had always been against abortion, she wondered if termination could be the right option for her. Speaking to *Cosmopolitan* magazine two years later, she admitted, 'I was so stressed out [about my family and Jay's reaction] that I got quite ill and was in hospital for four days. Even though I don't believe in abortion, I was in two minds about having her. I couldn't eat or drink. I usually weigh 8 ½ stone and went down to 7 stone, 7 pounds. I had no idea how to tell everyone, or what would happen to my career.'

Mutya finally resolved to tell her family and Jay, and, as she had suspected, her parents were upset. Her mother and father were concerned that she wasn't ready to be a parent, pointing out her incredibly busy lifestyle and penchant for partying. Instead of this turning her off the idea of becoming a mum, she became more convinced that this baby was meant to be. When Mutya went for her first scan and heard the foetus's heartbeat, she knew she couldn't go through with a termination. She said, 'The doctor played her heartbeat really loud on a speaker, and I was like, "Oh I can't get rid of her." I had thought to myself, Let me go and get a scan photo first, so that, if I do get rid of her, at least I've got a scan. That was my plan. Once I made the decision, I had to pull myself together, get healthy again and plan it – that was scary.'

After making her decision and telling Jay and her family, Mutya had to inform Sugababes' management as well as bandmates Keisha and Heidi. Once she had told her bosses, Mutya prepared to disclose her exciting news to her bandmates, but was shocked when she found out they already knew.

When Keisha discovered Mutya's pregnancy, she was

initially devastated and thought the band would have to split up. She recalled, 'I did think it was the end of the band. Heidi was more like, "Wooo, congratulations," but I was shocked and concerned. My whole thing was that I wanted her to tell me and Heidi personally. That was the only thing I was a bit funny about. She told management and they later told us and I was upset.'

After her stress-related illness and morning sickness, Mutya treated herself to a night out with her bandmates. The trio attended the launch of the latest Blackberry 7100v phone at the lavish Sanderson Hotel in London. Heidi and Keisha had brought their partners, Dave Berry and Zayne Alliluyeva respectively – the first time Keisha had taken her boyfriend to a media event. Mutya looked tired and drawn from all the turmoil she had been going through in recent months, but she continued to keep her baby news from the press until she felt physically better.

On 13 November, Mutya decided to go public with her pregnancy and, to an extent, her relationship. Fans didn't even know she had a boyfriend, so were stunned to find out she was expecting a child. She released a statement to the press: 'We are both so happy and I am looking forward to having my baby. I'll take a couple of months off when the baby is born before rejoining the band to promote our fourth album in June.'

All she revealed about the father was his first name, Jay, that he was 26 and that they had met through mutual friends. When the announcement appeared in the *Mirror*, Mutya was stunned to read the 3am girls, who had been so nasty to her in the past, had called her 'Sugababe beauty'.

The day after the big announcement, Sugababes woke up bright and early to go to Sir George Martin's Air Studios in Hampstead, north London. Two weeks earlier, they had been invited by the Band Aid Trust to sing on the Band Aid 20 re-recording of 'Do They Know It's Christmas?'. The trio were honoured to take part: only respected singers and musicians were being approached for the record and the fact that they had been given their own lines in the song made them feel even better. Given that Heidi and Keisha were only babies when the song came out and Mutya hadn't even been born, they felt comfortable admitting to the press that they didn't know much about the original Band Aid.

The whole track had to be recorded and mixed in one day so radio stations nationwide could play it two days later. When Mutya, Keisha and Heidi arrived at 9.20am that morning, they were stunned to find a queue of photographers outside. This was the first time they had ever been photographed going to a recording studio. Inside, they were informed by producers that they would be singing Simon Le Bon's line from the 1984 original version: 'There's a world outside your window. And it's a world of dread and fear.' They also sang another line: '...Is the bitter sting of tears' with Travis frontman Fran Healy, much to the delight of Heidi. She said, 'I like Travis, they're really nice.'

Along with other celebrities on the day, the Sugababes were enlightened to the plight for which they were raising money when Bob Geldof showed them a video of the horrific conditions in Africa. The trio admitted they were very upset by what they saw. Heidi said, 'It just brings home what it is all about because everyone can get a bit excited and carried away recording the song. But, after seeing that, everyone was really upset.'

When it came to recording and filming the chorus at the end of the track, Keisha was on the lookout for Bono. After meeting him at the Q Awards ten days earlier, she had decided she had a crush on the U2 frontman. Heidi revealed, 'I think Keisha should probably stand next to Bono [during the chorus] because when we were at the Q Awards she declared that she fancied him, so she'd probably be quite pleased.'

Unfortunately for Keisha, Bono arrived at the studio late at night to record his line, after most of the stars had gone home.

During the climax of the track, the artists involved were given the chance to play an instrument. Jamelia, who compiled a diary of the day for the *Mirror*, was impressed by Sugababes' drumming skills, after they had practised the instrument in Linda Perry's home while recording *Three* a year earlier. She wrote, 'The Sugababes were on real drums and were pretty good – they have discovered a new talent but I surely haven't.' Keisha was also given a confidence boost when Coldplay singer Chris Martin told her his wife Gwyneth Paltrow was a fan. 'We got told the other day that we're the only pop band Gwyneth listens to. She really rates us. It's so flattering.'

As expected, the song reached Number One on 5 December and remained there for four weeks, including Christmas Day. The track sold 72,000 copies in its first 24 hours on sale and went on to sell over 1 million copies in its first few weeks. On 17 December, the BPI certified the release double Platinum and it was confirmed as the best-selling single of 2004.

The day after the song was recorded, the Sugababes flew to Atlanta, Georgia, to rejoin Dallas Austin at his mansion. There, they spent a month working on the five tracks that would appear on their fourth album. During their evenings and days off, Heidi checked out the malls of Atlanta, while Keisha partied downtown with friends. Meanwhile, Mutya was forced to take things easy and began to grow frustrated with her pregnancy. She missed drinking and socialising until the early hours and hated shopping, so just relaxed at Austin's mansion. She explained, 'I'm not really a shopper. When we go out, people are like, "Oh look, it's Mutya from Sugababes!"'

Keisha lamented, 'We can't believe her. She's even planned what her first clubbing outfit will be after the baby is born. She's said that a week-and-a-half after she gives birth she's going to have a large night on the tiles.'

Just before Christmas they returned home from Atlanta, but for Heidi it wasn't all smooth sailing. Not only did she have to endure a nine-hour flight, but also, when she finally stepped off the plane at Heathrow, customs officials stopped her at Arrivals. A self-confessed Christmas fanatic, Heidi admitted she had gone overboard buying Christmas decorations and presents in the US and didn't realise she would have to pay duty. She moaned, 'I couldn't believe it. They wanted to take away my Christmas decorations!'

Fortunately she paid the duty and was able to bring her new additions back home to Liverpool.

CHAPTER 16

Everything's Changing

FOR THE SUGABABES, 2005 was a year of great change. It would be their most relaxing year ever, but would also end in emotional turmoil when Mutya quit the group. It was no secret that the girls were taking time out so Mutya could enjoy her pregnancy, but the British press refuelled old speculation that Sugababes would split. Weeks into the New Year, the *Mirror* claimed Heidi was in talks to sign a solo deal with *Pop Idol* mogul Simon Cowell, after meeting him in Barbados, where he spends every Christmas. Heidi denied the reports, but said she planned to do solo work far into the future.

While Heidi's solo work was just rumours, Keisha did team up with east London rapper Crazy Titch. The grime MC, real name Carl Dobson, had met Keisha in Ayia Napa and she was a big fan of his music. Keisha was working in the studio on Sugababes' fourth album when a mutual friend told her that Dobson was looking for a female singer.

She explained, 'He was really quiet at first, a really sweet guy, really professional, funny and talented.'

Their collaboration appeared on the January 2005 compilation album *Garage Anthems 2005*. The pair struck up a friendship, and Keisha said she would like to work with him again. But a second duet looks unlikely – in November 2006, Dobson was sentenced to life imprisonment for the murder of 21-year-old Richard Holmes in Chingford, east London, a year earlier. Obviously, Keisha had no involvement in the incident whatsoever.

When the Brit Award nominees were announced on 10 January 2005, the Sugababes were dismayed to find that this time they had not received a single nomination. The categories were dominated by rock acts, such as Franz Ferdinand, Muse, Keane and Snow Patrol. They missed out on the Best Pop Act category, which featured Girls Aloud, McFly, Avril Lavigne, Natasha Bedingfield and Westlife. Just 11 days later, red-faced Brit bosses admitted they had made a mistake shortlisting songs for the Best Single category and were including an extra five tracks to the list, including Sugababes' 'In The Middle'. A spokesman said, 'It has been brought to our attention that the 2004 chart year comprised 53 weeks rather than 52. To avoid any ambiguity, and in the interest of accuracy and fair play, the Brits committee has decided to expand the nominations list to ten.'

All three members of the group united to attend the Brits on 9 February. It would be Mutya's last public appearance before she had her baby. While her bandmates flashed their toned flat torsos in their red-carpet outfits, at seven months' pregnant, Mutya wanted to stay low-key and comfortable and opted for a black vest and jeans. The trio lost out to Will Young's 'Your Game', but happily watched Scissor Sisters, one of Heidi's favourite groups, perform. After the ceremony ended, Mutya returned home to boyfriend Jay to rest her weary legs, while Heidi and Keisha partied into the night. They joined Scissor Sisters, Girls Aloud, Busted, Pharrell Williams, Gwen Stefani and Bob Geldof at the Universal Music Party at the Bluebird Restaurant on Chelsea's King's Road.

Sugababes were clearly revelling in their time out and, over the year, Keisha became a regular on the London showbiz-party circuit. In March, she attended the British premiere of *Be Cool* with her brother Shane. The siblings had become closer in recent years and Keisha knew her brother felt alienated by her success. She said, 'There are still times when my brother Shane feels a bit left out by the success I've had.' On the album sleeve for their next release *Taller In More Ways*, she wrote, 'Shane, I know it must be hard sometimes, but I want you to know that you are never in the shadow of me in my eyes. I'm proud of you.'

On the red carpet, Keisha was approached for an update on Mutya's progress. She was quoted in the *Mirror* saying: 'We've got our bags packed. Mutya looks ready to burst so it could happen any day. We're all going to be in the delivery room with her! We've ordered Mutya to take a two-month break once the baby's born – but she wants to return to work as soon as possible. She is just so stubborn. At the moment she's determined to start work two weeks after and bring the baby into the studio.'

After the film, the siblings joined Christina Milian, John Travolta and Keisha's friend Alesha Dixon at the after-party at nightclub Cirque.

At 3.30am on 23 March, Mutya gave birth to a 5-pound, 10-ounce baby girl in Worthing Hospital, West Sussex. The baby was just over a week early, but was healthy. Her bandmates were among the first to find out and, with Mutya's consent, announced the happy news at the Capital FM Awards that evening. Keisha and Heidi walked down the red carpet at London's Royal Lancaster Hotel clutching Winnie the Pooh balloons that read, 'It's a girl'. Heidi enthused, 'She had the baby this morning. It's all exciting; there's three Sugababes and a Sugababy now. We got a phonecall at 4am.'

Keisha added, 'It wasn't an easy delivery but Mutya's doing great now. She sent us a picture of the baby over her mobile phone. She's gorgeous, but so far there's no name. We're definitely not broody though. We've got a baby now, but we can give it back.'

When the pair were asked if they were there for the birth, Keisha recoiled in horror and explained she had been misquoted: 'I met someone at a premiere. She asked me how Mutya was doing and all I said was, "Fine" and that "I can't wait for her to give birth because we're gonna go down in the middle of the night and root for her outside the delivery room." No one said anything about actually being in the room, that's gross.'

Heidi continued, 'No way! She would have been embarrassed and so would we.'

Asked when the next album was coming out, Heidi and

Keisha said it all depended on Mutya. Heidi said, 'We wrote most of the album before Mutya took maternity leave. Since Mutya's been resting, Keisha and I are still going into the studio. We'll give her as much time as she wants. The new album depends on when Mutya wants to come back. We want Mutya to rest.'

While Heidi and Keisha were celebrating the new arrival, Mutya was recovering from the birth. She decided to name her daughter Tahlia Maya. Mutya choose Tahlia, because it means 'dew from God' in Hebrew – a perfect name for a baby born in the morning. The baby's second name – Maya – was Mutya's late sister's name. She explained, 'I just named her after my dead baby sister, and I just really liked the name. And it was handy, because I already have this tattoo of the name "Maya", so, if I ever forget my kid's name, I just peep at this, and it reminds me.'

Months after the birth, she added to her tattoo collection with 'Tahlia' written across her left arm.

Mutya plans to have four children in total, but is happy with just Tahlia at present. She said, 'The pain is horrible but it's great. I'd do it all over again because I know there's a baby coming at the end. When you have a baby you understand how much pain you can go through as a woman. You realise that you're a lot stronger than you thought you were.'

While Mutya was revelling in motherhood, it didn't take long before she was ready to return to the studio. Within weeks of the birth, the naturally skinny singer was back to her size-8 figure and told her record label she would be ready for a single release within months. She boasted, 'I never really had a big belly when I was pregnant. I was still wearing size 8 or 10. I don't know why, it just happened.'

The Sugababes, along with Mutya's baby Tahlia and boyfriend Jay, returned to Atlanta in June to continue work on the album. After getting to know Austin properly at the end of 2004, the producer felt ready to record a series of tracks for the album, including many more that didn't make the cut.

During her time in Atlanta, Keisha was 'on a break' from her on/off boyfriend Zayne. Austin had introduced her to a male artist with whom he was working and sparks flew. As a bystander to the fizzling chemistry, Austin was inspired to write 'Push The Button', a song warning a man to make a move before time runs out. Keisha explained, 'There was a cute boy that was a member of a group Dallas had signed. We both liked each other and there was some flirting going on but he was quite shy too so Dallas was playing cupid. I was chatting to him about it as this boy wasn't making a move to talk to me much or ask me out and he said, "Just go to him and say, 'If you don't get a move on and push my button, I'm gonna move on!'" I thought the boy was shy at first, but then I thought that maybe he was just a bit dumb and didn't see that I liked him. Dallas teased me all the time. That's where the song came from.' While Keisha refuses to name the mystery male, she admits they enjoyed a few dates, but the romance fizzled out and she reunited with Zayne when she returned to London.

The Sugababes formed a good relationship with Austin. He insisted on getting to know them properly so they could write honest song lyrics. Keisha said, 'Working with Dallas

Austin, who has done amazing people like TLC, Madonna; to be around someone who works with people we aspire to be like was very cool. We were the first girl band he has worked with since TLC. He said the reason he was able to write with them and for them was because he knew them so well. He wanted the same thing for us; he wanted to get to know us. For the first few months we didn't do any work at all. The record company were getting a bit worried. There was a lot more play than work.'

Austin had read lots of press cuttings on the group before they started working together and was shocked by the vicious rumours in the press. In particular, he found the cruel media descriptions of Mutya offensive. The cutting inspired him to write 'Ugly', a self-esteem-boosting song in the same vein as Christina Aguilera's 'Beautiful'. The trio were stunned when Austin sat down with them and wrote the lyrics in just ten minutes.

Keisha said, 'Dallas came across an article that said one of us was ugly. That's when he said, "That's rubbish. The girls do get along. They're not ugly." The song's about all the rubbish and nasty stuff that's been written about us, calling us the "Sugalumps", that sort of thing. It's about how everyone is different and we shouldn't judge people purely on their looks, and that everyone sees everyone else differently in some ways. Treating people differently because of how they look is a dangerous thing.'

Out of the group, Heidi felt the least comfortable with her body and regularly went to the gym to keep in shape. She admitted it really affected her when the press poked fun at her weight: 'The only time our weight became an issue was when they showed photos of us on holiday and called us "Sugalumps". That bothered me at the time because I was not feeling good about myself. At the time I had put a bit of weight on. It wasn't very nice because I wasn't feeling very good about myself and already had insecurities. But I'm comfortable with myself now. One of my favourite things to do is go to the gym.'

In 2005, Heidi had finally found confidence in her figure. She had started working out with a trainer and was proud of her toned abs. Keisha said, 'I wanted to show off my curves, Mutya has great legs and Heidi has this incredible washboard stomach and wants to wear crop tops.'

Heidi insists she eats properly after her fainting incident at the Ms Dynamite concert three years earlier, but burns off the calories at the gym if she eats too many carbs. She admitted, 'I do have pig-out days, but not every day. Parts of my body I don't like but I never draw attention to them. I have to work hard to keep slim and toned so I have a trainer and go to the gym. I try to walk everywhere. I also lift weights and do tummy exercises. It's vital not to stop as it's hard to get started again.'

The Sugababes took a line ('I grew taller in them in more ways') from 'Ugly' to name their new album: *Taller In More Ways*. The years of bad press about bullying and in-fighting, the unfair physical descriptions of the bandmembers and Mutya's transition from teenage clubber to adoring mother made the title all the more appropriate. Heidi admitted the new album was the first one in which she didn't 'hate any of the tracks. The title for the album, it means we've been through a lot as a band: the other girls lost a member, I joined, we got dropped, we got signed again, Mutya had a baby, the press were always saying we were splitting up. And we've overcome all of it. We haven't let any of it break us, and we're still here.'

While working with Austin, Sugababes recorded a series of R&B tracks. Having grown up listening to American artists like TLC, Mary J Blige and Monica, it was expected they would want to write similar songs to their idols. Despite enjoying the recordings, the group were well aware the music wouldn't go down so well in their native Britain and they would be accused of trying to sound American. Even though the US special edition of *Three* had fallen through a year earlier, the group kept the tracks aside in the hope of a potential US release. Keisha said, 'We recorded some R&B tracks. In Britain, we'd get slated for them. But there's no date for an American album. It's a different side to us, maybe a more urban side, but every single song we've released – from "Overload" to "Freak Like Me" to "Hole In The Head" to "Round Round" – has been completely different. To be honest, we felt we needed to give our fans what they wanted. They just want music that's very universal. We want to experiment with different sounds but at the same time we don't want to be something we're not and alienate people.

'Gwen Stefani is a great example of someone who can do R&B but it still represents herself. And the Americans do R&B very well already. I think we've definitely found ourselves with this album. This album is mature. You can definitely hear that we've all grown vocally, and it's a team effort. We're not just puppets on a string or the product of somebody else's imagination. This album is us.'

After being inspired by her late sister Maya on the last album, Mutya thought it only appropriate that she should write about her daughter. However, she is not the emotional type and didn't want a gushing 'ode to my daughter' track. Back in London, she teamed up with Jony 'Rockstar' Lipsey, who had co-written songs on all of the Sugababes' albums, including the powerful ballads 'Caught In A Moment' and 'Stronger'. Mutya said, 'Jony, who we did "Follow Me Home" with, said I should write something about Tahlia. I didn't want to make it corny so I wrote the first verse about her, but you can kinda relate it to other people as well.'

The trio also wrote 'Joy Division' with Lipsey and their longtime collaborator Cameron McVey. Heidi explained, 'There's another song that I love that Mutya's not very keen on, which is called "Joy Division". I really love that.'

The Sugababes spent longer working on *Taller In More Ways* than on any other album, yet they happily stepped back to let other songwriters take full credit for the songs. 'Gotta Be You', 'Ugly' and 'It Ain't Easy' were written without contributions from the trio, while 'Obsession' was a cover of a 1985 song by Animotion – a track that had been a rumoured duet between Heidi and Ashley Hamilton two years earlier. 'Gotta Be You', written by Tricky Stewart, Penelope Magnet and Terius Nash, was Mutya's favourite song on the album. Despite the Sugababes swearing they would never dance to their own songs in a bar or nightclub, she admitted she would make an exception: 'I guess if it came on in a club I wouldn't mind dancing to it.'

During the recording of the album, Keisha was keeping

track of Michael Jackson's child molestation trial in California. All her life she had remained a huge fan of the self-proclaimed King of Pop, but refused to judge him during his court case: 'I went through a phase when I was younger when I really fancied him, and wanted to be him. I was going to go to California to support him! But then I thought that might be a bit stalker-ish. I sat and watched the verdict live on *Sky News*. "Not guilty!" I was just like, "Ahhh," holding my heart. No one knows whether he did it or not – only God knows. If he did it, then that's no one's business, but it's something he'll have to answer to at some point in his life. And, if he didn't do it, everyone's just judging him for no reason. He's an inspiration.'

CHAPTER 17

Babes are Back!

AFTER THEY FINISHED recording the album, the Sugababes' schedule was relatively relaxed. They had decided to release 'Push The Button' as their first single and it wasn't scheduled until March 2006. For the first time the group wouldn't be doing the festival circuit so they actually got the chance to enjoy the British summer. They made an exception when Bob Geldof and Midge Ure approached them to sing at the final Live 8 concert: Edinburgh 50,000 – The Final Push on 6 July – the opening day of the G8 Summit at Gleneagles, Scotland. Sugababes accepted immediately; they had been following the problems in Africa and the campaign to end debt in developing countries since recording Band Aid the previous November. The month before, they had been involved in the 'Make Poverty History' campaign in the British press and were keen to give as much time as they could.

On the day, the trio dressed down in white shirts and

jeans. Unlike some American hip-hop stars who had 'blinged' themselves up for the Live 8 concerts days earlier, Sugababes joined the majority of artists who felt it was inappropriate to wear expensive jewels and clothing at an event raising awareness of poverty. The group sang 'Stronger' before exiting the stage for Keisha's crush Bono, who gave a message to the G8 leaders. Heidi got the chance to meet her idol Annie Lennox, who was also performing on the day: 'I met Annie Lennox at the show, which was great for me as I'm a big fan.'

Keisha admitted that when they first became involved they had been ignorant to the extent of the suffering in Africa. She said, 'We just learned so much. We've done things for charities before and all that stuff, but, with this particular one, we learned so much about it. I can't even remember the figures off the top of my head, but they were amazing. Appalling at the same time, because at the same time you're thinking, someone like Donald Trump, "Why on earth do you need so much money?" Don't get me wrong, people work hard for their money and they deserve it, but they should cough up the change too.'

Mutya declared motherhood had changed her and brought her more in touch with her emotions. She broke her tough media persona when she admitted she was incredibly angry and upset about the situation in Africa. 'When I see pictures of children starving it makes me want to cry. Since becoming a mum, these images upset me and I think, If that were my daughter, I'd want something to be done.'

After the Sugababes' contribution to Band Aid in November, they watched the DVD of the original Live Aid in July 1985. Keisha said, 'I watched the DVD and I saw, like, Boy George, Bananarama, all of that, but I didn't really know about the issues. Edinburgh, it was crazy to be part of something that'll go down in history, and you can look back at it when you're old and see that you did good.'

After their Live 8 gig, the Sugababes were free to return to their normal lives. Despite a photoshoot for their album cover and filming the video for 'Push The Button' in July, the trio were free agents. Keisha and Heidi finally learned to drive and rushed out to buy their own cars. Heidi said, 'I feel really positive and happy – I've also passed my driving test and ordered a brand-new Mini Cooper convertible, cream with black leather seats. It's really funny because I passed my theory test on April Fools' Day and passed my practical test on Independence Day.'

Summer 2005 was a year of great change for Keisha. She moved out of her family home and bought her own place, enthusing, 'I bought my own house recently, which is brilliant, isn't it? Of course, I've not bought it outright or anything. I have a mortgage just like everybody else, but that's OK, it keeps me normal.' Keisha also passed her driving test around the same time as Heidi and purchased a Beetle convertible. One of the first things she decided to do was to go on a girlie holiday to one of the Butlins resorts. Keisha said, 'My friend's dad, who is a driving instructor, took me out a few times. Now that I can drive, I like taking the roof down off my Beetle and going cruising with my friends to the countryside.'

In 2006, she admitted she had trouble keeping her foot off the accelerator when she first got behind the wheel:

'I've been caught speeding about four or five times but the cameras were hidden. If you're supposed to be driving at 20 miles-per-hour there should be big enough signs for people like me, who might need glasses to be able to see that. I was only at 30. It always happens to me on the same road. You go at, like, 35 and I think it's supposed be 20. It's not like it was really fast, but obviously it is compared to the speed limit you're supposed to be going.'

Despite all the time the Sugababes had spent in Atlanta recording the album with Austin, Keisha returned to the city with a group of girlfriends for a holiday. She loved the hot weather and the city's celebrity population: 'I've been there a few times and know some people over there. It's just a great atmosphere, everyone's always happy and it's got a lot of clubs – you just see Usher walking through them.'

During her vacation, Keisha bumped into Puerto Rican rapper Fat Joe, who had no idea who she was, but invited the singer and her friends to star in his 'Get It Poppin'' video. The song featured Nelly, one of Keisha and Mutya's favourite hip-hop artists and one of their celebrity crushes. Despite being offered a chance to sidle up to Nelly in the promo, Keisha declined to take up Fat Joe's offer when she realised they would have to dance around a swimming pool in bikinis. 'Fat Joe didn't actually know who I was. He was like, "Y'all should come down to the video shoot." We ended up not going, just in case we had to wear bikinis.'

Meanwhile, the 'Push The Button' single was released to radio stations and then the video a month later. The promo had been filmed in a studio in London's Shepherds Bush and directed by Matthew Rolston, who worked with

Sugababes on 'Hole In The Head' and 'In The Middle'. This time the video was set in an elevator of an apparently very tall building with the girls stepping out on the different floors to dance with a sexy male. Each of the Sugababes chose to flaunt their best feature in the video: Heidi was sporting her signature crop-top look, Keisha flashed her cleavage and butt in a short skirt and fitted cardigan, while Mutya was wearing a jumper and pants. Mutya felt sexier than ever after giving birth and wanted to show she had got her slender figure back into shape just a few months after Tahlia's arrival. She also chose to wear tiny bottoms to accentuate her backside, which was mentioned in her verse: 'My sexy ass has got him in a new dimension.'

When the Sugababes returned to their publicity duties, it was obvious to the media that time off had changed their attitude. They were refreshed and positive – at least Keisha and Heidi were. Mutya was finding it difficult to resume long days gigging and promoting, while caring for her five-month-old baby. She had become a calmer person and was less responsive to negative people: 'It has calmed me down a lot. From being someone who would go out from Monday to Saturday and get trashed out of my head, now I hardly ever drink. I was never an alcoholic but I did used to like a little drink.' She hoped the public would see her true personality and realise she wasn't the argumentative, moody celebrity the tabloids had presented: 'People find Heidi very approachable. She gives off a sense of being a smiley, happy girl. With me it's different. People seem to be intimidated by me, even small children. Like I'm going to chew off their heads. But I'm only horrible to someone if they're horrible to me. I've changed in a sense that I'll be completely calm around my child.'

Like all new celebrity mothers, she received a barrage of questions about her baby. She admitted it was a struggle trying to balance caring for her child and being a Sugababe, but insisted she was managing. In fact, privately Mutya was beginning to question her time away from Tahlia and only lasted four months in the group before quitting. She was grateful her partner Jay was so supportive and he travelled with her everywhere: 'It's been tiring and she's teething but I get a lot of support. It's about keeping a balance between her and work. Obviously, I'm a lot more tired, having to deal with her five times a night, getting out of my bed to make her a bottle. But it will get better.'

Her bandmates were supportive and loved spending time with Tahlia. Keisha assured Mutya she could work and be a parent at the same time after growing up with her own working mum Beverley. She said, 'There's such a negative spin on mothers who work, but my mum did. She raised two kids as a single parent. If you can handle it, go for it. Mutya no longer comes into work with hangovers. Now we know she's going to come in on time it's made us a lot tighter and everything's brighter.'

As the group prepared for their return to the charts, they were keen to let the public know they had grown up a lot in the past year. They referred to their Dublin argument in March 2004 as 'stupid'. Not only were they were getting on better than ever, but they had also begun to embrace elements of the job they had previously detested. Heidi said, 'One of the things we used to hate was going to

Europe to do press. We hated the travelling, the being away from home, we hated everything about it. This time around, before we started promoting the new album, we decided that we were going to enjoy it.'

After years of wishing for time off, Keisha began to get itchy feet during her time off and found she envied the success of Girls Aloud, with whom she had become friendly in late 2005. The rival group had enjoyed three Top 10 hits, including a Number One, during Sugababes' year out. Keisha said, 'It was tough watching Girls Aloud performing and doing so well – I wanted to be out there too.'

Ahead of the single's release, Sugababes appeared on *MTV Total Request Live* with Heidi's boyfriend Dave Berry. After reading a recent newspaper interview with the group, he was happy to hear his girlfriend had been dancing sexually with a gay guy. Interviewing the girls on *TRL*, Berry said, 'I hear all the boys on the "Push The Button" video are gay?' To which the girls replied, 'No.'

During the interview, Dave teased Heidi by feigning anger: 'What? What? This isn't the time or the place. What about the geeky one with the glasses that's with Heidi?' When Heidi declared her male co-star was heterosexual, Dave replied, 'Someone's gonna be in the spare room tonight.'

A week before 'Push The Button' was released, Sugababes joined Mariah Carey, Westlife and Sheryl Crow at the 'Tickled Pink' concert at London's Royal Albert Hall to raise money for breast cancer awareness. Since Band Aid, Sugababes had become much more involved in charity work and regularly offered their talents to help good causes. Heidi was delighted to be on the same stage as

Carey, who she had idolised since she was a child. On 26
September, the single was finally released to universal
praise by the critics. The *Mirror*'s Ian Hyland remained
consistent as ever: 'Girls Aloud might disagree but these
three young ladies are surely the biggest girl band in Britain
right now. And they've just come up with another slice of
pop genius that takes mere seconds to get under your skin.
And once it's there, it will never leave.'

MusicOMH.com's Tony Heywood wrote, '"Push The
Button" zips, bleeps, crashes and whirls like a PC in lust
with a Mac. The three voices melt into each like drinking
chocolate. The cyber groove is sassy and swings just right
side of rigid.'

It was no surprise when 'Push The Button' shot straight
to Number One on 2 October, knocking The Pussycat
Dolls' 'Don't Cha' off the top spot. While Girls Aloud and
The Pussycat Dolls were making their presence known in
the UK charts, Sugababes had something extra – they wrote
most of their own tracks and weren't using their sexuality
and dancing as primary marketing tools. 'Push The Button'
remained at the top of the charts for three weeks, making
it their most successful single to date. The 'Babes managed
to fight off competition from Robbie Williams's single
'Tripping', which entered at Number Two on 9 October.
Gracious Williams took his defeat well and sent the band
flowers. Keisha gushed, 'I think he's extremely talented and
attractive, I think he has charisma. I think he's got the x-
factor. He's a very nice guy, too. He sent us flowers when
we got the Number One.'

Besides the song's success in the UK, it also hit Number

One in Ireland, New Zealand, Austria, Poland and the European Chart. It reached Two in Germany and Norway, and Three in Belgium, The Netherlands, Switzerland and Australia. By the end of the year, the BPI confirmed the single was Number 12 in the Top 50 Best-selling Songs of 2005, just above Daniel Powter's 'Bad Day'. The single went Silver in its first week, selling over 200,000 copies in the UK. After three weeks ruling the airwaves, it was knocked off the top of the UK chart by rock newcomers Arctic Monkeys' 'I Bet You Look Good On The Dancefloor' on 23 October. Sugababes didn't mind, though – they soon became huge fans of Arctic Monkeys and five months later they covered the song on the B-side to 'Red Dress'.

When the Sugababes received word of their Number One, they weren't even together. Heidi was spending the day in London with boyfriend Dave Berry, while Keisha was on a city break in Amsterdam. After all the promotion of the past few weeks, Mutya was enjoying quality time at home with Tahlia and Jay. Of all the bandmembers, Heidi was always the one who got the most joy out of their Number Ones. Her mum hosted a family celebration up in Liverpool, but wasn't able to share the special day in person with her daughter. Karen said, 'She was celebrating in her flat in London with some friends. She had spent the day with her boyfriend, Dave, but he had to go to Manchester in the evening so her friends went round to have a drink with her. We phoned Heidi straight after the chart rundown. She was made up. She was just sorry she couldn't come home. Heidi says she can't celebrate any more or she'll become an alcoholic.'

sugababes

After the single's release, the Sugababes were straight on to album-promoting duties – *Taller In More Ways* was hitting stores just two weeks later. They performed tracks from the album at small gigs; at the opening of a new HMV store in Stratford, east London, and the G.A.Y. night at the London Astoria. Just two days before the album's release, the girls attended the Q Awards at London's Grosvenor House. While they hadn't been nominated, they had been asked to present KT Tunstall with a Best Track trophy for 'Black Horse And The Cherry Tree'. Keisha admitted the ceremony wasn't particularly enjoyable because there was tension in the air between Coldplay frontman Chris Martin and Oasis brothers Liam and Noel Gallagher. She said, 'Whenever Coldplay were up for something, the whole vibe in the room became very negative. I was wondering, Why am I the only one clapping?'

For the first time since *One Touch*, most critics loved the Sugababes' new album. It proved to the bandmembers that the longer they spent on an album, the better the final product. The *Guardian*'s Alex Petridis wrote, 'The single "Push The Button" sounds, rather marvellously, like the kind of record Abba might have made had they survived into the acid-house era: a melody as sweet and addictive as Smarties, atop clipped computer beats and buzzing electronics. "It Ain't Easy" is even better, Depeche Mode's "Personal Jesus" rewritten with its existential angst replaced by the travails of teen romance ... The album's strike rate is far higher than you might expect from a manufactured pop act's fourth album; it avoids the obvious pitfalls and its highpoints are genuinely high.'

The *Evening Standard*'s David Smyth wrote, 'There's a coherence running through these 12 sleek, funky tracks that means even the inevitable filler doesn't feel out of place. The bouncy electropop of this week's number one (their fourth), "Push The Button", stands out, but the equally huge choruses on self-esteem ballad "Ugly" and frantic party tune "Red Dress" come close.'

Meanwhile, the *Independent*'s Andy Gill praised Sugababes for managing to be one of the only girl groups on a fourth album: 'The fact that Sugababes have made it to their fourth album is quite an achievement. And this is by some distance their best effort yet.'

Following the huge response to 'Push The Button' and good reviews, the girls were ecstatic when the album went straight to Number One on 16 October. Not only was it their first-ever Number One album, they had also secured a chart double because 'Push The Button' was still ruling the UK singles charts. In the process, they knocked Franz Ferdinand's second disc *You Could Have It So Much Better* off the top of the album charts. Despite the dominance of rock acts in the album charts, Sugababes were one of the few pop acts selling well. The same week, Liberty X's third album X entered at a dismal 27. Two months later, their competitors Girls Aloud only managed to secure a chart position at 11 with their album *Chemistry*. *Taller In More Ways* was certified double Platinum ten weeks after its release.

The Sugababes' hectic schedule over the past two months meant Keisha was too busy to properly celebrate her 21st birthday on 30 September. She had spent her birthday weekend in Amsterdam, but decided to have a bigger celebration to coincide with the album's launch. The Sugababes, their management, family and friends gathered at London's Embassy nightclub for the bash. On the way into the party, Heidi was accosted by a concerned fan, worried she was still being bullied by her bandmates. Heidi said, 'We were all out for Keisha's birthday last week and a girl really upset me. She was saying, "Why don't you just leave the other two? I know they're really horrible to you and you're so pretty and you've got a great voice." It was horrible because she was trying to be so understanding but she got it completely wrong. We do row occasionally, but any three girls always will. If we didn't have that spark, we just wouldn't have such chemistry on our records.'

A *Mirror* reporter Sarah Tetteh was also at the party and claimed Keisha was jealous of the attention her boyfriend Zayne was getting. Tetteh alleged Keisha had been threatened by the presence of herself and her two friends and ordered security to remove them from the event. Tetteh wrote, 'It was so embarrassing! We'd done nothing wrong except chat to Keisha's bloke, but we were made to look like troublemakers.'

Contrary to Tetteh's report, Keisha insists she didn't have anyone forcibly removed from the party.

After the Sugababes' weeks of chart success, Island Records decided it was perfect timing to announce a 16-date UK tour for 2006, which would kick off in March. While the workload had been more manageable than previous years, Mutya still wasn't spending the amount of time she wanted with Tahlia. When the tour dates were booked, she realised she would be spending Tahlia's first birthday in Newcastle, where the group were scheduled to perform at the City Hall that night.

On 3 November, the Sugababes travelled to the Portuguese capital Lisbon to present a gong at the MTV Europe Music Awards. Unlike previous years when they had experimented with different looks, the group wowed the paparazzi with their sophisticated outfits. Mutya in particular gained a lot of attention in her figure-hugging red dress. The trio introduced the Best Pop Act nominees before presenting a trophy to The Black Eyed Peas at the Atlantic Pavilion gig. Just two weeks later, they were back in London at the last-ever Smash Hits Poll Winner Party. As well as performing 'Push The Button', the 'Babes were up for Best UK Band, Best Single, Best Album and Best Video, but went away empty-handed. Their set would turn out to be one of Mutya's last ever gigs with her bandmates.

In between the gigs and media interviews, the Sugababes were approached to do their most high-profile advertising campaign yet – becoming the faces, and legs, of hosiery firm Pretty Polly. The trio followed in the footsteps of Jamelia and Rachel Stevens and went on to star in the most high-profile Pretty Polly campaign to date. The firm even designed black 'Sugababes tights', which included the group's name written on pink strips down the legs. It was shot by French photographer Franck Sauvaire in a series of group and individual photos, featuring the Sugababes wearing a selection of knee-highs, stockings and tights. During the shoot Mutya and Keisha were more daring than Heidi and posed naked apart from their flesh-coloured tights. Heidi admitted, 'I was really nervous. I was physically shaking on the day that we were doing the pictures. It's probably the most nervous I've been in a shoot.'

Keisha said she was happy doing the raunchy shots: 'I was OK, because we had our people round us and the photographer made us feel really comfortable. It would have been different if I had to have my legs akimbo – I just had fun with it.' Since then she has even considered posing in her underwear for a men's magazine: 'As long as it's classy I'd do a lads' mag, but I'd never get my tits out. I don't mind the idea of them retouching my arse, though – that would be good.'

After receiving such good album reviews, 'Ugly' was chosen as the next single release. The Sugababes flew over to New York City to film the video in a warehouse. It was the first promo they had made outside the UK and, after initial sales of *Taller In More Ways*, it was clear they could use big budgets. The record label sent out a casting notice looking for 'an extrovert bunch of eclectic, inspiring performers'. Throughout the video, the trio took more of a backseat and watched performers of all races, backgrounds and ages show off their unique skills. During the video, Heidi attempted to copy a Bollywood dancer, Mutya tried Latin dancing and Keisha mimicked a mime artist.

Dallas Austin wrote the song, primarily for Mutya, who had been the target of unflattering tabloid comments, so it was only appropriate that she would look the most beautiful in the video. While the other girls may have been unaware at the time, Mutya was preparing for her last-ever Sugababes video. Keisha and Heidi were dressed fairly casually in a green shirt and brown skirt and trousers and crop top combo respectively. However, Mutya was wearing a sexy black number and pink bolero.

In one brief scene in the video, she was filmed sitting with her baby Tahlia on her lap as she watched the 'auditions'. ITV morning show *GMTV* joined Sugababes on location and it was obvious to the discerning viewer that Mutya was slowly slipping away from the group. She didn't talk as much as her bandmates and looked like her thoughts were elsewhere.

CHAPTER 18

Minus Mutya, Add Amelle

BY DECEMBER 2005, Mutya reached breaking point: she didn't want to be in the band any more. She had been a Sugababe for eight years and had been singing in public for 14 years. In that time she had achieved a Number One album, four Number One singles and countless Gold and Platinum discs. If she left the band now, she would be doing so on a high. She hadn't been getting the same buzz out of the gigs that she used to. Mutya made no secret of her dislike of photoshoots, and, when she was sitting still for hours on end, posing in front of a camera, she just wanted to be cuddling her daughter.

Sugababes were scheduled to perform at the Clothes Show Live in Birmingham in the first week of December – the same week 'Ugly' was released. The day of the gig arrived and Mutya didn't want to sing, so Heidi and Keisha had to perform as a duo. On Saturday, 10 December, Mutya performed for the last time with her bandmates on the

BBC talent contest *Strictly Come Dancing*. The trio were due to sing on rival channel ITV's *Record Of The Year* live final as well, but instead opted for *Strictly*, because they could sing live. Earlier that morning, Mutya had failed to show up for a recording of T4's *Popworld* so yet again her bandmates sang 'Ugly' as a duo. The following evening, the pair performed without her at the Nobel Peace Prize concert in Oslo's Spectrum in Norway. Just before they went on stage, they found out 'Ugly' had reached Number Three in the charts. It was bizarre for Keisha and Heidi to hear the chart rundown as a duo and not have the chance to celebrate it with Mutya.

Despite knocking The Pussycat Dolls off the charts three months earlier with 'Push The Button', this time it was the American six-piece stopping Sugababes from reaching a higher position with their ballad 'StickWitU'. The song charted well throughout Europe and Australasia, reaching Four in Denmark, Five in New Zealand and Seven in The Netherlands, Ireland and Norway.

But Mutya wasn't ill, she just wanted out. She took the management aside and told them she wanted to leave the group. Manager Mark Hargreaves broke the news to Keisha and Heidi and then decided to try to find another member. The group had only just released the second single of their new album, a UK tour was booked and they had also agreed to support Take That in concert the following summer. Sugababes couldn't split. Hargreaves had discovered Heidi when Siobhan left all those years ago and he was convinced he could find another talented female singer.

Mutya agreed to keep quiet about her exit until the

management could find a replacement. So, for two weeks, Keisha and Heidi fulfilled Sugababes' schedule as a duo. When anybody asked where Mutya was, they were told, 'Mutya's sick.' The two weeks not only gave Sugababes time to find a new member, but it also allowed Heidi and Keisha the time to deal with her exit emotionally before they would have to speak to the press.

When Heidi received the phone call to say that Mutya had left, she was devastated. Despite media assumptions, the two had grown close in the latter years – in fact, closer than Mutya and Keisha. She considered Mutya one of her best friends and couldn't believe that she didn't tell her herself: 'Mutya had problems and I was really close to her when she left the band. I wanted to help her through the problems and try to support her. I knew it was going to happen, but, when the call came through to say she'd actually done it, I cried. I don't know if it was because it was something that had been building for so long. I think she just wasn't happy doing it any more. She had a baby and she'd been in the band ever since she was 12. She felt it was time to move on. We'd always said that we'd never carry on doing it if we weren't enjoying it any more. In textbook terms, Mutya leaving when she did – well, it was probably the worst timing it could have been. But she never hated us. She never actually gave us a reason for quitting. She just went, that's all. She didn't tell us she was leaving. She told the management and that was it. I suppose people deal with things how they feel. Maybe she felt comfortable doing it like that at the time.'

Heidi waited in vain for a phone call from Mutya to

explain her departure. Over a year after she left the group, she admits she hasn't spoken to Mutya since just before her exit and she concedes that she still misses Mutya and her daughter Tahlia, of whom Heidi grew very fond. She explained, 'I haven't spoken to Mutya because she didn't tell me she was leaving and she's never called. It doesn't mean I don't like her or I'm angry with her. I hope she's good and she's enjoying what she's doing.'

Keisha had suspected for ages that Mutya would leave, but, when her thoughts became a reality, she wasn't prepared for the emotional turmoil. Having been friends since the age of nine, Keisha and Mutya had shared so many experiences together: their first bras, first periods, first love ... Mutya's first child. Keisha said, 'We knew that she wasn't happy and she'd leave at some point. It happened gradually. We did drift apart, but there weren't many rows. Me and her had history together. There was love there, but no friendship. Her and Heidi were very, very, very, very close.

'She felt like she'd been in the group for a century and a half. It was hard for me. I was in tears all the time because I'd lost a friend. I'd been with her practically every day since I was nine. We were like twins. But I had to get over it, realise that Heidi was still there, and that I still wanted it. After she split, we talked about what we were going to do. We weren't sure whether to keep going as a twosome or to recruit someone. It was devastating when Mutya quit. But, in our little world, we move very quickly. We need to carry on. Sugababes is a business; the band is not about one person. When someone leaves, you have to bounce back.

Life goes on. It's quite selfish, but you have to think about what's best for you.'

While Heidi had been hurt by Mutya's departure, she put on a brave face and carried on smiling, just as she had been taught at stage school so many years ago. She had survived her parents' divorce and the tough first year of being in Sugababes, so she knew she would get over Mutya's exit with the support of her family and boyfriend Dave.

Meanwhile, Keisha felt like she'd lost an arm: 'Heidi's bounced back and just got on with it. It's taken me a long time. I'd wake up crying my eyes out every single day – not because I wanted Mutya back, but because not to have her there was really hard. I was a frigging emotional wreck. I'd be on the phone to the management and the record company every other day saying, "I can't come into work." Which was really bad.'

But the girls were determined to keep the group going and gave their managers their blessing to find someone else. They insisted on having the final decision over who joined and they were all prepared to host auditions, when Mark Hargreaves mentioned he had someone in mind. Two years after meeting Amelle, Hargreaves remembered her singing talent and good looks. He knew she would be perfect for the band. Keisha said, 'It all happened really fast, and the first thing Heidi and I were thinking was, OK, next chapter – let's hold some auditions. But management were like, "Before we go into auditions, we remember this girl we saw years ago at a showcase in LA and really liked her …"'

Amelle, meanwhile, was working at the Funky End bar on Aldershot's Station Road when she received a phonecall

from her agent's office. She remembers, 'They said, "I've got
something big for you but I'm not going to tell you what it
is. Come to London tomorrow." Mark picked me up in his
car and told me what it was about. It was a complete shock
– I almost had a heart attack, I was speechless. I literally had
to go and do the new vocals on the album straight away,
that's how mad it was.'

Hargreaves got Amelle straight into the studio to record
Mutya's verses and the choruses of 'Push The Button',
'Ugly' and 'Follow Me Home'.

Following another Sugababes' gig as a duo, Keisha and
Heidi were approached by Hargreaves who said he'd met
up with this mystery singer. He summoned the pair to a
listening session so they could hear Amelle's strong, husky
singing voice. Heidi said, 'He put a CD on in the car. Keisha
was in the back and I was in the front. He played four songs
and we didn't say anything until after the fourth when I
said, "What do you think, Keisha?" She said, "She's really
good, isn't she?" Mark said he had a video recording. We
thought, It'll be one of two things: either she's completely
ugly or a six-foot-five model who'll make the two of us
look like dwarves.'

Fortunately, Heidi and Keisha liked the look of Amelle
and agreed, 'She's the new Sugababe.'

Amelle was bursting with excitement with the
opportunity she had been offered, but Hargreaves told her
she had to keep it a secret from everyone, including her
family and boyfriend Freddie Fuller. They had managed to
keep Mutya's departure out of the media for now and
wanted to give Amelle time to adjust to her new

bandmembers. Amelle explained, 'I stayed in a hotel and wasn't allowed to go back home, which was quite hard. I couldn't tell my family until the day before it came out in the newspaper. I had to tell them a story Mark and I made up, that I was doing some songwriting for some group from Norway. Freddie wanted to come and visit, but I said, "No, sorry. I'm busy." He thought I was having an affair.'

Five days after the audition, it was time for Amelle to meet her new bandmates. She was terrified because of the press rumours – would they be bullies? Would they be bitchy to each other? Little did she know that Keisha and Heidi were just as nervous as she was. They were keeping their fingers crossed they would have a natural chemistry with her so they could keep Sugababes going. Keisha recalled, 'I was asking Heidi beforehand how to sit. I didn't know whether to lean back, or if that looked too casual, or lean forward, which could have looked too intense. I didn't want her to come in the room and get the wrong idea.'

With Amelle secured as Mutya's replacement, it was time to let the group's fans and the world know what was happening. Rumours started circling on 13 December when Mutya failed to turn up for the 'Live from London' gig at the Apple Store in London's Regent Street. The group's spokesperson laughed off speculation Mutya had left, saying, 'All the girls have a month off for Christmas. Mutya had a cold on Tuesday and couldn't make the Apple show.'

On 21 December, the band and Mutya released a statement, admitting she was leaving: 'My decision is based purely on my personal reasons. It was a very difficult decision, not a snap decision. I've enjoyed an unbelievable career so far and I'm so proud of what we've achieved with Sugababes.'

The following day, Amelle was unveiled as the new Sugababe and tabloid columns invited the public to contact them with information on her. Amelle's joining statement read, 'For years I've dreamed of breaking into the music business but never did I dream of waking up one day to be the third Sugababe! They're the biggest girl group in the country and absolutely the only band I would ever have thought about joining … Like millions of girls my age, I've grown up with Sugababes' music as a soundtrack to my life and I've been a fan of theirs for years. I still can't believe my luck.'

CHAPTER 19

Growing Even Taller

AFTER BREAKING FOR Christmas and New Year, it was all go for the third version of Sugababes. Before the UK tour started in March 2006, Island Records decided to release a new version of *Taller In More Ways* with Amelle's vocals. However, due to lack of time, they only managed to re-record 'Red Dress', 'Follow Me Home', 'Gotta Be You' and a new song – 'Now You're Gone' – written by Pete Kirtley and Tim Hawes at Jiant, the songwriters who had spent two years working with Amelle before she joined the band.

When the girls were back in the studio, word reached the press that Mutya had signed a recording deal with their record label Island. The report immediately triggered negative media criticism, accusing Mutya of leaving Sugababes for her own career, rather than for motherhood. However, Mutya insisted young Tahlia prompted her departure and her solo career was an after-thought. She explained, 'My main reason for leaving Sugababes was motherhood. There's no point in having a child if you're not going to look after it. I didn't think, Ooh, I want a solo career. I didn't believe that my record company would have the confidence to take me on, but they did. It's really nerve-wracking when you're so used to have two girls either side of you. Leaving was very painful but one of the best things I've ever done – I needed to be there for my daughter.'

With the drama surrounding Mutya's exit and Amelle's arrival, the Sugababes were delighted when they started the year off with a Brit nomination. The trio's song 'Push The Button' was up for Best Single, alongside Coldplay's 'Speed Of Sound', James Blunt's 'You're Beautiful', Shayne Ward's 'That's My Goal' and Tony Christie ft Peter Kaye's 'Is This The Way To Amarillo?'. They were happy with their single nomination until they saw the acts up for Best Pop Act. Surprisingly, McFly, Girls Aloud and Sugababes – some of the biggest pop acts around – weren't in the category at all, instead it fell to singer/songwriters Blunt and Katie Melua. Heidi complained, 'I'm surprised we've not been nominated. It would've been nice as we are a pop band, after all. I was shocked that McFly weren't in the category either and it's James Blunt and Katie Melua. Maybe they've changed the way of doing things. I'm not expecting to win, though. Although it would obviously be fantastic, I wouldn't be disappointed – I don't have my hopes up.'

As well as studio time, the Sugababes also had to film a new video. Following the line-up change, they had received a lot of press and needed to release a single quickly to capitalise on it. The next release would be 'Red Dress'. It was funky and fun, and the label hoped the Xenomania production on the track would continue the tradition of providing the Sugababes with good chart positions. Tim Royes, who directed Holly Valance's 'Kiss Kiss' and Rachel Stevens's 'Sweet Dreams My LA Ex' promos, was called in to direct a sexy video to complement the song's lyrics. In the video, the Sugababes continued with the new sophisticated wardrobe they had begun to cultivate with 'Push The Button' and even managed to feature Pretty Polly tights too.

Amelle couldn't wait to film her first video: 'We're really looking forward to it as there are going to be lots of costume changes. It's going to have a catwalk-show theme with lots of mad outfits – very over the top and extravagant – we can't wait!'

On 28 January 2006, Amelle made her official debut as a Sugababe on the German TV show *Wetten, Dass...?* Before performing 'Push The Button', the trio had a sit-down interview and she couldn't help nervously wringing her hands and fiddling with her dress. She admitted, 'I'm really nervous, but I'm also really excited at the same time.'

During the interview, Amelle and Heidi couldn't stop smiling, while Keisha looked visibly sad – she was still reeling from Mutya's departure.

On 2 February, Amelle made her red-carpet debut at the Meteor Ireland Music Awards at Dublin's Point Theatre. The trio were performing and presenting an award. When Amelle started her verse, the whole audience applauded, as if giving her the seal of approval. Five days later, Sugababes were in the Italian Alps for the Winter

Olympics. They performed 'Push The Button' and 'Red Dress' to a crowd of young Italians and sports fans from around the world for a special *Top Of The Pops* broadcast. Amelle was enjoying the travel; she hadn't seen much of the world while growing up and was revelling in the opportunity. She enthused, 'I haven't seen much of Europe so it's nice to be able to go. We did a performance at the Winter Olympics in Turin and that was wicked; it was really beautiful up in the mountains.'

Less than two weeks later, she was glammed up again on the red carpet for the Brit Awards at London's Earls Court. It was then that the realisation of the past two months hit her. She was standing in an expensive outfit with dozens of paparazzi shouting at her to look their way – she'd made it!

Later that evening, Heidi and Amelle shrugged off their loss in the Best Single category to Coldplay, but Keisha was gutted. She revealed, 'I wanted to be nominated for Best Pop and not winning Best Single was disappointing. But Coldplay are a great band and deserved their Best Single win. We have had such a great year and this would have been a bonus. I wanted to walk away with that award, with that little gold man.'

During the ceremony, Amelle spent more time looking at her fellow diners and drinkers in the star-studded audience than she did on stage. She admitted, 'At the Brits, it hit me. I was just sitting down having my dinner and I looked around. Paris Hilton was one table away and the Kaiser Chiefs were to our left. Me and Heidi were really starstruck when we saw Madonna there. She smiled at us and we froze. We just kept staring at her, we couldn't even go up to her, it was that bad. I wouldn't have known what to say anyway. It was mad to see her.'

Fortunately for Amelle, her boyfriend Freddy Fuller kept her down-to-earth. When she took him to a Universal Records party at the Nobu Berkeley restaurant later that night, he was completely unfazed by the celebrities in the room. Amelle explained, 'There was Paris Hilton in one corner and Prince in the other and he didn't give a crap. He's very down-to-earth.'

Three days after the Brit Awards, the trio introduced Amelle to British TV viewers on ITV's morning show *CD:UK*. Mutya decided to travel down to the Riverside Studios in London to meet Amelle and wish her luck. The girls were interrogated by the programme's host – Lauren Laverne – who wanted to know if Heidi and Keisha were still friends with Mutya. Keisha said, 'She just came down to support us.'

While Keisha discussed Mutya's departure and her plans for the future, Heidi looked solemnly at the ground. Clearly, she was hurt by Mutya's exit and, despite agreeing with Keisha that they were 'all friends', she didn't talk to her backstage. Amelle's introduction with Mutya went well, but it would be the first and last time they would see each other. Amelle said, 'She came down to say hello and wish me luck and that. It was really nice to see each other actually. She was quite interested in me, what I'd be like, and me the same with her. So it was just really nice to have a chat and see what she's going to do soon and about her baby. It was just really nice to see the person you're filling. She's just a really nice girl and she's doing her own thing and she's doing really well at the moment and doing her solo stuff.'

Despite going home empty-handed from the Brit Awards, it didn't take long before the group got their hands on another gong. The trio attended the *Elle* Style Awards at the Old Truman Brewery on Brick Lane in East London and were given the Music Star Award for being the best-dressed singers in the charts – the same prize they had been awarded four years earlier. For hosiery manufacturers Pretty Polly, the *Elle* win justified their decision to choose the Sugababes as their new spokesmodels. As soon as they heard Mutya had left, they called in Heidi, Keisha and Amelle to reshoot the campaign. It seemed Heidi had got more courageous since the initial photos with Mutya and agreed to go nearly-nude for the photos to advertise the transparent tights range. However, while Amelle and Keisha flashed the flesh, Heidi was strategically placed behind a chair. The Pretty Polly reshoot was only the second shoot Amelle had ever done with her new bandmates, so she was pretty nervous. When she was told she would have to pose in nothing but a pair of nude tights, she asked, 'What the hell is going on?'

The re-release of *Taller In More Ways* hit the stores on 27 February, with a new cover and four tracks featuring the vocals of Amelle, including a brand-new song. The re-release entered the charts at Number 18 and remained in the Top 40 for another six weeks. On the album sleeve, Amelle paid tribute to Mutya and promised to try hard to match up to her singing standards. She said, 'Good luck with your future – you've given me a lot to live up to.'

After 'Push The Button' was toppled from the top spot in the UK charts by Arctic Monkeys the previous year, Sugababes thought they would cover 'I Bet You Look Good On The Dancefloor' for the B-side of the 'Red Dress' single. Heidi admitted, 'We loved it, even though it knocked us off Number One! It was our A&R guy that suggested to us Arctic Monkeys and we really loved the song anyway. So we went in the studio and recorded it. There was a big thing about it when it came out; everyone had their opinion about it.'

Two weeks before 'Red Dress' was released, Sugababes performed their Arctic Monkeys cover at the *NME* Awards at London's Hammersmith Palais. The trio were incredibly nervous because they had read the response to news of the cover on the *NME* message boards. When they realised the rock newcomers would actually be in the audience at the ceremony, their nerves tripled. Heidi said, 'I was shaking for ten minutes after we did it, but we thought it went well.'

Besides their performance, the group also presented the Best Solo Artist award to Kanye West, who took a shine to Amelle. When he arrived on stage to accept his trophy, he put his arms around Amelle, shouting, 'I thought she was my prize! Can I have her instead?'

A gracious Amelle laughed off the attention. 'I spoke to him after and he said I was beautiful. I'm flattered but there's no way I'd do anything – I love Freddie.'

Just before 'Red Dress' was released, Sugababes performed at one of their favourite London venues – G.A.Y. at Astoria and Amelle received a huge response from the group's fans. She was relieved Sugababes' fans had accepted her: 'At first I thought they'd be chucking things at me and stuff. I really did, but surprisingly they haven't.'

When 'Red Dress' was finally released on 6 March, it entered the UK charts at Number Four. The song also received a good response across Europe and Australasia, charting at Seven in The Netherlands, 12 in Ireland, 14 in Norway and 16 in New Zealand.

After the single's release and all the interviews introducing Amelle to the fans, Sugababes were back on the road. It was the first time they had toured since 2004. On the second night in Liverpool, Heidi introduced Amelle to her friends and family, and hosted a post-gig party in the city's Baby Blue bar on the Royal Albert Dock.

Their 16-date tour went ahead without a hitch and Heidi and Keisha enjoyed it more than previous tours. As much as they loved being in Sugababes, after all the years, they occasionally weren't in the mood. They credited Amelle's arrival with bringing a new enthusiasm to the group. Keisha explained, 'Amelle adds a touch of sophistication, a classy element. Mutya brought more of a street element. When Mutya was in the band, there was something edgy about it, whereas with Amelle it's more slick; people say we look more united now. Amelle is kicking us back into shape because she's so enthusiastic. We were pulling too many sickies and slacking off, so she's like a breath of fresh air.'

After their last concert in London on 10 April, Sugababes were ready to have fun. While Heidi wanted to spend quiet nights in with her boyfriend Dave Berry, Keisha introduced Amelle to her new celebrity lifestyle and together they attended the premiere of *Rollin' With The Nines*. Keisha had split from Zayne Alliluyeva in February and was enjoying her new single status. Much to her horror, some uncouth male fans decided to use the band's latest Number One as a chat-up line, however. She explained, 'When "Freak Like Me" came out, there were a couple saying "I'll be your freak," but "Push The Button" has been the worst. "I'd like to push your button" and "Are you gonna push my button?" and, "Oooh! I wanna push your button." That whole pushing the button thing, fellas, please, stop it! It's embarrassing.'

Following their successful Pretty Polly campaign, Sugababes were approached and agreed to star in a Polish mobile-phone network commercial. The ERA Tak Tak advert told listeners their phones would play Sugababes' songs whenever their phone rang. In the video, the trio walk into a store and start singing 'Push The Button' every time the geeky assistant's phone rings. Heidi was given the most comedic role in the ad and stepped out of a changing room with her head in a polo neck. She admitted she found it embarrassing: 'Every time they played "Push The Button" I had to stumble out of a changing-room cubicle with a polo-neck jumper half on, jump up and push a button on a giant fake phone hanging above our heads – it was pretty bizarre.'

During their time in Eastern Europe, they also shot the video for their final single from the *Taller In More Ways* album – 'Follow Me Home' – in the neighbouring Czech Republic. Sugababes' fans thought the song was an odd choice for a post-Mutya release, considering she had written it about her daughter. However, the group were following their tradition of releasing two up-tempo and two slower tracks from every album. The video starred the trio as 'honeytrappers' in 1970s Poland, who used their feminine wiles to secrete information from military personnel. They were wrapped up in fur hats and coats, but assured fans it was faux fur.

While they were starring in ads for a mobile-phone company, they also signed a deal with O2 to appear in an interactive mobile reality show *Get Close To*. The episodes followed the group around Copenhagen, Vienna and Zurich on promotional tours and also saw them meet Britain's Royal Family at the Prince's Trust 30th Live. Instead of the huge line-ups at the previous Prince's Trust Party In The Park events, just ten acts were selected to perform at the Tower of London on 20 May. The girls were introduced to Prince Charles and Camilla and Princes William and Harry. They admitted getting very flustered and forgot to say, 'Your Royal Highness'. Heidi gushed, 'William says he knows our music!'

During the summer, the girls announced they would be releasing a *Greatest Hits* album, which of course, refuelled the old rumours they were going to split. Amelle was horrified: 'I'm just getting started!' Over her first six months as a Sugababe, she had slowly got used to the bad press, but wasn't expecting to be treated differently when she visited her family in Aldershot. She said, 'Even my friends treat me differently now. To tell the truth, there's a lot of creeping and people seem a bit fake. I'm getting more wary of people now. I wonder if they want something from me. Even my family make a big fuss of me. They say, "Oh,

Amelle, you're home." I just want to be normal Amelle. To be able to say, "Hello, Mum, you all right?" And be treated normally. But everything has changed in that way.'

She was also frustrated when an unnamed 'friend' told the *Sun* that she used to date an armed robber. Amelle confirmed the report that she had dated Garri Collins – but only for three months and their relationship ended three years before he was imprisoned. She lamented, 'I was a little shocked and a bit down, but Keisha and Heidi have warned me about everything that would be happening. I was with him for about three months, split up, and then three years later he went to prison. It has nothing to do with me now.'

When 'Follow Me Home' was released on 5 June, it received little response from the public. It entered the charts at Number 32, making it the lowest-charting Sugababes' song ever. Critics believed fans were protesting against the song because it was written for Mutya's baby and thought it was inappropriate to release it after her departure. Despite the poor response, Keisha rated the video their 'greatest', adding, 'That director is amazing.'

While Keisha thought the video was amazing, her former bandmate Mutya was not so impressed as she watched it at home. She was surprised that they had chosen the song she had written for her daughter as their next single. She explained, 'My verse was talking about my daughter, it was personal and then the video was awful.'

Sugababes started off the summer winning yet another trophy at the *Glamour* Women of the Year Awards on 6 June. The trio went on to beat their close pals Girls Aloud to the Band of the Year title at a star-studded bash in London's Grosvenor Square. Eleven days later, they joined their idols Take That on a six-date stadium tour. Out of the three bandmembers, Amelle was the biggest Take That fan and had a huge crush on Gary Barlow. She had spoken of her passion for him during a lot of the TV interviews, but wasn't prepared to meet him in the flesh. Amelle approached Gary for an autograph for one of her friends and was stunned by his reaction. 'I remember the first Manchester date, I knew how many people were going to be there, but I just didn't see it. And me and Keisha went out to go and see Beverley Knight, on the top near our dressing rooms, and I nearly had a heart attack. Literally I was like, "Oh my God!" But once we got out there it was absolutely brilliant and the boys were really nice. Except one ... he was just really rude and just horrible. I had been a big fan of Take That – I think everyone was at that sort of age. I was a big fan of Gary Barlow so I was excited to meet him. But he wasn't nice to me; he was really rude. He was up his own arse. He was like, "See you later, love, and why are you even speaking to me?" All I had done was ask him to sign a CD for me. He was my first crush so I was devastated.'

After performing over the summer with Take That, and on the festival circuit, the Sugababes returned to the studio to record some new tracks for their *Greatest Hits* album. After singing Mutya's lines for most of the year, studio time was a chance for Amelle to contribute lyrically to the sound of the group. She enthused, 'I'm looking forward to writing for the album, to put my stamp on the band. There'll be

three or four new tracks that I've helped to write, so I'm
pleased about that. I write a lot of ballads.'

Their record label teamed them up with George
Astasiois and Jason Pebworth from Californian band Orson
– who share the same parent record label as Sugababes.
Orson wrote two songs for the girls – 'Good To Be Gone'
and 'Easy'.

While Amelle and Keisha liked the electro-pop track
'Easy', Heidi wasn't sure: 'At first I just didn't like the song
at all. We also recorded a song called "Good To Be Gone". I
really liked that. But we went in to do "Easy" and when I
came out of the studio I phoned the girls and told them, "I
don't like that song at all. I'm not into it." They really liked
it, though. The next day I went back in and listened to it,
and I loved it. Now it is probably one of my favourite songs
out of all we've ever done.'

The song includes the raciest lyrics the Sugababes have
ever sung, full of sexual innuendo.

The song was announced as the next single, but Heidi
and Keisha couldn't believe it when they heard Mutya had
recorded a duet with George Michael entitled 'This Is Not
Real Love', that would be released on the same day.
Despite this, the girls insisted they were happy for their
former bandmember, because Michael had wanted to work
with her for years. Heidi said, 'He's a really big fan of
Mutya and she's got a fantastic voice.'

Interestingly enough, Michael had attended the same
primary and secondary school as Mutya and Keisha, albeit
some decades earlier.

Just six days before the trio filmed the video for 'Easy',

Keisha bumped into Mutya at the MOBO Awards. Keisha admitted it was awkward: 'I'm the only one who has seen her since she left the band, but only twice. Our friendship's gonna take a lot of time because it's really weird for her at the moment.'

After the success of the 'Red Dress' video, Sugababes again enlisted the directorial skills of Tim Royes. They needed an extra-sexy promo to match the raunchy lyrics of 'Easy'. The video featured the girls dressed in latex and dancing in a public toilet. Their fans, particular the male ones, loved the video and Sugababes kept hold of the latex look for their G.A.Y. gig at the London Astoria two months later.

On 3 October, the group hosted a small gig in the capital's famous jazz spot, the 100 Club, to showcase their forthcoming album *Overloaded: The Singles Collection* to a select audience of media, family, friends and competition winners. The intimate gig featured the trio and their live band playing on a small stage. It provided the perfect opportunity to remind the press that they could sing live and had a string of hits under their belt. Although the gig started an hour late due to technical problems, they wowed the crowd singing all the group's hits, from 'Overload' to the forthcoming 'Easy'.

A few days later, Sugababes earned themselves a place in the history books. According to research by *The Guinness Book of World Records*, the group were the Most Successful Female Act of the 21st Century. In over six years, the 'Babes – in all their line-ups – had secured 16 hits. *Records'* expert David Roberts said, 'Britain has a tradition of creating great girl groups. Bananarama dominated the Eighties, the Spice Girls were huge in the Nineties, but the Noughties belong to the Sugababes.'

In fact, the Spice Girls only had ten hits in the space of four-and-a-half years – not a patch on the 'Babes!

Towards the end of the month, Sugababes were honoured by the invitation to sing with the late James Brown at the BBC Electric Proms. The trio joined the Godfather of Soul at London's Roundhouse for a performance of his 1958 hit 'Try Me'. The 76-year-old introduced the girl group, saying, 'We've got gospel, we've got jazz, we've got James Brown, we've got pop, you've got a little bit of Janice Joplin, you've got a lot of things tonight and you've got the Sugababes. I'm very happy to be here.' While the Sugababes were thrilled to be performing with such a legend, they realised they had been doubly privileged to sing with him when he died just two months later. Had the gig been scheduled a few months down the line, the trio would have missed out on the chance to share the stage with the music veteran.

Two nights after their night of funk with legend Brown, the girls had their own audience during a special one-off gig at London's Dominion Theatre to promote the *Greatest Hits* album. They performed all the group's hit songs and their cover of the Arctic Monkeys. A host of celebrity guests turned up to see Sugababes in action, including Avid Merrion, Shane Lynch, Roxanne McKee, Holly Willoughby, Lady Isabella Hervey and Kate Thornton.

November was awards season again and the Sugababes had been lined up to present a lot of trophies. They weren't nominated in many categories and ended up going home empty-handed, but their presence was still good publicity for the *Overloaded* album. In early November, they flew to Copenhagen, Denmark, for the MTV Europe Music Awards. Upon arrival at the city's airport, Keisha suddenly realised she had lost her passport somewhere between London and Copenhagen, and panicked. Fortunately for Keisha, an honest citizen handed it in. She said, 'I was so embarrassed and I started to panic. I heard my name being read out over the Tannoy and thought the airline had lost my luggage.'

Meanwhile, superstar Kanye West hadn't forgotten Amelle since meeting her at the *NME* Awards earlier that year and he was determined to have her all to himself. At the Awards, the hip-hop star, renowned for his self-confidence, approached her and told her he expected to see her at his hotel later. What transpired days later horrified the new Sugababe: 'He had two other women hanging off each arm but he didn't care and told me he wanted me to go to his hotel room later. I was polite but said it wasn't going to happen. But he's not used to that and clearly thought I was joking. When I didn't show up he must have just flipped. I had forgotten all about it, but when I was at home the other night I got the call from Kanye's assistant. She said she was calling on behalf of Kanye, who said he was furious because I had offended him by not dating him. I told her that Kanye knew I had a boyfriend, but she wasn't having any of it. She said he was not used to being treated like that, and I should be more considerate next time I see him.'

On 6 November, Sugababes' 'Easy' and George Michael and Mutya's 'This Is Not Real Love' went on sale. That week, neither won the coveted Number One spot – Westlife secured their 14th place at the top of the charts with 'The Rose'. 'Easy' entered at Eight, while Michael and Mutya entered at 15. As soon as 'Easy' charted, Sugababes were free to concentrate on promoting the *Overloaded* album, which was released the next day. Despite press rumours to the contrary, Amelle and Heidi did not re-record over Mutya and Siobhan's vocals in the songs that had been released with their voices on. The album received good reviews because it featured the group's best songs and entered the album charts at Number Three.

After releasing their album, Keisha was mentally preparing herself to meet her ultimate pop idol: Michael Jackson. He was reported to be performing 'Thriller' at the World Music Awards, where he would accept a Diamond Award for his contribution to music. Ahead of the ceremony, an overexcited Keisha gushed, 'He's definitely my idol. I was one of those kids that watched his videos and cried. I couldn't wait to see him tonight. I woke up like a big kid on Christmas today. I was so excited, I woke up so early – like 7am. I swear, if I see him, I'll pass out.'

Unfortunately for Keisha, Jackson's appearance was a huge anti-climax. His performance included just a few lines of 'We Are The World'. Keisha didn't get the chance to meet him and was disappointed she didn't get to see a proper set.

As 2006 drew to a close, the Sugababes were thrilled they'd pulled it off. When they substituted Amelle for

Mutya, they had received some mean comments from the media, but she proved herself. They had performed live as often as possible and even proved they could be humble by supporting Take That. Not only this, they experimented with new sounds and looks and finally found their fashion feet after years of style disasters on the red carpet. One fashion critic even cried out for the return of their crazy ensembles, claiming they were 'playing it safe' with their newly glam award outfits.

After spending Christmas at home with their families, the Sugababes flew to Berlin to welcome in 2007 with Scissor Sisters. The girls, Heidi in particular, were huge fans of the New York group. Heidi said, 'I really want us to do collaboration with Scissor Sisters. I'm such a huge fan. They would fit really well with our sound.'

Sugababes and Scissor Sisters performed to an amazing 1.2 million partygoers – their biggest audience ever – at the city's Brandenburg Gate, which formed part of the five-city Nokia New Year's Eve celebration.

Following their pyrotechnic-laden introduction to 2007, the Sugababes finally had a holiday. Amelle and boyfriend Freddie Fuller had had a tough Christmas and were hoping to escape to Barbados.

Meanwhile, Keisha and a group of girlfriends spent two weeks partying in Miami Beach, Florida, where she was snapped by the paparazzi wearing just a bikini.

After their recuperation, it was back to work. The last week of January was incredibly busy and saw the girls perform in Dublin for a Childline charity gig, before heading back to London to launch their new single. Comic Relief had approached Sugababes and Girls Aloud to do a duet of Aerosmith and Run DMC's 'Walk This Way' to benefit the charity's annual fundraising event. Despite both groups being pitted as rivals in the charts – which they were – the eight girls had formed a strong friendship and the 'Babes had even been invited to Girls Aloud beauty Cheryl Tweedy's wedding to football ace Ashley Cole the previous July.

Recording of the song was tricky due to clashing schedules, but talented video editors meshed the tapes together so it looked as if all eight girls were present. The Sugababes persuaded Dallas Austin – who had produced many tracks on their previous studio album – to produce the song. The video placed Sugababes and Girls Aloud in separate rooms, banging on the walls between as they keep interrupting each other. Girls Aloud members Kimberley Walsh and Nadine Coyle shared the first verse, while Heidi and Keisha shared the second. Amelle and Cheryl shared ad-libbing throughout the song, while Sarah Harding and Nicola Roberts got the chance to rap towards the end.

Despite a mixed response from critics, the song went straight to the top of the UK charts upon its 12 March release. The track became the Sugababes' fifth UK Number One and their 18th Top 40 hit. 'Walk This Way' sold over 65,000 copies, raising thousands of pounds for disadvantaged people living in the UK and Africa. The two girl groups united to perform the song for the first time with all eight members present during the live Comic Relief telecast on 16 March.

Ahead of the single's release, Heidi and Keisha joined Girls Aloud member Kimberley Walsh on a charity trip to South Africa. Despite the Sugababes' international jet-setting, they had never stepped foot on the African continent before and weren't prepared for the poverty they were to encounter. The three singers spent two days in the Durban townships of Richmond Farm and Tafelkop, visiting families affected by HIV and AIDS.

Heidi, Keisha and Kimberley were profoundly affected by what they saw. During their brief few days in South Africa, the girls experienced a combination of joy and sorrow. They were ecstatic to experience the cultural exchange of music and dance with the joyful locals, but were saddened when they learned of the residents' tragic personal histories. The trio admitted they felt ungracious for complaining about simple things back home, like running out of hot water, after meeting people who couldn't even access cold clean water.

Heidi said, 'I didn't realise how dependent people here are on charities. They don't have any water, they don't have any food and they don't have support from family members.'

Keisha formed a special bond with 12-year-old Nokwanda, who was abandoned by her family after being raped. The singer later admitted she felt compelled to adopt after meeting so many parentless children and is determined she will do so later in life. Keisha said, 'Meeting children like her makes me understand why Madonna felt compelled to adopt. It is definitely something I would consider one day.'

Following the release of the single, Keisha admitted she

wasn't so sure about duetting with Girls Aloud when the opportunity first presented it. Despite her two-year-long friendship with a lot of the bandmates, including neighbour Kimberley, Keisha saw her group as a different, credible alternative to Girls Aloud, who had been put together in ITV talent show *Popstars: The Rivals*.

She explained, 'It was great working with them, but I won't lie – we were sceptical because we have worked so hard for our credibility. We wanted to make sure we could come across how we are as a band and did the best we could vocally. They did their thing and we made sure we kept our choreography as minimal as possible while they had their full-on dance routine. I definitely think in the video you can see we are two separate bands.'

CHAPTER 20

What Siobhan Did Next...

WHEN SIOBHAN DONAGHY arrived home at the end of August 2001, she had had enough. Much as she loved to sing, she had decided she hated the record industry. She'd spent years being told what to wear, how to dance and hanging around with two girls with whom she didn't have much in common and who wanted to make different music to her. When she left Sugababes, she was so angry with the music industry that she declared she wouldn't sing professionally again: 'I wasn't gonna do music again. I'd completely and utterly had it. I never wanted to be famous anyway. Our whole thing was, "Let's just make music that we wanna listen to."'

Though Siobhan waited to experience the elating feeling of freedom she expected following her exit from Sugababes, it never came. She had just taken control of her destiny by removing herself from a situation she was unhappy in, yet she still felt miserable. She didn't want to leave her bed, let alone her house. Instead, she just stayed at home and cried constantly.

Siobhan had to decide what to do with her life. She was 17 and her friends were all at college, doing A levels and planning their futures. A year ago, she had her adult life all mapped out for her, but now she didn't know what to do. After passing seven GCSEs in summer 2000, she started four A levels, but earlier that year had slimmed down to one – fashion design – before eventually dropping out altogether. She had always seen further education as part of her future, but, after leaving the band, Siobhan couldn't think straight.

Despite her confusion about her career path, word came from the Sugababes' camp that she had left to pursue a career in fashion or photography. She fumed, 'They said I was going to study fashion photography, or some bollocks. Nobody knew what I was going to do, because nobody phoned to find out. But, for the foreseeable future, I thought I wasn't going to do anything, so that's what I did. A lot of people said I was doing fashion photography or styling, doing lots of things, but really I didn't know what I was gonna do.'

For two months after leaving the band, Siobhan withdrew into herself. Her parents thought she was just a bit down and encouraged her to socialise with friends. Siobhan explained, 'I was clinically depressed. I couldn't get out of bed. It got very bad and I couldn't cope. It was very taboo and I couldn't really talk about it with my family. My family were like, "Go out for a drink with your friends and you'll be fine" or "Get a hobby", but that wasn't good enough – I needed help.'

One morning when all her family were at work, Siobhan woke up and decided she couldn't stand being miserable any more. She went to the doctors and was stunned to be told she was suffering from clinical depression and was having a breakdown. The GP also told Siobhan that a skin medication she was taking could be contributing to her fragile emotional state. The drug has been linked to teenage depression, but Siobhan admitted she hadn't been told of the possible side effects when she was first prescribed it.

The doctor prescribed Siobhan antidepressants and counselling, but she couldn't bring herself to tell her friends and family. She admitted, 'When I went on antidepressants I was really ashamed. I didn't tell my mum at the time. I was taking medication for my skin, which is notorious for making teenagers really aggressive. Even though it was nothing to be ashamed of, I couldn't tell anyone. Secretly I started taking the tablets to see if they made a difference. After a couple of weeks I wasn't crying so much and two months later I was back to normal. At this point I felt strong enough to tell everyone. To my surprise they understood.'

Siobhan joined her paternal granddad in Omagh, Northern Ireland. Following the death of his wife a year earlier, he was lonely and Siobhan just needed time and space away from London. She said, 'I just hung out with my granddad. He needed the company, and people were just cool enough over there to leave me alone.'

Just as she went on the antidepressants, her boyfriend Ted May dumped her. She hadn't been herself for months and her emotional problems had obviously put a strain on the relationship. Fortunately, one of her sisters swooped in and told her she was taking her to Ibiza for some sun and relaxation. The sisters got a last-minute £99 deal and were soon on a plane to the Balearics. Siobhan explained, 'My sister was like, "Right, we're getting on a plane and we're going to Ibiza and we're gonna have some fun." We didn't really go out partying, we just sunbathed and relaxed.'

While in Ibiza, she was stunned to bump into Jony 'Rockstar' Lipsey, with whom she had worked on the *One Touch* album. It was the first time she had seen anyone related to the group since quitting. Siobhan recalled, 'He saw I was in a bad way and, when I saw him, I burst into tears.'

After seeing Siobhan in Ibiza, Lipsey phoned Cameron McVey – another songwriter-producer from the Sugababes' first album – and told him about her. McVey soon got in touch and admitted he had suspicions Siobhan wasn't happy in the band years before. He told her he had every confidence that she was a talented singer and songwriter and urged her to continue music: 'Cameron's got kids my age and he knew what was going on in the band from way back when. He got me back writing, told me it would be therapeutic, and got me in the studio again. There was no pending release date, there was no management – I was just kinda writing for therapeutic reasons. I do love making music and I think I'd forgotten that. It didn't have to get as complicated as it did.'

McVey teamed Siobhan up with his son Marlon Roudette and another producer named Pretesh Hirji. She said, 'Marlon and Pretesh were similar ages and we were really timid and kind of awkward and … perfect for each other! It was wicked, wicked tunes and I was excited to be writing again.'

After getting back in touch with McVey, life became better. Siobhan reunited with her former boyfriend and started to enjoy herself. The antidepressant tablets were working and she was feeling better by herself. However, while she was relieved to be out of her depressive state, she was concerned about how long she would have to remain on the tablets.

In summer 2002, Siobhan had made a heap of new material inspired by her time in Sugababes and was ready to try a solo career. She signed up with CMO Management – who had directed the careers of Blur, Morcheeba and Turin Brakes – after sending them a five-track demo. She enthused, 'They were so different to my old management. I thought, I'll stick with these boys.'

It didn't take long before CMO found Siobhan a deal with her old label London Records – who had dropped Sugababes nearly a year earlier. The confidence the label and her management had in her was enough for Siobhan to determine she could come off the antidepressants. 'The pills did me some good but they come with their own set of problems. For the first time I felt I was in safe hands so I decided to stop taking the antidepressants. Looking back I have no regrets and I don't feel any shame about seeking help for my depression. I am now anti-narcotics, I just want to make it on my fucking own.'

In 2003, Siobhan was ready to start her solo career. She was adamant she wanted to take things slowly, so she began performing at small gigs around the UK under the name

'Shanghai Nobody' – an anagram of her name. She enthused, 'I missed out all the scummy venues such as Dublin Castle, in Camden, as a Sugababe, and, to be honest, it has helped me deal with my stagefright. I can't sing in shoes. I need to be grounded, earthbound. It is about breathing and mobility. I wore proper stilettos as a Sugababe, 45 minutes at a time.'

In March 2003, she released the single 'Nothing But Song' under the name Shanghai Nobody because she didn't want people to know her as 'the girl that left Sugababes'. The track was only released as a 7" so failed to chart.

After slowly gaining confidence on stage, Siobhan was ready to release music under her own name again. In June 2003, she released 'Overrated' – a song about her time in the group. The video was filmed in east London's Brick Lane, an area she loved to socialise in. She wanted to show herself as a normal teenager on a night out with her girlfriends – the social activity she had desperately missed out on during her time in Sugababes. In the video, she is seen kissing a mystery man during a party scene, who she later revealed was her boyfriend May. 'He didn't want to do it and he was a bit embarrassed, but as soon as they said, "Well, it will have to be someone else," he was like, "I'll do it!"'

'Overrated' entered the UK charts at Number 19 on 29 June 2003 – the same day Siobhan played in the New Band Tent at the Glastonbury Festival. She couldn't believe the coincidence when she learned her former band were on the Main Stage at the exact same time. Siobhan didn't see the Sugababes during the festival weekend. Following her gig, she pitched a tent with her boyfriend and friends, and 'roughed it'. She just wanted to fulfil her dreams of having a normal teenage life and live a student lifestyle like her friends. She enthused, 'Glastonbury was an amazing buzz. For me, the band and my backing singer Hannah, we'd never done it before. As a singer-songwriter, that's your ultimate goal – you want to play Glastonbury.'

When 'Twist Of Fate' was released in September, it missed out on the Top 40 altogether and charted at a dismal 52. Two weeks later, it was time to release her album, *Revolution In Me*. Most of the critics were impressed, just as they were with *One Touch*, but would good reviews be enough?

The *Mirror*'s Ian Hyland loved Siobhan as much as he loved the Sugababes, declaring *Revolution In Me* was 'the best album by a former girlband member this week. 9/10.'

The *Independent*'s Tim Perry wrote, 'The ex-Sugababe lends her hard-working, but indistinct voice onto some beat-ridden studio trickery from Cameron McVey [Massive Attack, Portishead] without producing anything catchy. Ordinary.'

Meanwhile, the *Guardian* said Siobhan had talent, but criticised London Records' marketing campaign: 'Sugababes accused London Records of wrecking their career with a snooty marketing campaign and left. Siobhan Donaghy stayed with London, who persist with their too-cool-for-school routine. Yet behind the clunky marketing, *Revolution in Me* is a fine album: not as self-consciously angsty as Avril or as fearlessly buoyant as Busted, but a rounded meditation on the teenage psyche. And if London are committed to Siobhan, they won't drop her when this album flops – they'll wait until album three for payday. Won't they…?'

Due to lack of marketing and the fact that Dido's second album *Life For Rent* came out the same week, Siobhan's album charted at 117. After the commercial failure of her music and the subsequent reshuffling at the record label she was dropped. In retrospect, she didn't mind. 'Everyone was dropped, everyone! But I like London Records – they signed me when I was 14, with the girls, they kept me on solo and let me make whatever kind of record I wanted to make. So I got it out of my system. And I decided from then on I'd just take everything on the chin. Much worse things in life can happen!'

Just weeks after she left London Records, her three-year relationship with May came to an end. He had been Siobhan's first love and she was devastated. She admitted, 'It overshadowed everything: I was heartbroken, I loved him desperately.'

Despite lacking a record label, Siobhan had the confidence to keep going with her music and CMO Management were convinced they would find her a record deal.

Having been released from her record contract, Siobhan went backpacking with friends in Europe, the United States and Thailand. She found the experience therapeutic and gave her plenty of inspiration for her next record. She teamed up with producer James Sanger at his studio in northern France and started recording tracks which would later form part of her second solo album *Ghosts*.

She started writing more songs, many of which dealt with her broken relationship, and, in November 2005, she approached Parlophone – who handed her a deal. Siobhan enthused, 'There can be a lot of rejection in this industry so it was a real confidence booster. They really find the time to have a relationship with their artists. They've been working with me, not against me. It doesn't feel corporate, it feels like an indie label.'

With her new record label, Siobhan has also been able to use the skills of her make-up artist sister Roisin, who she was not allowed to employ during her time with Sugababes. She has kept her friend Hannah as her backing singer, which means she always has a pal with her.

As well as recording *Ghosts*, Siobhan repaid Marlon Roudette and Pretesh Hirji for their work on *Revolution In Me* by singing for their own material. The pair had started to release music under the name 'Mattafix' and asked Siobhan to sing on their single 'To & Fro', which appeared on their 2005 album *Signs Of A Struggle*.

After taking her time with the album and enjoying plenty of life in between, Siobhan hopes 2007 will bring her musical success. As well as singing and songwriting, she found another way to cultivate her love of music – DJ-ing at London bars. After several delays, she announced 'Don't Give It Up', the first single of her second solo album *Ghosts* would be released in April 2007 and the album would follow two months later. Only time will tell if she will match the success of Sugababes ...

CHAPTER 21

Sugababes and their Sugapies

AS THE SUGABABES have grown up in the public eye, their fans have watched the group fall in and out of love. Not only have the bandmembers' relationships given them much needed support during their busy lifestyles; they also provide them with material for their songs.

During the early years of Sugababes, Keisha and Mutya were boy-crazy. They were always talking about the opposite sex and their celebrity crushes. In 2002, they admitted they were dating two dancers, but, being 18 at the time, predictably the relationships didn't last.

Following the success of 'Freak Like Me', the Sugababes became regular features in the tabloid gossip columns, thanks to their alleged romances. The group were linked to all the members of Blue throughout the year, but always insisted they were 'just friends' with the boy band.

Both Heidi and Keisha were alleged to have enjoyed brief

romances with former 5ive singer Richard 'Abs' Breen. Throughout 2002, Heidi was presented as 'a prize' in a battle between Breen and 3SL singer Steve Scott-Lee. While the tabloids claimed Heidi had eventually plumped for Breen, later that year she declared she had been single for ages. In an interview with *Smash Hits* magazine, Heidi and Keisha both admitted to kissing Breen. Keisha said, 'He's a bad one. I kissed him once and he slobbers.'

A more tactful Heidi added, 'I've snogged Abs – I think we all know that.'

In summer 2003, Heidi was romantically linked to Northampton Town striker Steve Morison. The papers claimed she had been seeing him for six months and was 'heartbroken' when they split in August. But the relationship was news to Heidi: 'I went to a bar with my sister and a few days later in the press it said I was bumping and grinding with some footballer. Apparently, he was on the same table as us with his girlfriend but I didn't even chat to him.'

At the end of 2003, all three of the Sugababes began their first long-term relationships and fell in love for the first time. Mutya began dating a 25-year-old named Jay from her local area, who she met through friends. She remains fiercely protective of him and refused to disclose his surname in a bid to keep him out of the gossip columns she hates so much. In March 2005, they welcomed their daughter Tahlia and remain together still.

Keisha embarked on a rocky on-off relationship with Namibian-born basketball player Zayne Alliluyeva, who was brought up in east London. In 2005, during promotional activities for 'Push The Button', she fuelled rumours she was engaged after she was spotted flashing a big ring on her engagement finger. It was only after the couple split in February 2006 that she admitted she had been engaged. She said, 'Zayne's one of my best friends but things hadn't been right with us for ages. We've always been quite on and off and that was going on for the past year. It didn't end badly; it pretty much just dried up. We went through a lot together and we'll always love each other but we just weren't connecting. In between those ages you're learning so much about yourself and that's where you do your most vital growing and you become different people. I was engaged, but during that time I was focusing on the album and just doing the work – I think guys are a lot of hassle.'

Months before Heidi started dating Dave Berry, Keisha tried to fix the couple up. She approached Berry at a film premiere to find out if he had a girlfriend – which he had at the time. Keisha recalled, 'He was like, "Hi." I was like, "Do you have a girlfriend?" I think he thought I was asking for me, which was really embarrassing. He was like, "Yeah, nice to meet you."'

A few months later, Heidi appeared on Berry's MTV show. The presenter had since split with his girlfriend and sparks flew. After enjoying their first date, the couple's romance was made public on 25 October. Berry admitted, 'Heidi came on the show and it was pretty much love at first sight. For the first couple of dates, it was more like, "Wow, I am dating a Sugababe!" but that soon wore off. But that's why I know I am so lucky because I would never have had a chance to meet Heidi if I didn't do the job I do, and we are really happy together. She has a gorgeous flat in Kensington and I live just across the road from my mum and dad in east London but we spend a lot of time together.'

Heidi is equally fond of Berry, and, despite rumours of an engagement, the couple insist they are not ready to wed just yet. She gushed, 'I have found my true love and I know I always want to be with him – I see us being together, getting married, the whole thing. I have never been happier. I really want to have children.'

When Amelle joined the band in December 2005, Heidi was stunned to discover her new bandmate had started dating her boyfriend Freddie Fuller on the exact same day as she and Dave had got together. During Amelle's first few weeks as a Sugababe, the British tabloids were eager to find out as much about her as possible and quickly discovered she was dating a traveller.

Amelle was disgusted by some of the media's response to Fuller's background and did an interview with the *Sun* confirming their relationship. She said, 'I don't care what people think about me seeing a traveller. He's always treated me like a princess. He's just so happy for me. He's been such a good support. He has a normal job. He's so laidback and chilled out. Freddie's been great with how everything's changed for me. I know he'll always keep me grounded. I'm not looking for anyone else. I love my boyfriend. I'm not the sort of person who'd go looking for someone else just because this has happened. He's the one I want.'

However, by late January 2007, Amelle and Freddie had split up and Amelle has denied press reports of a subsequent reunion.

After seven years in the charts, five bandmembers and two record labels – the Sugababes are stronger than ever in 2007 and promise fans they still have ambitions to fulfil and big plans for the future.

Epilogue

AFTER THEIR BRIEF journey as part of a charity supergroup with Girls Aloud, Sugababes returned to work as a trio in spring 2007. Working in proximity to the energetic, all-dancing Girls Aloud had made the trio question their live act ahead of their UK and Irish tour. Before the girls kicked off their tour in Dublin's Point Theatre on 27 March, they asked themselves if there was enough action on stage.

Keisha explained, 'For a second, we did think that we can't entertain properly because we don't dance about and stuff. Girls Aloud did a big, full-on routine in the video, plus on tour they have loads of dancers. Our tour is going back to basics – the Sugababes was always about three girls, three voices in harmony and we want to show that.'

As the 'Babes began their three-week arena tour, which concluded at London's Wembley Arena on 13 April, their former bandmate Mutya Buena was also promoting her debut solo single 'Real Girl', which sampled Lenny Kravitz's 1991 hit 'It Ain't Over Til It's Over'. Mutya's debut solo album, also entitled *Real Girl*, is scheduled to hit stores three weeks before Siobhan Donaghy's second album *Ghosts* is released in June.

In the early stages of Mutya's promotion, she revealed she hadn't spoken to Heidi since quitting the group. Laidback Mutya claims she tried to speak to Heidi at Amelle's first UK TV performance on *CD:UK* in February 2006, but her attempts were fruitless. Nevertheless, Mutya has moved on: 'I wasn't allowed to see them because apparently Heidi was shocked and upset, I made Amelle feel out of place and put them all off their performance. It took me to get up out of my bed to come and show there's no hard feelings and I got it pushed back right in my face, so I thought, Forget it. I was in a great band. I've got no issues. I've got my daughter now, my own album, I'm living my life.'

So, as far as Mutya's concerned, a peace-making session with former close pal Heidi looks out of the question. However, her second attempt at friendship with Siobhan is going swimmingly. Mutya was devastated when the redhead quit the group in 2001, comparing it to 'losing a sister', and the pair are now in regular contact through the social networking site MySpace.com.

While Mutya and Siobhan will be launching their solo albums over the summer, Sugababes will be back in the studio recording their fifth studio album. The disc, scheduled for release in the autumn, will be the first album new member Amelle can lyrically and vocally contribute to fully, after her appearance on only four songs on the *Taller In More Ways* re-release.

A long-delayed plan to launch Sugababes dolls will also come to fruition, after the trio signed a deal with toy giant Mattel UK. The deal first appeared in the press in late 2005, when Mutya was still with the band, but was apparently put on hold following her departure. After Mattel saw new member Amelle's smooth transition into the group, they created specially designed Barbie dolls, modelled after the singer and her bandmates.

Mattel UK Managing Director Jean-Christophe Pean enthused, 'This exciting collaboration will bring another hot band into the Barbie portfolio, building on the success that we had with Girls Aloud in 2005. Barbie is yet again at the cutting edge of what is hot in a girls' world; her interests, aspirations and dreams. Sugababes are the top-selling female act of the century, what better company is there for the top-selling doll?'

Family and friends predict Heidi's relationship with Dave Berry will go from strength to strength and an engagement announcement over the next couple of years is likely. Meanwhile, single girl Keisha now has a nightclub companion in Amelle following her January split from long-term love Freddie Fuller. Together with their party-loving pals from Girls Aloud, there's a host of males in London just waiting for the chance to wine and dine the sexy singers.

With a hit charity collaboration and yet another sell-out UK tour behind them, Sugababes' success looks to continue on in 2007. With their likenesses appearing in all

sugababes

good toy shops, and their forthcoming album hitting download websites, Sugababes can only keep growing bigger and better.

But for how long they will remain as a group before embarking on their as-yet unrealised dreams of having solo careers only time will tell.

Sugababes Discography

SINGLES		
Title	**Release Date**	**Highest UK chart position**
'Overload'	6 November 2000	6
'New Year'	18 December 2000	12
'Run For Cover'	9 April 2001	13
'Soul Sound'	16 July 2001	30
'Freak Like Me'	22 April 2002	1
'Round Round'	12 August 2002	1
'Stronger/Angels with Dirty Faces'	11 November 2002	7
'Shape'	10 March 2003	11
'Hole In The Head'	13 October 2003	1
'Too Lost In You'	15 December 2003	10
'In the Middle'	22 March 2004	8
'Caught In A Moment'	23 August 2004	8

SINGLES

Title	Release Date	Highest UK chart position
'Push The Button'	26 September 2005	1
'Ugly'	5 December 2005	3
'Red Dress'	6 March 2006	4
'Follow Me Home'	5 June 2006	32
'Easy'	6 November 2006	8
'Walk This Way' (Sugababes Vs Girls Aloud)	12 March 2007	1

ALBUMS

Title	Release Date	Highest UK chart position
One Touch	27 November 2000	26
Angels With Dirty Faces	26 August 2002	2
Three	27 October 2003	3
Taller In More Ways	10 October 2005	1
Taller In More Ways (Reissue with Amelle Berrabah's vocals)	27 February 2006	16
Overloaded: The Singles	13 November 2006	3